THEORETICAL SERIES.—No. 7.
NOVELLO'S LIBRARY FOR THE DIFFUSION OF MUSICAL KNOWLEDGE.

"Studies serve for delight, for ornament, and ability. * * * There is no stond or impediment in the wit but may be wrought out by fit studies."—*Lord Bacon.*

A TREATISE

ON

MODERN INSTRUMENTATION

AND

ORCHESTRATION

(DEDICATED TO FREDERICK WILLIAM IV., KING OF PRUSSIA)

TO WHICH IS APPENDED

THE CHEF D'ORCHESTRE

BY

HECTOR BERLIOZ.

TRANSLATED BY

MARY COWDEN CLARKE.

NEW EDITION, REVISED AND EDITED BY

JOSEPH BENNETT.

LONDON: NOVELLO, EWER & CO.,
1, BERNERS STREET (W.), AND 80 & 81, QUEEN STREET (E.C.)
BOSTON, NEW YORK, AND PHILADELPHIA: DITSON & CO.
1882.

INTRODUCTION.

At no period in the History of Music has *Instrumentation* been more discussed than at the present time. The reason is doubtless to be found in the recent development of this branch of the Art; and perhaps, also, in the multitude of criticisms, opinions, different doctrines, judgments, rational and irrational arguments spoken or written, for which the slightest productions of the most inferior composers form a pretext.

Great importance seems now attached to the art of Instrumentation, which was unknown at the commencement of the last century; and the advance of which, sixty years ago, many persons who passed for sincere friends of Music endeavoured to prevent. There is an effort, nowadays, to place an obstacle in the way of musical progress upon other points. It has always been thus; therefore we ought not to feel surprise. At first, music was only acknowledged as a series of *consonant* harmonies, intermingled with discords of suspension; and when Monteverde attempted to add the chord of the seventh on the dominant without preparation, blame and invective of all kinds were levelled at him. But this seventh once admitted, in spite of opposition, to companionship with the discords of suspension, there were not wanting those among so-called learned authorities who held in contempt all compositions of which the harmony was simple, sweet, clear, sonorous, natural. It was absolutely requisite, to please these gentry, that music should be crammed with chords of the second major and minor, with sevenths, ninths, fourths, and fifths, employed without reason or intention, unless that of being as frequently as possible harsh to the ear. These musicians took a fancy for dissonant chords, as certain animals have a predilection for salt, prickly plants, and thorny shrubs. It was the exaggeration of reaction.

Melody was not to be found among these fine combinations; when it appeared, it was cried down as the ruin of Art, the neglect of time-honoured rules, &c., &c. All was apparently lost. Nevertheless, melody maintained its ground; and a reaction of melody, in its turn, was not long in appearing. There were fanatical melodists, to whom every piece of music in more than three parts was insupportable. Some of them asserted that, in the majority of cases, the subject should be accompanied by a bass only, *leaving to the hearer the delight of imagining the complemental notes of the chords.* Others went still further, desiring to have no accompaniment at all, affirming that harmony was but a barbarous invention.

Then came the turn of modulations. At the time when modulation was only into relative keys, the first who ventured to pass into a foreign key was treated with contumely—as might have been expected. Whatever the effect of this new modulation, masters severely objected to it. The innovator vainly pleaded :—"Listen to it; observe how agreeably it is brought in, how well worked, how adroitly linked with that which precedes and follows, and how deliciously it sounds!" "*That's not the question!*" was the reply. "This modulation is prohibited; therefore it must not be made!" But as, on the contrary, that is the sole question throughout, modulations into foreign keys did not fail soon to appear in high-class music, producing effects no less felicitous than unexpected. Almost immediately arose a new order of pedantry; some composers thinking themselves degraded by modulating into the dominant; and frolicking sweetly, in the smallest rondo, from the key of C natural to that of F♯ major.

Time, little by little, has put each thing in its proper place. A too rigid adherence to custom has been distinguished from the reactions of vanity, folly, and obstinacy; and it is now pretty generally agreed, as concerns harmony, melody, and modulation, that whatever produces a good effect *is good*; that whatever produces a bad effect *is bad;* and that the authority of a hundred old men, even if they were each a hundred and twenty years of age, cannot make ugly that which is beautiful, nor beautiful that which is ugly.

As for instrumentation, expression, and rhythm, that is quite another affair. Their turn for being discerned, denounced, admitted, fettered, freed, and exaggerated, not having come until much later, they have not yet attained the point reached by other branches of the Art. It may be said that instrumentation, as first in order, is at the stage of exaggeration.

It requires much time to discover Musical Mediterraneans; and still more to master their navigation.

CHAPTER I

Every sonorous body employed by the composer is a musical instrument. Hence, the following division of the means now at his disposal —

- Stringed instruments
  - Their vibration effected by the bow
    - Violins
    - Violas
    - Violes d'amour
    - Violoncellos
    - Double basses
  - Played by hand
    - Harps
    - Guitars
    - Mandolins
  - With keys—Pianoforte
- Wind instruments
  - With reeds
    - Hautboys
    - Corni Inglesi
    - Bassoons
    - Bassons de quinte
    - Double-bassoons
    - Clarinets
    - Corni di bassetti
    - Bass-clarinets
    - Saxophones
  - Without reeds—Flutes, great and small
  - With keys
    - Organ
    - Melodium
    - Concertina
  - With mouthpiece, and of brass
    - Horns
    - Trumpets
    - Cornets
    - Bugles
    - Trombones
    - Ophicleides
    - Bombardons
    - Bass tubas
  - Voices of men, women, children, and artificial soprani
- Instruments of percussion
  - Of definite sonorousness
    - Kettle-drums
    - Ancient cymbals
    - Set of bells
    - Glockenspiel
    - Keyed harmonica
    - Bells
  - Of indefinite sonorousness, and producing various characteristic noises
    - Drums
    - Long-drums
    - Tambours de basque (or Tambourine)
    - Cymbals
    - Triangles
    - Gongs
    - Pavillon Chinois

The employment of these various sonorous elements, and their application,—either for *colouring* the melody, harmony, and rhythm, or for producing peculiar impressions (originating or not in an intention of expression) independently of all aid from the three other great musical powers,—constitutes *the art of instrumentation*.

Considered in its poetical aspect, this art is as little to be taught as that of inventing beautiful subjects, fine successions of chords or original and striking rhythmical forms. That which suits various instruments, that which is practicable or not for them, easy or difficult, dull or sonorous —may be indicated; it may also be pointed out, that such and such an instrument is more fitted than another, to produce certain effects, and to express certain sentiments; but as for combining them in groups in small orchestras or large masses, —as for the art of uniting them, mixing them, in such a way as to modify the sound of some by that of others, giving to the *ensemble* a particular tone, which could neither be produced by one of them singly, nor by joining it to instruments of its own species,—this can only be done by instancing the results obtained by masters in the Art and tracing their mode of procedure; results which, doubtless will be again modified in a thousand ways, for good or ill, by such composers as shall reproduce them.

The object of this work is, first,—the indication of the *extent*, and certain essential parts of the *mechanism* of instruments; next, the study (hitherto much neglected) of the *quality of tone* (*timbre*), particular *character*, and powers of expression, pertaining to each of them; and lastly, the best known methods of proceeding, in order to group them appropriately. Any endeavour to step beyond this would be an attempt to set foot on the domain of inspiration; where genius alone is capable of making discoveries, because to genius alone is reserved the right of traversing it.

CHAPTER II

INSTRUMENTS PLAYED WITH A BOW

The Violin.

The four strings of a violin are usually tuned by fifths, thus —

1st String
2nd String
3rd String
4th String

The highest string, E, is also called the *chanterelle*; and generally known as such.

These strings, when the fingers of the left hand do not modify the sound by shortening more or less the portion set in vibration by the bow, are called *open* strings: the notes which are played on an open string being indicated by an O placed above them.

Some eminent composers and performers have not chosen to hold themselves restricted to this method of tuning the violin. Paganini, in order to give more brilliancy to the instrument, occasionally raised all the strings half a tone —

and consequently transposing his part, he played in D♮, while the orchestra was in E♭, and in A♮, while the orchestra was in B♭, &c, thus keeping the majority of his strings *open*—the sonorousness being greater when open, than when pressed by the finger—in keys where, with the ordinary method of tuning, that would not have been possible.

De Beriot frequently raises merely the G a whole tone in his concertos.

Baillot, on the contrary, sometimes lowers the G half a tone, in order to produce softer and deeper effects.

Winter has even employed F♮ instead of the G with a similar intention.

Having regard to the degree of skill at present attained by our young violinists, this is about the extent which may be assigned to the violin in a well-constituted orchestra.—

The great performers carry the range of the violin several notes higher, and even in the orchestra, a much greater degree of acuteness may be obtained by means of *harmonics*—of which mention will be made hereafter

Shakes are practicable on all the steps of this vast ladder of three octaves and a half, but the extreme difficulty of those which occur on the three topmost notes—A, B, C, is to be dreaded; and in the orchestra, it would be prudent not to employ them

The minor shake on the fourth string, from G to A♭, should be avoided as much as possible — It is harsh, and its effect is scarcely agreeable.

Chords of two, three, or four notes, which may be ***struck*** or *played in arpeggio*, on the violin, are very numerous, and the effects they produce extremely various

Chords of two notes, resulting from what is called the *double-string*, are well suited to melodic figures, to sustained phrases either *forte* or *piano*, to ***accompaniments*** of all kinds, and to the *tremolo*

Chords of three or four notes, on the contrary, produce rather a bad effect when played *piano*, they seem rich and energetic only when played loud and boldly, as the bow can then strike the strings sufficiently together to make them vibrate simultaneously

It should not be forgotten, that, of these three or four notes, two at most can be sustained, the bow being compelled to quit the others immediately after they are struck It is therefore useless, in a slow or measured movement, to write thus —

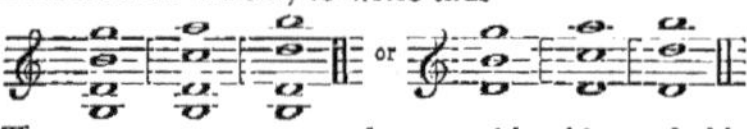

The two upper notes are alone capable of being held, hence it is better to indicate the passage in this way.—

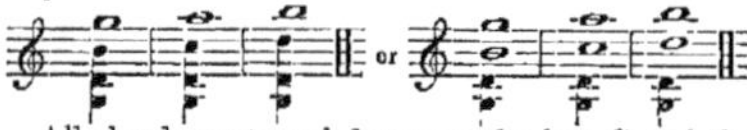

All chords contained between the low G and the low D are evidently impossible since there is only a single string (the G) to produce the two notes. When there is need of harmony in this extreme point of the scale, it can be obtained in the orchestra only by dividing the violins This division is indicated by the Italian word *divisi*, or by the French words *divisés* (divided), and *à deux* (in two), written over the passage.—

The violins are then separated, that one set may play the higher part, and the other the lower Beginning with D (3rd string) all intervals of a second, a third a fifth, a sixth, a seventh, an octave, are practicable But they become more and more difficult in proportion as they advance upon the high strings

The unison is sometimes employed on a double string, but although it can be done upon many other notes, it is well to limit it to D, A, E, because they are the only ones that offer, with the facility necessary to good execution, variety of *timbre*, and a sonority due to the fact that one of the strings is *open* —

there being no open string, their execution becomes rather difficult, and consequently, their strict intonation very rare.

A bass string can cross an upper open string, by pursuing an ascending movement while the open string remains as a pedal —

It will be seen that the D, here, remains open, while the ascending scale is executed throughout upon the fourth string

The intervals of a *ninth* and a *tenth* are feasible, but much less easy than the preceding it is much better not to write them for the orchestra, unless the lower string is *open*, in which case there is no danger :—

Care should be taken to avoid, as excessively difficult—not to say impossible—such leaps of a double string as demand an immense displacing of the hand:—

In general, such leaps should not be written, unless the two upper notes belong to a chord of four notes which may be struck together :—

This is feasible, because the four notes may be struck at once :—

In the following example, however, though the four notes can only be struck at once with some difficulty (those of the last chord alone excepted), the leap from low to high is not less easy,—the two lower notes being on open strings, and the two others with the first and third fingers :—

Among chords of three, and particularly of four notes, the best and most sonorous are always those which contain most open strings. I even think that if none of these strings can be had for a chord of four notes, it is better to rest contented with a chord of three notes.

Here are those most used ; the most sonorous, and the least difficult :—

It is better in all the chords marked thus * to let them remain with three notes, and to omit the lowest sounds :—

Easy in a movement of moderate speed :—

All these chords *linked in this manner* are not difficult. They may be executed in arpeggio ; that is to say, by letting their notes be heard consecutively, from which frequently results the most agreeable effects—in a *pianissimo* especially:—

Nevertheless, there are designs, similar to the preceding, of which the four notes cannot, without extreme difficulty, be played at once, yet which are easily executed in arpeggio, by means of the first and second fingers passing from the fourth string to the first, in order to produce the low note and the high note :—

By omitting the high note or the low note of the preceding examples, so many chords of three notes are obtained. There must be superadded those which result from the various notes produced by the E string above the two centre *open* strings, or by the E and the A, above the open D only :—

If it be required to strike an isolated chord, in D minor or major, the disposition of the A should not be made too difficult when not led up to; it is better to take the following, which is quite easy, and more sonorous, on account of the effect of the two open strings:—

It may be seen by the preceding examples that all chords of three notes are possible for the violin; if care be taken, in those which contain no open string, to spread the parts sufficiently to allow an interval of a fifth or sixth between them. The sixth may be found either above or below, or both:—

Certain chords of three notes being practicable in two ways, it is always better to choose that which contains an open string:—

Double shakes in thirds may be made, beginning with the first B♭ below:—

But as they are more difficult of execution than simple shakes, and as the same effect may be obtained more neatly by means of two separate violin-parts, it is better, in general, to abstain from them *in the orchestra.*

The *tremolo,* simple or double, by many violins, produces several excellent effects; it expresses trouble, agitation, terror, in the respective shades of *piano, mezzo-forte,* and *fortissimo,* when it is placed on one or two of the three strings, G, D, and A, and when it is not carried much above the middle B♭:—

It has something of a stormy, violent character, in the *fortissimo* on the middle of the first or second string:—

It becomes, on the contrary, aerial, angelic, when employed in several parts, and *pianissimo,* on the high notes of the first string:—

Occasion may here be taken to mention that the custom is to divide the violins into two sets; but there is no reason why they should not be subdivided into two or three sets, according to the object which the composer has in view. Sometimes, it is even advantageous to carry the number of violin parts up to eight, either for the sake of isolating from the grand mass eight single violins (playing in eight parts), or in order to divide the whole of the first and second violins into four equal portions.

To return to the tremolo. The chief point, in order to ensure its complete effect, is that the movement of the bow shall be sufficiently rapid to produce an actual tremulousness or quivering. The composer must therefore write it with precision, keeping in view the nature of the movement in which the *tremolo* occurs; for the performers, delighted to avoid a mode of execution which fatigues them, will not fail to profit by any latitude allowed in this respect.

Thus, in an *Allegro assai,* if the following were to be written for a tremolo— which produces the tremulousness would certainly exist; but if the tremolo of an *Adagio* were indicated also by semiquavers, the performers would strictly keep to semiquavers; the result of which would be, instead of tremulousness, an effect of heaviness and flatness the most detestable. In such a case the composer should write—

and even, if the movement be slower than an *Adagio:*—

The *tremolo* on the lower and middle notes of the third and fourth string, is much more characteristic in *fortissimo* if the bow strike the strings near the bridge. In large orchestras, and when the performers take pains to give the full effect, it produces a sound like that of a rapid and powerful cascade. This mode of execution should be indicated by the words: *near the bridge.*

A fine application of this kind of tremolo occurs in the scene of the oracle, in the first act of Gluck's *Alceste.*

The effect of the tremulousness of the second violins and violas is there much enhanced by the grand and emphatic progression of the double-basses, by the blow struck from time to time by the first violins, by the successive introduction of the wind instruments, and lastly by the sublime *recitative* which this surging of the orchestra accompanies. I know nothing of this kind more dramatic or more terrible.

However, the idea of the tremolo *near the bridge,* not having been expressed by Gluck in his score, cannot be ascribed to him. The honor of it reverts entirely to M. Habeneck, who, when directing the studies of the Conservatoire pupils in this stupendous scene, required the violins to try this energetic style of execution—the advantage of which, in such a case, is incontestible:—

No. 1.
Alceste.—(GLUCK.)
Violins.
Violas.
High Priest.
Double Basses.
Animated.
Recitative.
A-pol-lo has re-gard to our distressful pray'rs,
Apol-lon est sen-sible à nos gemis-se-ments,
and with portends sure conveys to me th'as-surance
Et des si-gnes cer-tains m'en donnent l'assu-ran-ce
Hautboys.
Moderato.
Fill'd by the ho-ly fire, attendant on His presence, I am rais'd by his pow'r far above mortal man.
plein de l'esprit di-vin qu'inspire sa pré-sen-ce je me sens é-le-ver audessus d'un mor-tel.
See where the flame brightly stream-ing, sur-rounds with light the sta-tue,
Quelle lumière é-cla-tan-te en-tou-re la statu-e

and on the altar burns,
et bril-le sur l'au-tel
all proclaims to my soul that the God comes in
tout m'an-non-ce du Dieu la pré-sen-ce su-
per-son, and of our fu-ture fate to speak him-self the purport. Feelings of a Ho-ly surrounding
prê-me ce dieu sur nos des-tins veut s'ex-pli-quer lui-mê-me l'horreur d'une sainte épouvan-te
Flutes.
fills my mind with awful dread;
se répand autour de moi,
the ground beneath my step seems to be falling
la ter-re sous mes pas fuit et se préci-

from me.
pi - te,
Mar-ble it-self has life.
le mar-bre est ani-mé,
Clarinets in C.
Horns in G.
Trombones.
The ho-ly tripod trembles.
le saint trépied s'a-gi-te,
Terror pervades on ev'ry side.
tout se remplit d'un juste ef froi

He now will speak. Bent low with fear and dread respect, peo-ple ob-serve a per-fect
il va par - ler. Sai - si de crainte et de res-pect peu-ple ob-serve un profond si -
silence. O Queen, quit at his coming these the empty trappings of thy power. Trem - ble!
- len-ce. Rei-ne dépose à son as-pect le vain orgueil de la puis-san-ce. Trem - ble!
cres.
p

For certain dramatic accompaniments of an agitated character, advantageous use is made of the *broken tremolo*, occasionally upon one string—

sometimes upon two strings:

Lastly, there is another kind of tremolo, never employed nowadays, but of which Gluck has made admirable use in his recitatives. It may be entitled the *undulating tremolo*, and consists of a not very rapid utterance of bound notes on the same tone; while the bow never quits the string.

In these *non-measured* accompaniments, the performers cannot precisely hit the same number of notes in each bar,—some playing more, others fewer; and from these differences results a sort of fluctuation, or indecision in the orchestra, perfectly adapted to express the uneasiness and anxiety of certain scenes. Gluck wrote thus:—

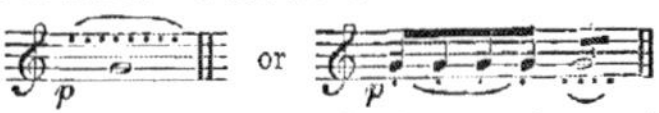

The different kinds of *bowing* are of great importance, and exercise a singular influence on sonority and on the expression of peculiar features and melodies. They should therefore be carefully indicated —according to the nature of the idea which is to be conveyed—by the following signs:—

For *slurred* notes, two and two:—

For *extended slurs*:—

For *staccato*, or *lightly detached* notes, simple or double, which are to be executed during a single drawing of the bow, by means of a succession of small strokes that move it as little as possible:—

For *markedly detached* notes, which are to give to the string all possible sonority, by permitting it to vibrate alone after the bow has vigorously struck it, and which particularly suit pieces of a haughty, grand character, and of moderate movement:—

Notes reiterated two, three, and four times (according to the rapidity of the movement), give more force and agitation to the sound of the violins, and suit many orchestral effects, in all kinds of *nuances*:—

Nevertheless, in a phrase of broad movement and vigorous character, simple notes *markedly detached*, produce a much better effect, when a true tremolo is not employed upon each note. Thus the following passage—

would be,—taking into consideration the slowness of the movement—of an incomparably more noble and more powerful sonority, than this one:—

Composers would be considered too minute, probably, were they to indicate the movements of the bow in their score; still, it is well, when a passage demands lightness or extreme energy or amplitude of sound, to indicate the mode of execution by these words:—"With *the point* of the bow;" or "with *the heel* of the bow;" or "with the *full length* of the bow, upon each note." So the words—"On the bridge," and "On the finger-board," designating the spot nearer or farther from the bridge, where the bow should strike the strings, might be used in the same manner. The metallic sounds, slightly rough, which the bows draws forth when near the bridge, differ greatly from the soft veiled sounds which are generated when it is passed across the finger-board.

In a symphonic piece, where the terrible mingles with the grotesque, the back of the bow has been employed in striking the strings. The use of this whimsical means should be very rare, and have a decided purpose; moreover it has perceptible effect only in a large orchestra. The multitude of bows then falling precipitately on the strings, produce a sort of snapping noise, which would be scarcely noticeable if the violins were few in number, so weak and short-lived is the sound thus obtained.

Harmonics are those sounds which are generated by touching the strings with the fingers of the left hand, so as to divide them in their length, yet not with sufficient pressure to place them in contact with the finger-board, as is the case for ordinary sounds.

These *Harmonics* possess a singular character of mysterious softness; and the extreme acuteness of some of them afford the violin, in the upper part, an immense compass. They are *natural*, or *artificial*.

Natural harmonics are those which are produced by touching certain points of open strings. Here are some which may be produced most surely and with the greatest sonority upon each string.

The black notes represent the real harmonics; and the white notes indicate the notes touched upon the open string :—

Artificial harmonics are to be obtained very distinctly throughout the extent of the gamut by means of the first finger; which, firmly pressed upon the string, while the other fingers touch it, serves for a movable nut.

Here is the table of touched intervals, and of the real harmonics which they produce :—

The touched octave gives its unison: With the chromatic intervals. This fingering is little used, excepting for the 4th string, on account of its inconvenience.

The touched fifth gives its octave above : This fingering is more easy than the preceding, and less so than the following.

The touched fourth gives its twelfth above :

This fingering is the most easy, and is that which should be preferred for the orchestra, when the object is not to obtain as a real harmonic the twelfth of an open string, for in that case the fingering by fifth is preferable. Thus, in order to sound singly a B in alt :

it is better to employ this position :

on account of the open E, of which the touched fifth (B) gives its octave above; and is more sonorous than a string upon which the first finger must be pressed; as for example:—

which gives equally :—

The fingerings of the touched major third and minor third, are very little used; the harmonics being thus produced much less well :

The touched major third gives its double octave above :

The minor third gives its major seventeenth above.

The touched major sixth gives its twelfth above. This fingering is less used than that of the fourth; it is nevertheless tolerably good, and often useful:—

The positions of touched fourth and fifth are undoubtedly the most advantageous.

Some performers sound double strings in harmonics; but this effect is so difficult to obtain, and, consequently, so hazardous, that composers can never be advised to write it.

The harmonics of the fourth string, have something of the quality of a flute; they are preferable for delivering a slow air. Paganini employed them with wonderful success in the prayer of *Moïse*. The harmonics of the other strings acquire more delicacy and tenuity in proportion as they are higher; it is precisely this character, and their crystalline quality, which renders them appropriate to chords that may be called fairy-like,—that is to say, to those effects of harmony which inspire brilliant musings, and carry the imagination towards the most graceful fictions of the poetical and supernatural world. However much they may have become familiar, nowadays, to our young violinists, they should never be employed in a lively movement; or, at least, care should be taken not to give them rapid successions of notes, if their perfect execution is to be ensured.

It is lawful for a composer to write them in two, three, and even in four parts, according to the number of violin parts. The effect of such chords, sustained, is very remarkable, if it be warranted by the subject of the piece, and well mingled with the rest of the orchestration. I have employed them for the first time, in three parts, in the scherzo of a symphony, above a fourth violin part not in harmonics, which *shakes* continually on the least high note. The great delicacy of the harmonics is still more enhanced in this passage by the use of mutes; and thus deadened, they issue from the extreme heights of the musical scale, which it would be impossible to reach with ordinary sounds.

It would be well, in writing such chords in harmonics, not to neglect designating by notes of different shape and size, placed one above another, *the note for the finger touching the string*, and that of the *real harmonic* (when touching an open string) and *the note of the finger pressing*, that *of the finger touching the string*, and that of the *real harmonic*, in the other cases. It is therefore sometimes necessary to employ three signs together for a single sound; as without this precaution the execution might become an inextricable muddle, in which the author himself would have difficulty in recognizing his own production.

No. 2.

Romeo and Juliet.—Berlioz.

Solo 1mo.—*Allegro.*
Flutes.
Solo.
Corno Inglese.
Clar. in B♭.
1st Harps.
2nd Harps.
1st Violins divided.
Real harmonic. - - - 8ve.
8ve.
Finger touching the string.
Finger pressed.
Harmonics.
Real harmonic. - - 8ve.
8ve.
Finger touching the string.
Finger pressed.
2nd Violins divided.
Harmonics.
Real harmonic. - - 8ve.
Finger touching the open string.
Harmonics.
Soli.
Violas.
1st Violoncelli.

Harmonic.
Harmonic.
8ve.
Real harmonic. - - 8ve.
Finger touching.
Finger pressing.
Soli.
ppp
8ve.

Sordines (or *mutes*) are little wooden implements which are placed on the bridge of stringed instruments in order to deaden their sonorousness; and give them at the same time a mournful, mysterious and softened tone, which is frequently felicitous in all styles of music. Sordines are most often used in slow pieces; but they serve scarcely less well, when the subject of the piece admits it, for rapid and light designs, or for accompaniments of hurried rhythm. Gluck has effectually proved this in his sublime monologue of the Italian (*"Alceste"*) "Chi mi parla."

The custom is, when employing *sordines*, to cause them to be used by all the band of stringed instruments; nevertheless, there are certain circumstances, more frequent than is generally believed, under which *sordines* placed in a single part (the first violins, for instance) will colour the instrumentation in a special way, by the mixture of clear sounds and veiled sounds. There are others also, where the character of the melody is sufficiently dissimilar from that of the accompaniments, which render the use of the sordine advisable.

The composer, when introducing sordines in the middle of a piece (which is indicated by the words "*con sordini*"), should not forget to give the performers time to put them on; consequently, he will be careful to arrange a previous rest for the violin parts about equivalent to the duration of two bars in four time (*moderato*).

A rest of such length is not necessary, when the words "*senza sordini*" indicate they are to be removed; this operation requiring much less time. The sudden transition from sounds deadened in a mass of violins, to sounds clear and natural (*without sordines*), is often immensely effective.

No. 3.

SCHERZO—Prestissimo.
Romeo and Juliet.—BERLIOZ.
Flutes.
Hautboys.
Clarinets in B♭.
1st. Violins divided.
2d Violins divided.
Violas.
Violoncelli divided.
Double-Basses.
Con Sordini.
Pizz.
Arco.
pp
poco f
Divided.

Arco.
pp
Arco.
pp
Arco.
pp
Andante non molto.
Con Sordini. 6
No. 4.
Alceste. (Gluck.)
Violins.
Con Sordini. 6
Con Sordini. 6
Viola.
Hautboys.
This instrument is obsolete and quite unknown at the present day
Chalumeau.
Bassoons.
Alceste.
Chi mi par - la!
Che ris -
Violoncellos.
Con Sordini.
Double-Bass.

The *Pizzicato* is still in general use for instruments played with the bow. The sounds obtained by vibrating the strings with the finger produce accompaniments approved by singers, since they do not cover the voice; they do well also for symphonic effects, even in vigorous orchestral sallies, either in the whole band of stringed instruments, or in one or two parts only.

Here is a charming example of the employment of the *Pizzicato* in the second violins, violas, and basses, while the first violins are playing with the bow. These contrasted effects of sound blend here, in a truly marvellous style, with the melodious sighs of the clarinet, the expression of which they serve to heighten:—

No. 5.

cres.
p
cres.
Pizz.
p
Pizz.
Pizz.
f
p
3
6
cres.
Arco.
Arco
Arco.

If the pizzicato be employed in a *forte*, it should be written, generally, neither too high nor too low: the extreme upper notes being shrill and wiry, and the deeper ones too dull. Thus, in a strenuous tutti of wind instruments, a remarkably striking effect will result from a pizzicato like this, assigned to all the stringed instruments :—

Violins together. Pizz. *ff*

Violas and Basses. Pizz. *ff*

Pizzicato chords of two, three, and four notes, are equally valuable in a fortissimo; the single finger which violinists use, then traverses the strings so rapidly that they seem struck altogether, and vibrate almost simultaneously.

Figures of accompaniment, pizzicato *piano*, have always a graceful effect; they afford a sense of repose to the hearer, and impart—when not abused—variety to the features of the orchestra. In future, doubtless, more original and striking effects will be secured from pizzicato than have hitherto been obtained. Violinists, not considering pizzicato as an integral portion of violin-playing, have studied it but little. Even yet, they have only cared to use the thumb and forefinger in playing pizzicato; so that they have never been able to execute passages or arpeggios more rapid than the semiquavers of a bar in four-time of very moderate speed. Whereas, if, laying down their bow, they were to use the thumb and three fingers, letting the little finger support the right hand, by resting upon the violin, as when playing the guitar, they would soon obtain facility in executing passages such as the following, impossible at present :—

The figures placed above the notes, show the fingers of the right hand that are employed; a + indicating the thumb.

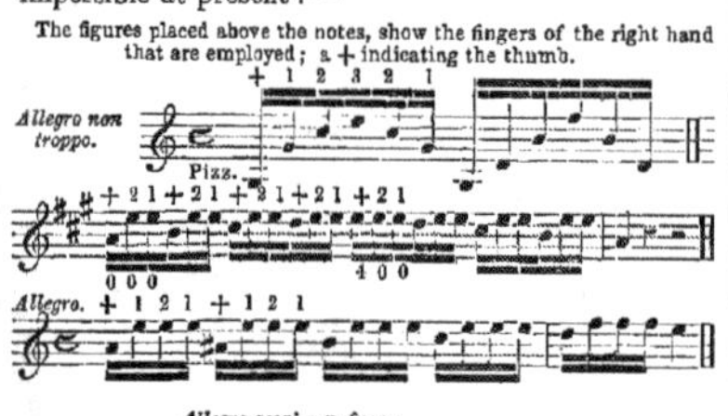

The double and triple iteration of the upper notes, in the two last examples, become extremely easy, by the successive use of the first and second finger on the same string.

Small bound notes are not impracticable in pizzicato. The following phrase from the Scherzo of Beethoven's Symphony in C minor, containing some of them, is always well executed :—

Some of our young violinists have learned from Paganini to execute descending scales in rapid pizzicato, by plucking the strings with the fingers of the left hand resting on the neck of the instrument; and pizzicato passages (still with the left hand), with a mixture of strokes from the bow, even serve as accompaniment to an air played by the bow. These various feats will doubtless become, in course of time, familiar to every violin-performer; and then will be available in composition.

Violins are able, nowadays, to execute whatever they will. They play up to the extreme height as easily as in the middle; passages the most rapid, designs the most eccentric, do not dismay them. In an orchestra where they are sufficiently numerous, that which one fails to perform is done by others; and the result is that, without any apparent mistake, the phrase is delivered as the author wrote it.

In cases, however, where the rapidity, complication, and height of a passage make it too hazardous, or if only for the sake of greater sureness and neatness of execution, it should be dispersed; that is to say, the mass of violins should be divided, and one part of the passage given to some, the rest to others. In this way the music of each division is sprinkled with little rests unperceived by the hearer; allowing, as it were, breathing-space to the violinists, and affording them time to take carefully the difficult positions, and thus to obtain the necessary firmness for a vigorous attack :—

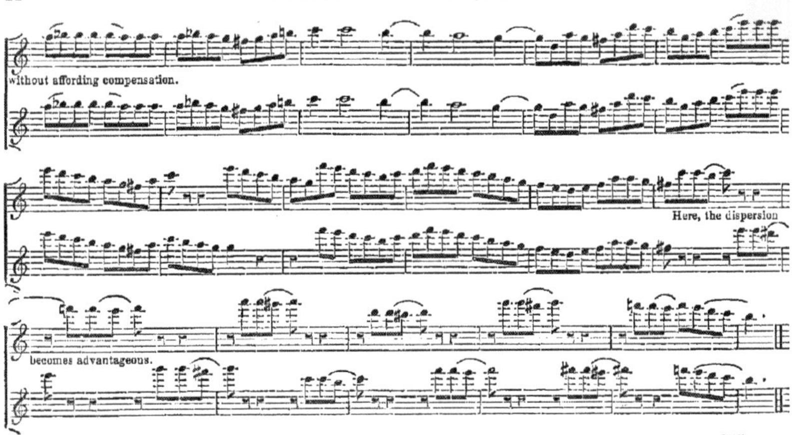

If it be desired to have a similar or still more difficult passage played by the whole mass of violins, it will be always better, as in the preceding example, to divide the first violins into two sets, and the second violins also, causing these latter to double the two parts of the first violins, than to allow all the first violins to play one portion, and all the second violins another; for the distance of the two *points of departure* of the sounds, will break the unity of the passage, rendering the join too apparent. Whereas, the same division occurring on both sides among the two sets of violins, and between the two performers who read from the same desk, one playing the first part and the other the second, it follows that the divided sets are so near each other that it is impossible to perceive the dispersion of the passage, and the hearer may imagine it to be executed entire by all the violins. It should therefore be written thus:

Moreover, this mode of procedure is applicable to all the parts of the orchestra which possess in themselves analogies of quality of tone or lightness; and it should be employed in all cases where a phrase is too difficult to admit of being well executed by a single instrument, or single set of instruments.

I think there might be made in the orchestra better use than hitherto of phrases on the fourth string; and, for certain melodies, of the high notes of the third string. When use is thus made of a particular string, it should be indicated with precision whereabouts this string is employed exclusively; otherwise the performers will certainly yield to habit and to the facility of passing from one string to another, by playing the phrase in the usual way:—

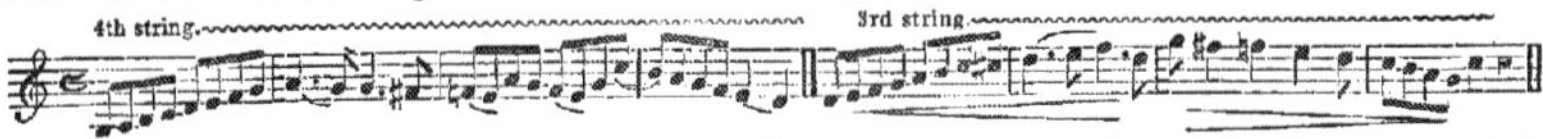

It frequently happens that, in order to give a passage greater energy, the first violins are doubled by the second violins an octave lower; but, if the passage do not lie excessively high, it is better to double them in unison. The effect is thus incomparably finer and more forcible. The overwhelming effect of the peroration of the first movement in Beethoven's C minor Symphony is attributable to the unison of the violins. It happens, even in such a case, that if, the violins being thus together, additional force should be sought by subjoining the violas in octaves, this weak lower doubling, on account of the disproportionate upper part, produces a futile murmuring, by which the vibration of the high violin notes is rather obscured than assisted. It is preferable, if the viola part cannot be made prominent, to employ it in augmenting the sound of the violoncellos, taking care to put them together (as much as the low compass of the instrument will permit) in the unison and not in the octave. This is what Beethoven did in the following passage :—

No. 6.

Symphony in C minor.—BEETHOVEN.

Violins are more brilliant, and play more easily in keys which leave them the use of the open strings. The key of C, alone, appears to form an exception to this rule, as regards its sonorousness, which is evidently less than that of the keys of A and E, although it keeps four open strings, while A keeps but three, and E two only. The *timbre* of the various keys for the violin may be thus characterized; together with their greater or less facility of execution:—

MAJOR.

Key	Facility	Timbre
C.	Easy.	Grave; but dull and vague.
C♯.	Very difficult.	Less vague; and more elegant.
D♭.	Difficult; but less so than the preceding.	Majestic.
D♮.	Easy.	Gay, noisy, and rather commonplace.
D♯.	Almost impracticable.	Dull.
E♭.	Easy.	Majestic; tolerably sonorous; soft; grave.
E♮.	Not very difficult.	Brilliant; pompous; noble.
F♭.	Impracticable.	
F♮.	Easy.	Energetic; vigorous.
F♯.	Very difficult.	Brilliant; incisive.
G♭.	Very difficult.	Less brilliant; more tender.
G♮.	Easy.	Rather gay; and slightly commonplace.
G♯.	Nearly impracticable.	Dull; but noble.
A♭.	Not very difficult.	Soft; veiled; very noble.
A♮.	Easy.	Brilliant; elegant; joyous.
A♯.	Inpracticable.	
B♭.	Easy.	Noble; but without distinction.
B♮.	Not very difficult.	Noble; sonorous; radiant.
C♭.	Almost impracticable.	Noble; but not very sonorous.

MINOR.

Key	Facility	Timbre
C.	Easy.	Gloomy; not very sonorous.
C♯.	Tolerably easy.	Tragic; sonorous; elegant.
D♭.	Very difficult.	Serious; not very sonorous.
D♮.	Easy.	Lugubrious; sonorous; somewhat commonplace.
D♯.	Almost impracticable.	Dull.
E♭.	Difficult.	Very vague; and very mournful.
E♮.	Easy.	Screamy; and slightly commonplace.
F♭.	Impracticable.	
F♮.	Rather difficult.	Not very sonorous; gloomy; violent.
F♯.	Less difficult.	Tragic; sonorous; incisive.
G♭.	Impracticable.	
G♮.	Easy.	Melancholy; tolerably sonorous; soft.
G♯.	Very difficult.	Not very sonorous; mournful; elegant.
A♭.	Very difficult; almost impracticable.	Very dull, and mournful; but noble.
A♮.	Easy.	Tolerably sonorous; soft; mournful; rather noble.
A♯.	Impracticable.	
B♭.	Difficult.	Gloomy; dull; hoarse; but noble.
B♮.	Easy.	Very sonorous; wild; rough; ominous; violent.
C♭.	Impracticable.	

Instruments played with a bow, of which the combination forms what is somewhat improperly termed the quartet, are the base and main constituent element of the orchestra. From them are evolved the greatest power of expression and an incontestable variety of different qualities of tone. Violins particularly are capable of a host of apparently inconsistent shades of expression. They possess (in a mass) force, lightness, grace, accents both gloomy and gay, thought, and passion. The only point is, to know how to make them speak. Moreover, it is not needful to calculate for them,—as for wind instruments—the duration of a *holding-note*, and to contrive for them occasional rests; they are sure never to be out of breath. Violins are faithful, intelligent, active, and indefatigable servants.

Slow and tender melodies, confided too often now-a-days, to the wind instruments, are nevertheless never better rendered than by a mass of violins. Nothing can equal the touching sweetness of a score of first strings made to sing by twenty well-skilled bows. That is, in fact, the true female voice of the orchestra,—a voice at once passionate and chaste, heart-rending, yet soft, which can weep, sigh, and lament, chant, pray, and muse, or burst forth into joyous accents, as none other can do. An imperceptible movement of the arm, an almost unconscious sentiment on the part of him who experiences it, while producing scarcely any apparent effect when executed by a single violin, shall, when multiplied by a number of them in unison, give forth enchanting gradation, irresistible impulse, and accents which penetrate to the very heart's core.

CHAPTER III.

The Viola.

The four strings of the viola are generally tuned in fifths, like those of the violin, and at a fifth below them:—

Its ordinary compass is at least three octaves:—

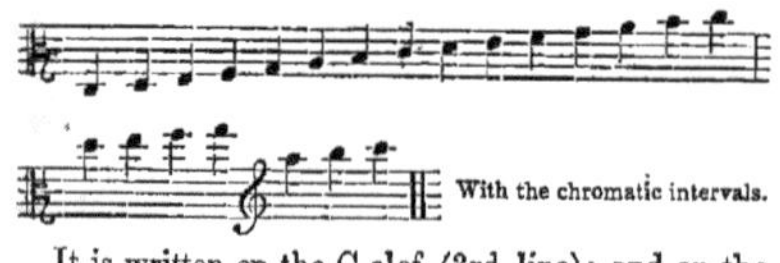

It is written on the C clef (3rd line); and on the G clef, when it extends high.

What has been said in Chapter II. on the subject of shakes, bowing, chords struck together or played arpeggio, harmonics, &c., is throughout applicable to the viola,—considered as a violin a fifth lower.

Of all the instruments in the orchestra, the one whose excellent qualities have been longest misunderstood is the viola. It is no less agile than the violin, the sound of its low strings is peculiarly telling, its upper notes are distinguished by their mournfully passionate accent, and its quality of tone altogether, profoundly melancholy, differs from that of other instruments played with a bow. It has, nevertheless, been long neglected, or put to a use as unimportant as ineffectual,—that of merely doubling the bass part an octave above. Several causes have operated to bring about the unjust treatment of this noble instrument. In the first place, the majority of the composers of the last century, rarely writing four real parts, scarcely knew what to do with it; and when they did not readily find some filling-up notes in the chords for it to play, they hastily wrote the fatal *col Basso*,— sometimes with so much heedlessness, that it produced a doubling in the octave of the basses irreconcilable with the harmony or the melody, or with both one and the other. Moreover, it was unfortunately impossible, at that time, to write anything for the violas of a prominent character, requiring even ordinary skill in execution. Viola-players were always taken from among the refuse of violinists. When a musician found himself incapable of creditably filling the place of violinist, he took refuge among the violas. Hence it arose that the viola performers knew neither how to play the violin nor the viola. It must even be admitted that, at the present time, this prejudice against the viola part is not altogether destroyed; and that there are still, in the best orchestras, many viola-players who are not more proficient on that instrument than on the violin. But the mischief resulting from forbearance towards them is daily becoming more felt; and, little by little, the viola will, like other instruments, be confided only to clever hands. Its quality of tone so strongly attracts and captivates the attention that it is not necessary to have in the orchestra quite so many violas as second violins; and the expressive powers of this quality of tone are so marked, that, on the rare occasions which the old masters afford for its display, it never fails to answer their purpose. Instance the profound impression produced by that movement in the *Iphigenia in Tauride*, where Orestes, overcome with fatigue, panting, oppressed with remorse, grows more tranquil as he repeats: "Composure lulls again my heart!" while the orchestra, deeply agitated, utters sobs and convulsive sighs, attended throughout by the fearful and persevering mutter of the violas. Although, in this unspeakably fine piece of inspiration, there is not a note of voice or instruments without its sublime intention, yet it should be observed that the fascination exercised over the hearers, and the sensation of horror which causes their eyes to dilate and fill with tears, are principally attributable to the viola part, to the quality of its third string, to its syncopated rhythm, and to the strange effect of unison resulting from the syncopation of the A, abruptly broken in the middle by another A in the basses marking a different rhythm:—

No. 7.

Andante.
Iphigenia in Tauride.—GLUCK.
Violins.
Violas.
Orestes.
Basses.
p
p sf
sf sempre
Hautboys.
Com - po - - sure
Le cal - - me
lulls a - gain my heart,
ren - tre dans mon cœur,
my woes at
mes maux ont
length pre - vail To stay Hea - - ven's dis - plea - - sure,
donc lus - sé la co - lè - - re cé - les - - te
My term . . . . to for - mer pain is come,
je tou - - - - che au ter - me du mal - heur

Once more a mo - ment's pause is vouch - saf'd vile O -
vous lais - sez res - pi - rer le par - ri - - ci - de O -
- res - - tes. Heavn's jus - tice, Heavn's . .
- res - - te. Dieux jus - tes, Ciel . . .
. . . ven - geance! Yes, yes, com -
. . . ven - geur! oui, oui, le
po - - - sure lulls a - gain my heart.
cal - - - me ren - - - tre dans mon cœur.

In the overture of *Iphigenia in Aulide*, Gluck has made them sustain alone the lower part of the harmony; not so much, in this case, for the sake of producing an effect arising from the peculiarity of their quality of tone, but in order to accompany as softly as possible the air of the first violins, and to make more impressive the entrance of the basses upon the *forte* after a considerable number of rests. Sacchini has also given the lower part to the violas alone, in the air of Œdipus:—"Your court became my refuge;" without intending, however, to prepare an outburst. On the contrary, the instrumentation here gives to the phrase of melody it accompanies a most delicious calm and freshness. Melodies on the high strings of the viola have a marvellous beauty in scenes of a religious and antique character. Spontini was the first to conceive the idea of assigning the melody to them in several passages of his admirable prayers in the *Vestale*. Méhul, allured by the sympathy existing between the tone of the viola and the dreamy character of Ossianic poetry, constantly availed himself of them, even to the exclusion of the violins, in his opera of *Uthal*. Hence arose what the critics of the time called an intolerable monotony detrimental to the success of the work. It was in reference to this that Grétry exclaimed:—"I'd give a guinea to hear a *first string!*" This quality of the viola,—so choice when it is judiciously employed, and skilfully contrasted with the *timbres* of violins and other instruments,—necessarily soon palls; it is too unvaried, and too much imbued with mournfulness, for any other result. It is not unfrequent, at the present day, to divide the violas into first violas and second violas; and in orchestras like that of the opera, where they are sufficiently numerous, there is no difficulty in writing for them thus; but in others, where there are at most four or five violas, division only serves to diminish the effect of a body already weak in itself, and which the other instruments are ever tending to overwhelm. It should also be remarked that the majority of violas at present used in our French orchestras are far from possessing the requisite degree of power; they have neither the size, nor consequently the strength of tone of veritable violas—being almost violins strung with viola strings. Musical directors should absolutely prohibit the use of these mongrel instruments; the weak sonority of which impairs one of the most interesting parts in the orchestra by depriving it of energy and of its fine depth of tone.

When the violoncellos play the air, it is sometimes excellent to double them in unison by the violas. The tone of the violoncellos then acquires additional roundness and purity, without becoming less predominant. As an example of this, take the theme of the Adagio in Beethoven's C minor Symphony:—

No. 8.

CHAPTER IV.

The Viole d'Amour.

This instrument is rather larger than the viola. It has almost universally fallen into disuse; and were it not for M. Urhan—the only player of the instrument in Paris,—it would be known to us only by name.

It has *seven catgut strings*, the three lowest of which—like the C and G of the viola,—are covered with silver wire. Below the neck of the instrument, and passing beneath the bridge, are seven more strings, *of metal*, tuned in unison with the others, so as to vibrate *sympathetically* with them; thereby giving to the instrument a second resonance, full of sweetness and mystery. It was formerly tuned in several different whimsical ways; but M. Urhan has adopted the following mode of tuning in thirds and fourths,—as the most simple, and the most rational:—

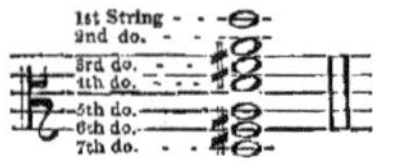

The compass of the viole d'amour is three octaves and a half, at least. It is written—like the viola,—on two clefs:—

It may be seen, from the arrangement of its strings, that the viole d'amour is peculiarly appropriate to chords of three, four, or more notes, whether played arpeggio, or struck, or sustained; and above all to melodies of double notes. Only it is evident that in designing *harmonies* for this instrument, a different plan must be pursued from that employed for violins, violas, and violoncellos, which are tuned by fifths; and that care must be taken in general to avoid the notes of chords beyond a third or fourth, unless the lower string be an open string. Thus, the A of the second octave gives every latitude to the high D, to extend its scale above itself:—

It is needless to observe that the chords of the minor third and the second—

are impracticable below, since the sounds that constitute them are necessarily on the D string. A moment's reflection shows similar impossibilities on the lowest string of all instruments played with a bow.

Harmonics have an admirable effect on the viole d'amour. They are obtained precisely in the same way as those of the violin and viola; excepting that its seven open strings, being disposed as a common chord, give the viole d'amour great facility in producing with rapidity the arpeggios of its chord of D major, in the octave and double octave above; those of the chord of A major in the twelfth above; and those of the chord of F♯ major in the seventeenth above:—

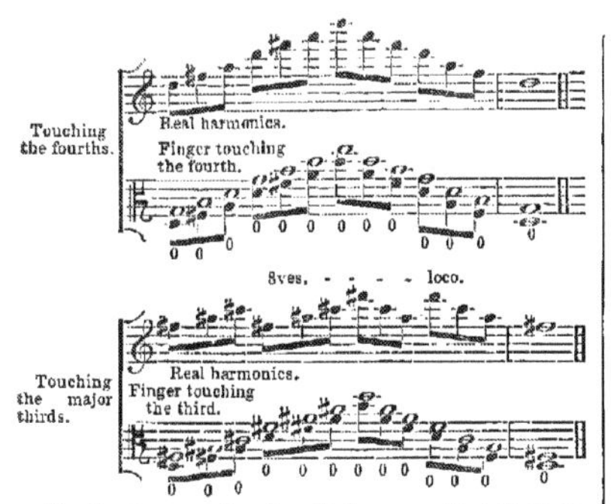

By these examples it will be seen that if it be proposed to use the charming arpeggios of the viole d'amour, the keys of D, G, A, F♯, or B♮, are those which will best allow of so doing. As these three chords would doubtless not suffice for accompanying unintermittingly an air somewhat modulated, there is no reason why a set of violes d'amour should not be had, tuned in a different way: in C, for example; or in D♭; according to the chords required by the composer for his piece. The extreme charm of these arpeggio harmonics on the open strings quite deserve that every pains should be taken to render them available.

The quality of the viole d'amour is faint and sweet; there is something *seraphic* in it,—partaking at once of the viola, and of the harmonics of the violin. It is peculiarly suitable to the legato style, to dreamy melodies, and to the expression of ecstatic or religious feelings. Mons. Meyerbeer has felicitously introduced it in Raoul's Romance, in the first act of the *Huguenots*:—

No. 9.

But this is merely a solo effect. What would not be that, in an andante, of a mass of violes d'amour playing a fine prayer in several parts, or accompanying with their sustained harmonics a melody of violas, or violoncellos, or corni inglesi, or of a horn, or a flute in its middle part, mingled with harp arpeggios! It would really be a great pity to allow this choice instrument to become lost; and any violinist might learn to play upon it by a few weeks' practice.

CHAPTER V.

The Violoncello.

Its four strings are tuned in fifths, and precisely an octave lower than the four strings of the viola :—

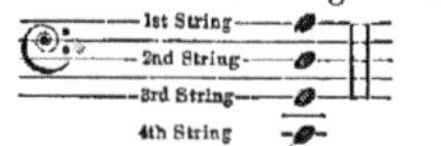

Its compass may be, even in the orchestra, three octaves and a half :—

The great performers go still higher; but, in general, these extreme upper notes—which have no beauty excepting in the conclusion of slow passages—are seldom given in natural sounds; they are mostly taken in harmonics, which are produced more easily, and are of better quality. It may not be amiss, before going farther, to warn the reader of the double sense given to the G clef in violoncello music. When it is written from the commencement of a piece, or immediately after the F clef, it presents to the eye the octave above the real sounds :—

It has its full value only when succeeding the C clef (on the fourth line); in which case it represents the real sounds, and not their octave above :—

This custom, which there is nothing to justify, leads to errors the more frequent because certain violoncellists refuse to conform to it, and choose to receive the G clef in its true acceptation. In order to avoid all misconception, it will be here employed only after the C clef, and when that clef would lead us too far beyond the stave; the G clef will then always represent the real sounds, as in the preceding example.

That which has been said respecting double strings, arpeggios, shakes, and the bowing of the violin, applies equally to the violoncello. It should, however, never be lost sight of, that the violoncello strings, being longer than those of the violin, demand a wider extension of the fingers of the left hand: whence it follows that passages of tenths on a double string, practicable on the violin and viola, are not so on the violoncello; and that an isolated tenth cannot be struck, unless the lower note is on an open string.

The following tenths would be impossible :—

The violoncello, on account of the depth of its *timbre* and the thickness of its strings, is not susceptible of the extreme agility belonging to the violin and viola. As to the natural and artificial harmonics —of which frequent use is made on the violoncello in solo passages,—they are obtained by the same means as those of the violin and viola. The length of its strings even contributes to render the extreme upper notes in harmonics, which are produced near the bridge, much more easy and more beautiful than those of the violin. Here is a table of those which are best obtained from each string :—

The best way of obtaining artifical harmonics is that which consists in touching the fourth, while the first finger or thumb, strongly *pressed*, forms the factitious movable nut :—

This fingering is almost the only one practicable on the violoncello; the position of the *fifth touched* could hardly be used, excepting in the upper part of the string, because the distances and the proportions becoming much smaller than in the lower, and the extension of the left hand proportionably less, they then allow of the fifth being touched with the fourth finger, while the thumb serves for the nut.

(The sign ♁ indicates that the thumb is to be placed transversely across the strings.)

Scale of natural and artificial harmonics :—

Harmonies in harmonics on the violoncello would doubtless have a charming effect in the orchestra with soft and slow music; nevertheless, it is easier, and consequently less hazardous, to obtain the same result by means of divided violins playing high on the first string *with sordines*. These two qualities of tone resemble each other so closely as to be almost undistinguishable.

Example of harmonics :—

The same passage reproduced exactly, and more easily, in usual sounds, by violins :—

In the orchestra the part of the double-bass is ordinarily given to violoncellos, which they double an octave above or in unison: but there are many instances when it is advisable to separate them, either to let them play, on the high strings, a melody or melodious phrase; or to take advantage of their peculiar sonorousness on an open string for producing an effect of special harmony, by writing their part *below* the double-basses; or, lastly, to assign them a part nearly like that of the double-basses, but giving them more rapid notes, which the latter could not well execute :—

Here the part of the violoncellos, more agitated and turbulent in its movement, has nevertheless nearly the same notes as that of the double basses, the design of which it follows almost throughout. In the following example, on the contrary, the violoncellos are entirely distinct from the double-basses, and go beneath them, in order to obtain the tremendous conflict of the minor second below, and at the same time the rough vibration of the C—the fourth open string of the violoncello—while the double basses grind out against the high octave of this C, the B♮, which they take forcibly on their first string :—

No. 10.

Requiem.—BERLIOZ.
Flutes.
Hautboys.
Clarinets in A.
Bassoons.
Horns in E♮.
Horns in D.
Horns in A♮ high.
Horns in C.
Violins.
Violas.
Sopranos.
Flam - - - mis a - - - - - cri - bus a - - -
Tenors.
Flam - - - mis a - - - - - cri - bus a - - -
Basses.
Flam - - - mis a - - - - - cri - bus a - - -
Violoncellos.
Double string.
Double-basses.

The composer should never without an excellent reason—that is to say, without being sure of producing thereby a very marked effect — entirely separate the violoncellos from the double-basses; nor even write them, as many have done, a double octave above. Such procedure has the result of considerably weakening the sonority of the fundamental notes of the harmony. The bass part, thus forsaken by the violoncellos, becomes dull, bald, extremely heavy, and ill-connected with the upper parts, which are held at too great distance by the extreme depth of tone of the double-basses. When it is required to produce a very soft harmony of stringed instruments, it is, on the contrary, often well to give the bass to the violoncellos, omitting the double-basses, as Weber has done, in the accompaniment to the *Andante* of Agatha's sublime air in the second act of the *Freyschutz*. It is worthy of remark, in this example, that the violas alone supply the bass beneath a harmony of violins in four parts; the violoncellos only coming in, a little later, to double the violas:—

No. 11.

Andante.
Adagio.
Der Freyschütz.—WEBER.
Flutes.
Oboes.
Clarinets.
Bassoons.
Violins.
Divisi. con sordini.
Divisi. con sordini.
Viola.
AGATHA.
Oh love - - - - ly night
Ray - on - - - - ne aux Cieux
Soft - ly sighs the
Ma pri - è - re
Basses.
cres.
voice of ev' - ning, steal - ing thro' yon wil - low grove, While the
prends des ai - les vers les sphères e - ter - nel - les ô pha -

stars, like guar - di - an spi - rits, Set their night - ly watch a - bove

- lan - ges im - - mor - tel - les ê - - le - vez ma voix au Roi des Rois.

Thro' the dark blue vault of æther Silence reigns with soothing pow'r But a storm o'er yonder mountain, Darkly

Quel beau ciel et que d'étoi-les dans les vou - tes de l'a-zur mais quoi sous de sombres voi-les l'hori -

Violoncellos together, to the number of eight or ten, are essentially melodious; their *timbre*, on the upper strings, is one of the most expressive in the orchestra. Nothing is more voluptuously melancholy, or more suited to the utterance of tender, languishing themes, than a mass of violoncellos playing in unison upon the *first string*. They are also excellent for airs of a religious character; and the composer ought, in such a case, to select the strings upon which the phrase should be executed. The two lower strings, C and G, especially in keys which permit the use of them as *open strings*, are of a smooth and deep sonorousness, perfectly appropriate; but their depth scarcely ever permits of giving them any other than basses more or less melodious—the actual airs being reserved for the upper strings. Weber, in the Overture to *Oberon*, has, with rare felicity, caused the violoncellos to *sing* above; while the two clarinets in A, in unison, make their lower notes heard beneath them. The effect is both new and striking:—

No. 12.

Although our violoncello-players of the present day are very skilful, and well able to execute all sorts of difficulties, yet it is seldom that rapid passages of violoncellos do not produce some confusion in the lower part. As for those which require the use of the thumb, and lie among the higher notes, there is less to be expected; they are not very sonorous, and are always of dubious precision. In modern orchestras of large resources, where the violoncellos are numerous, they are frequently divided into firsts and seconds; the firsts executing a special part of melody or harmony, and the seconds doubling the double-basses, either in octave or in unison. Sometimes even, for accompaniments of a melancholy, veiled, and mysterious character, the bass is left to the double-basses alone, while above them are designed two different parts for the violoncellos, which, joining the viola part, give a low four-part harmony. This method is rarely well-contrived; and care should be taken not to misuse it.

No. 13.
Romeo and Juliet.—(Berlioz.)
Adagio.
Flutes.
Corno Inglese.
Clarinets in A.
Violins.
Violas. con Sordini.
1st Violoncellos. con Sordini.
2nd Violoncellos. con Sordini.
Double-basses.
Solo.
Expr.
Pizz.
1st and 2nd Bassoons.
3rd and 4th Bassoons
1st Horn in E♭.
2nd Horn in F.
3rd Horn in A♭, high.

The tremolo in *double string*, and *forte* arpeggios, suit violoncellos perfectly; they add greatly to the richness of the harmony, and augment the general sonority of the orchestra. Rossini, in the introduction of the overture to *Guillaume Tell*, has written a quintet for five *solo* violoncellos, accompanied in pizzicato by the other violoncellos, divided into firsts and seconds. These deep-toned *timbres*, all of the same kind, are there of excellent effect; and serve to make still more impressive the brilliant orchestration of the succeeding Allegro.

The *pizzicato* of the violoncello cannot have much rapidity, and the means proposed for improving the execution of that of violins cannot avail in this case, owing to the thickness and tension of the strings, and to their too great elevation above the finger-board of the instrument. According to the procedure generally in use, players seldom exceed, in pizzicato, the rapidity of *eight quavers* in a bar in two-time (Allegro non troppo), or that of *twelve semiquavers*, arpeggio, in a $\frac{6}{8}$ bar (Andantino).

CHAPTER VI.

Double-basses.

There are two kinds; those with three, and those with four strings. Those with three strings are tuned in fifths:—

Those with four, are tuned in fourths:—

The sound of both is an octave lower than the note written. Their compass in the orchestra is two octaves and a quarter; allowing, for three-stringed double-basses, two notes less below.

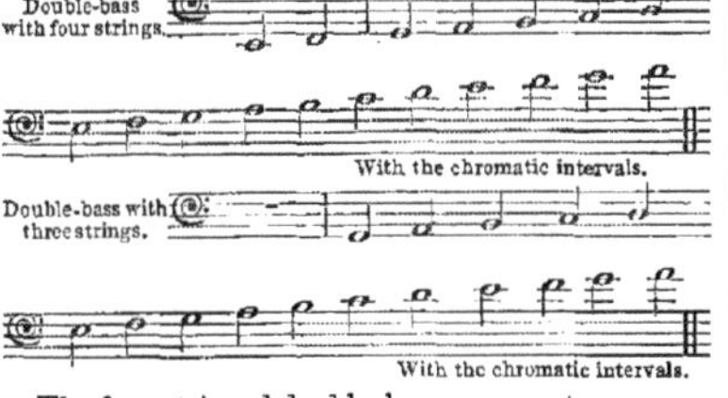

The four-stringed double-bass appears to me preferable to the other: first, on account of facility in execution,—tuning in fourths not compelling the performer to *shift* in playing the scale; and next, because of the great utility of the three low sounds, E, F, and F♯, which are wanting in double-basses tuned in fifths, and the absence of which frequently disturbs the order of the best-designed bass passages by enforcing for these notes an ungraceful and unseasonable transposition above. These observations are especially applicable to English double-basses; which, although tuned in fourths, have, nevertheless, only three strings, A, D, G:—

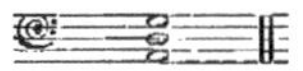

In a well-constituted orchestra there should be several four-string double-basses, tuned in thirds and fifths:—

Thus there would be—the other double-basses tuning in fourths—an increase of open strings and of sonority.

To double-basses belong, in the orchestra, the lowest sounds of the harmony. In a preceding chapter it has been shown in what cases they may be separated from the violoncellos. The defect which arises for the basses out of this disposal may be amended to a certain extent by doubling them, in octave or in unison, with the bassoons, the corni di bassetto, the bass clarinets, or the ordinary clarinets in the extreme lower notes. But, for my part, I detest the use which certain musicians make on such occasions of trombones and ophicleides—the quality of tone of which, having neither sympathy nor analogy with that of double-basses, of course mixes very badly with it. There are cases where the harmonics of the double-basses may be successfully introduced. The extreme tension of the string, their length and distance from the finger-board, do not permit, however, of having recourse to artificial harmonics. Natural harmonics come out very well, particularly commencing from the first octave, occupying the middle of the string; they are the same, in the octave below, as those of violoncellos. Strictly speaking, chords and arpeggios may be used on the double-bass; but it must be by giving them two or three notes at the utmost, of which one only should be fingered.

The *intermittent tremolo* may easily be obtained, thanks to the elasticity of the bow, which causes it to re-bound several times on the strings, when a single blow is somewhat sharply struck.

This does not hold good in the following passage; which is only rendered *p* by means of the *continuous tremolo*, with some trouble, and by striking the strings with the end of the bow, which lacks force, and brings out little tone.

Allegro moderato.

The *continuous tremolo* of double-basses, rather less close than this last, is nevertheless of excellent dramatic effect, and nothing gives a more menacing aspect to the orchestra; but it should not last too long, since the fatigue it occasions the performers *who are willing to take the trouble* of doing it well soon renders it impossible. When it is needful thus to disturb the depths of an orchestra during a long passage, the best way is to divide the double-basses, not giving them a real *tremolo*, but merely quick repercussions, mutually disagreeing as rhythmical values, while the violoncellos execute the true *tremolo* :—

The semiquavers meeting only at the comencement of each accented part of the bar with the quavers in triplets of the other part, produce a dull murmur something like the *tremolo*, which is thus tolerably well supplied. On many occasions, these different rhythms, thus heard together, are even preferable. Rapid diatonic groups of four or five notes have frequently an admirable effect, and are readily executed, provided the passage contain at least one open string :—

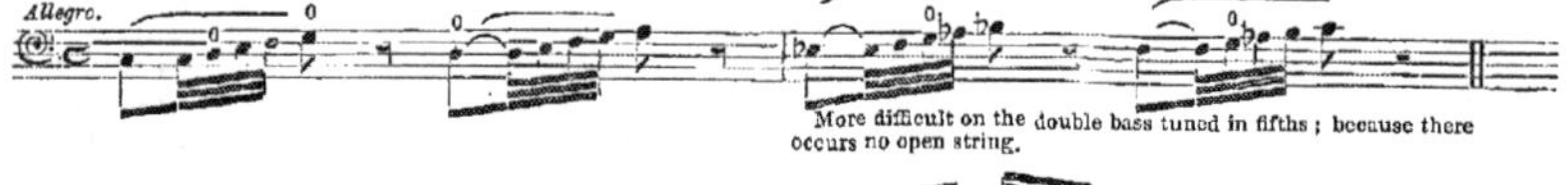

If a long rapid passage be absolutely requisite for the double-basses, the best way is to divide them, and apply the dispersing process recommended for violins; at the same time, taking great care not to remove the first double-basses from the seconds.

Some are so injudicious, now-a-days, as to write, for the heaviest of all instruments, passages of such rapidity that violoncellos themselves would find difficulty in executing them. Whence results a serious inconvenience: lazy or incapable double-bass players, dismayed by such difficulties, give them up at the first glance, and set themselves to *simplifying* the passage; but this simplifying of some, not being that of others,—since they have not all the same ideas upon the harmonic importance of the various notes contained in the passage,—there ensues a horrible disorder and confusion. This buzzing chaos, full of strange noises and hideous grumblings, is completed and heightened by the other double-bass players, who, either more zealous or more confident of ability, toil away in ineffectual efforts at executing the passage just as it is written. Composers should therefore take care to ask of double-basses no more than possible things; of which the good execution shall not be doubtful. It is enough to say that the old system of simplifying double-bass passages—a system generally adopted in the ancient instrumental school, and of which the danger has just been demonstrated—is at present utterly renounced. If the author have written no other than passages suitable to the instrument, the performer must play them, nothing more, and nothing less. When the blame lies with the composer, it is he and the audience who take the consequences; the performer being no longer responsible.

Flights of little notes, before large ones:—

are executed by sliding rapidly on the string, without paying attention to the precision of any of the intermediate sounds; and have an extremely good effect. The furious shock given to the whole orchestra by the double-basses coming upon the high F, by four little preceding notes, B, C, D, E, in the infernal scene in *Orfeo*, on the words, "At the dire howling of Cerberus," is well known. This hoarse barking,—one of the finest inspirations of Gluck,—is rendered the more terrible, by the author having placed it on the third inversion of the chord of the diminished seventh (F, G♯, B, D); and, for the sake of giving his idea all the effect and vehemence possible, he has doubled the double-basses in the octave, not only with the violoncellos, but with the violas, and the entire mass of violins:—

Beethoven, also, has availed himself of these scarcely articulate notes; but (contrary to the previous example), by accenting the first note of the group more than the last. He has done so in a passage of the Storm in the Pastoral Symphony; which so well depicts the raging of a violent wind and rain, and the muffled rumblings of the gust. It is to be observed that Beethoven, in this example, and in many other passages, has given to the double-basses deep notes, beyond their power of executing, which leads to the supposition that the orchestra written for possessed double-basses descending as low as the C, an octave below the violoncello C. Such instruments are no longer to be found.

No. 15.

Allegro. Met. 𝅗𝅥 = 80.
Pastoral Symphony.
BEETHOVEN.
Flutes.
Hautboys.
Clarinets in B♭.
Horns in F.
Trumpets in E♭.
Bassoons.
Kettle-drums in F.
Violins.
Violas.
Violoncellos.
Double-basses.
pp
sf
fp
p
cres.
f

f f fp
f Più. f fp
Più. f
f Più f fp
f
p
Più. f
sf f
f fp
f Più. f fp
f Più. f
f Più. f
pp
pp pp
pp

Sometimes it has a fine and dramatic effect to give the violoncellos the real bass, or, at least, the notes which determine the chords and mark the accented parts of the bar: while beneath them, the double-bass has an isolated part, the design of which, interrupted by rests, allows the harmony to rest upon the violoncellos. Beethoven, in the admirable scene of *Fidelio*, where Leonora and the jailer dig Florestan's grave, has displayed all the pathetic and gloomy sadness of this mode of instrumentation. He has, however, given in this case the real bass to the double-basses:—

No. 16.

Fidelio.—BEETHOVEN.

Andante con moto. Imo.

Hautboys. pp

Clarinets in D. pp

Bassoons. pp

Horns in C. pp

Tenor Trombone pp

Bass Trombone. pp

Double Bassoon. Col Contra-Basso.

1st Violins with sordine. pp

2nd Violins with sordine. pp

Violas with sordine. pp *divisi.*

Violoncellos. pp

Contra-basso.

fp
fp
fp
fp
fp
fp
fp
fp
fp
fp
fp
fp
fp
fp
sf p
sf p
sf p
sf p
sf p
sf p
sf p
fp
fp
fp
fp
fp

pp
pp
pp
pp
pp
pp
pp
decres.
pp
decres.
pp
Rocco.
Come dig away, for time flies quick - ly, the go-venor will soon be
Ne tardons point travaillons vi - te, le gouverneur bientôt vien -
decres.
pp

LEONORA.
Your zea - lous toil should well con -
Du zèle ar - dent qui nous a -
here; . . . . come dig a - way, The governor will soon be here.
- dra . . . . le gouver - neur, le gou-verneur bien -tôt vien-dra.
pizz.
pizz.
pp

cres.
Col. C. B.
-tent him; my wil - ling aid you shall not lack.
- gi - te sans doute un jour il vous paie - ra.
Come dig a-way, for time flies quickly, the go-ver -
ne tardons point travaillons vi - te le gou-ver -
Arco.
D

Your zea-lous toil should well con - tent him; My will-ing aid you shall not
Du zèle ar - dent qui vous a - gi - te sans doute un jour il vous paie -
- nor . . . will soon be here.
- neur . . . bien tôt viendra.
Pizz.
Pizz.

pp
pp
Col. C. B.
lack.
- ra.
Quick here your hand, to help me lift this bur - den.
Viens donc m'ai - der en-le-vons cet - te pier - re
Arco.
Arco.

cres.
cres.
cres.
cres.
fp
fp
fp
f
my fa - ther, my
mon pè - re, mon
'tis well,
fort bien,
'tis well.
fort bien,
Do not give way!
soutiens la bien
cres.
fp

cres.
fp
p
fa - ther, I'll do my best to give as-sist - ance. It moves!
pè - re est - ce bien là ce qu'il faut fai - re voy - ons
push steadily. 'Tis
ren - ver - se fort

One effort more
en - co - re
Ah! what a load!
ah quel fardeau
Ah! what a load
fort bien, fort bien.
welt.
bien.
Do not give way.
soutiens la bien
'Tis done at last.
je la sou-tiens.

With the view of expressing a lugubrious silence, I have in a cantata divided the double-basses into four parts; causing them thus to sustain long pianissimo chords, beneath a decrescendo of all the rest of the orchestra.

No. 17.

The 5th of May, or, the Emperor's death.—BERLIOZ.

Un peu retenu.
Unis. sf p
Unis.
p Coups de canon lointain.
Cannon in the distance.
He is dead! He! O glo - ry, lone - ly wi - dow;
lui mourir! lui! O gloi - re quel veu - va - ge;
He is dead! He O glo - ry, lone - ly wi - dow!
lui mourir! lui! O gloi - re quel veu - va - ge!

Unis.
poco sf p
poco p
sf p
poco sf p
p
pp
around I see, around I see, tears e'en from e - ne - mies.
au-tour de moi autour de moi, pleu - rent ses en - ne - mis.

Imo Solo.
ppp
Imo Solo.
ppp
Dim. sempre.
Dim. sempre.
Sotto voce.
pp
Far from that rock
let us hurry in si - lence;
star of the day,
cease to shine in the
Loin de ce roc
nous fuyons en si - len - ce,
l'astre du jour,
abandon - ne les

ppp
ppp
Put on sordini.
Put on sordini.
Double string.
Put on sordini.
sky,
Cieux,
Star of the day,
l'astre du jour
cease to shine in
a-ban - don - ne
the sky.
les Cieux.
sotto voce.
ppp
Ah!
Ah!
sotto voce.
ppp
Ah! . . . .
Ah! . . . .
sotto voce.
ppp
Ah! . . .
Ah! . . .
Double string.
ppp
Put on sordini.

The pizzicato of double-basses, either loud or soft, is of good sonority, unless it be employed on very high sounds; but it changes character according to the harmonies beneath which it occurs. Thus, the famous pizzicato *A*, in the overture to *Freyschutz*, is big with threats and infernal accents, only because of the reflex of the chord of the diminished seventh, (F♯, A, C, E♭,) the first inversion of which it resolves on the unaccented part of the bar. Let it become the major tonic, or dominant, produced mezzo-forte, as in the case in question, and this *A* would no longer have anything strange in its effect. Sordines are employed on double-basses, as on other instruments played with a bow; bnt the effect they produce is little marked: they only diminish somewhat the sonority of double-basses by rendering it more gloomy and vague. A Piedmontese artist, M. Langlois, who played in Paris about fifteen years ago, obtained with the bow, by pinching the high string of the double-bass between the thumb and forefinger of the left hand, instead of pressing it on the finger-board, and by rising thus, nearly to the bridge, high sounds of singular acuteness, and incredible power. If there were need to introduce in the orchestra, a loud female cry, no instrument could better utter it than double-basses employed in this way. I doubt whether our artists are acquainted with M. Langlois' method of producing acute sounds; but they would soon be able to make themselves familiar with it.

Stringed Instruments played with the hand.

The Harp.

This instrument is essentially anti-chromatic; that is to say, successions by half-tones are almost impossible to it. The reason of this will be presently stated. Its compass was formerly but five octaves and a sixth:—

This scale, it will be seen, belongs to the key of E♭; and in this key all harps were tuned, when the skilful manufacturer Erard, seeking to remedy the inconveniences of the system, invented the mechanism which removed them, and proposed tuning the harp in C♭; a course adopted by all harp players of the present day. The chromatic intervals can be obtained on the ancient harp only by means of seven pedals, put in motion by the player, and fixed *one after the other* with the foot, each of which heightens by half a tone the note to which its mechanism applies, but throughout the extent of the scale, and not singly. Thus the F♯ pedal cannot sharpen an F, without sharpening all the other Fs in the scale by the same action. Hence it results, that every chromatic scale (unless in an excessively slow movement), every progression of chords proceeding chromatically, or belonging to different keys, the majority of florid passages containing appoggiaturas with accidentals, or small chromatic notes, are all impracticable, or, at best, extremely difficult, and detestably ugly. There are even, on the harp in E♭, three chords of seventh major, and three chords of ninth major, totally impossible to play; and which ought therefore to be banished from the composer's store of harmonies. These are they:—

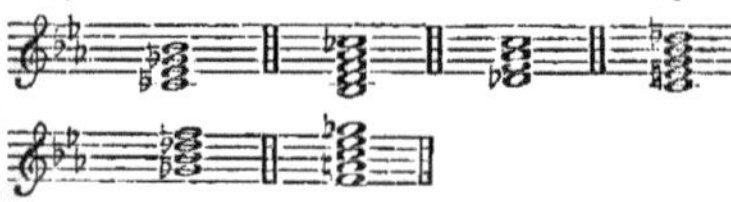

It is, in fact, evident that every chord in which C♭ is to be heard simultaneously with B♭, cannot be possible; since (the harp being tuned in E♭, and the pedals raising each string only a half-tone) C♭ can only be produced by taking the B♮ pedal, which immediately destroys all the B♭s in the scale. The same is the case with the D♭, which results from raising the C♮; and with the G♭, produced by the raising of the F. The mechanism of the pedals of the harp in E♭, only serving to restore the three flattened notes (B, E, A) to their natural state, and to sharpen four other notes (F, C, G, D), it follows, that this harp can only be prepared in eight keys; namely, E♭, B♭, F, C, G, D, A, E. The flattened keys are only produced in harmonics, and by taking and leaving quickly one or more pedals. In A♭, for instance, the D♭ is only the harmonic of C♯; and the player should quit this C♯ pedal immediately he has taken it; otherwise, he will not be able to make the C♮ heard,—the major third of the key in which he is playing: and moreover, he must skip a string (D♮) when ascending diatonically, which is so inconvenient, that the use of such scales may be considered impracticable:—

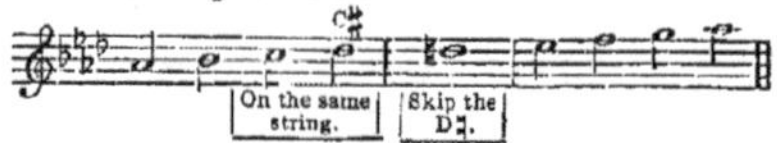

This inconvenience and difficulty are doubled in D♭ and in G♭—both keys nearly inaccessible, except for certain chords. Again, the key of G♭, like that of C♭, presents another difficulty, —that of compelling the player to an actual transposition for some notes of his scale, since he must strike the F♯ string when the written note is G♭; the B♮ string when the note is C♭; and the C♯ string when the note is D♭. As for the key of C♭, it becomes more practicable if written in its other form,—that of B♮; but all the pedals being taken, there still remains to be overcome in this scale (as in that of A♭) the horrible difficulty of skipping a string, and of quitting a pedal to retake it again, for the leading note (in harmonic) and the tonic, which occur upon the same string:—

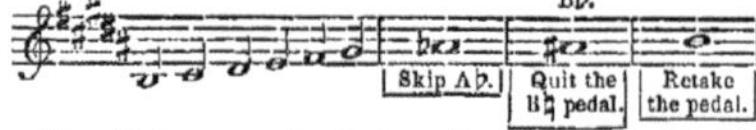

It will be perceived that, for the execution of a chromatic scale of two octaves' extent like this—

it is necessary to put in action five pedals, rapidly and in succession, for the first octave only; and also that they must all be very promptly quitted, in order to replace in their primitive condition those notes which they raised, and which are to recur in the upper octave, to be again retaken as in the first octave. Such a scale therefore, even in a movement of moderate time, is impossible for *any harp.* If the object be a succession of chords belonging to different keys, the impossibility becomes still more evident; because, in that case, several pedals will have to be taken at once and successively:—

Certain appoggiaturas and ornaments containing chromatic successions, may, in fact, be executed after a fashion: but the majority of these ornaments, as I have already observed, are scarcely practicable; and those which form the exceptions produce a very indifferent effect, on account of the influence which the movement of the pedal taken and quitted at the same instant, exercises over the sonority of the string :—

The following example, on the contrary, and all those, which, like it, contain several semitones in a short space, and in a quick movement, are next to impossible :—

It should now be stated that the harp, being played with two hands, is written for upon two lines. The lower line usually has the F clef and the upper one the G clef; but if the height of the bass notes or the depth of the treble notes demand it, the G clef or the F clef may find themselves on the two lines at one and the same time.

It will be seen that this disposal renders the inexecutable passages still more numerous for the harp in B♭; since a passage that may be easy for the right hand becomes impossible if the left hand wish to strike certain notes of accompaniment which are altered by a pedal in the melody, while the harmony admits of them only in their ordinary condition :—

The two chords marked with a cross cannot be played; since they contain an F♮, sharpened in the upper part. In such a case, therefore, the note which thus presents itself under a double aspect, must be suppressed in one or other of the parts. In the preceding example, it is better to mutilate the chord in the left hand, and leave out the F♮.

When a melody already played by other instruments is to be repeated on the harp, and contains chromatic passages either impossible or hazardous, it should be dexterously modified, by substituting for one or more of the altered notes, other notes comprised in the harmony. Thus, instead of giving to the harp the following air, as previously played by the violins

the author should have written it in the following manner :—

The nature of the harp's mechanism requires the sacrifice of the four successive semitones in the third bar.

Struck with the important obstacles just cited, M. Erard invented, some years ago, the mechanism which has given to instruments so constructed the name of *double-action* harps. Of what it consists, and wherefore it allows the harp, if not to play chromatic successions, at least to play in all keys, and to strike or arpeggio all chords, I will now show.

The double-action harp is tuned in C♭, and its compass is six octaves and a quarter :—

The seven pedals with which it is furnished are made so that the player may, by means of each of them, raise at option each string a tone, or a semitone only. By taking in succession the seven semitone pedals, the harp in C♭ can therefore be set in G♭, in D♭, in A♭, in E♭, in B♭, in F, or in C♮. In still farther raising each string another semitone, by means of the second action of the pedals, the seven notes of the natural scale will become sharpened; since the seven pedals produce F♯, C♯, G♯, D♯, A♯, E♯, and B♯, which gives to the harp the power of playing in the keys of G, D, E, B, F♯, and C♯.

These, then, are all the keys accessible to the harp; only, the minor scales cannot be *set*, unless by treating them, in ascending as in descending, without regarding the usage adopted with respect to the sixth and seventh notes; otherwise, two pedals must be taken and quitted :—

By adopting the interval of the augmented second between the sixth and seventh note, the minor scale can be set, and the accidental use of the pedals will not be necessary; which is a considerable advantage, and should suffice to make this scale preferred :—

As for the chords interdicted to the harp in E♭, it will be seen that the double action renders them possible.

Nothing is more easy than to produce  these four notes being in the scale of the harp in C♭.

The chord, 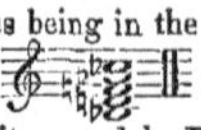 merely requires the use of the two semitone pedals, D♮ and F♮;  wants only two also, F♮ and C♮;  must have three, C♮, E♮, and G♮;  need have but one, F♮; and 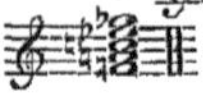 requires three, F♮, A♮, and C♮.

All this is done without difficulty. Even the chord which seems to contain at once C♮ and C♭, is equally practicable :—

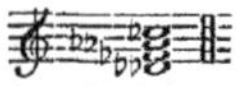

The D♭♭ (or C♮) is gained by means of the pedal raising the C♭ a semitone, and the C♭ is produced by the pedal which raises the B♭ a semitone. The A♭♭ comes from the G♭ raised a semitone, and the F♭ has no need of a pedal, being in the scale of the harp in C♭. This chord, such as I have just written it, will therefore be played under this singular form :— 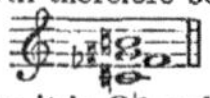 wherefore, it would be better to write it in C♮ major, and under the following aspect :— 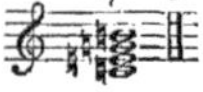 If double-action harps have to be employed in an orchestral piece set for other instruments in B♮ major, it would be much better for sonority and convenience of execution to write their music in the key of C♭ :—

Composers should have a care, in writing harp parts, to forewarn the player, a little in advance, of the change he will have to make, and of the pedal soon to be used, by placing, a few bars before the occurrence of the modulation, such words as :— *Prepare the G♯, prepare the key of C♮, &c.*

The nature of the instrument having been explained, we proceed now to the fingering, confounded by many composers with that of the pianoforte, which it nowise resembles. Chords of four notes may be struck with each hand if the two extreme notes do not extend beyond an octave :—

Also, by a great stretch of the thumb and little finger, chords of a tenth may be reached; and consequently, such chords as these are possible :—

But this position is less convenient, less natural, and therefore less sonorous; since none of the fingers can attack the string with as much force as in the ordinary position. Incidentally, let us note that chords lying in the extreme lower part of the instrument, form groups without sonorousness, and produce confused harmonies that should be avoided :—  These deep sounds are only fit for doubling a bass in the octave below :—

The successive execution of the notes of a chord, either ascending or descending, is perfectly in the character of the harp; it is even after its Italian name, *arpa*, that these passages have obtained the title of *arpeggios*. Generally speaking, they should not exceed an octave in extent; particularly, if the movement be quick; otherwise, they would necessitate a change of position of extreme difficulty.

The note which exceeds the extent of an octave should never be written but for the termination of a phrase; as thus :—

The following is very easy; because the change of position, occurring from below to above, does not require the use of the fourth finger, which can be little employed, nor does it demand two consecutive notes with the third :—

Care should be taken, in general, not to write for the hands too near together, but to keep them separated by an octave or a sixth at least, otherwise they interfere with each other.

Moreover, if the two hands play an arpeggio chord in thirds with each other, the same string being retaken by the finger of one hand, at the moment when that of the other hand has just played it, it necessarily follows that the string has not time to vibrate, and that its sound is stifled as soon as born :—

All successions which oblige the same fingers to skip from one string to another can only be written for a movement in very moderate time.

When a rapid series of diatonic octaves is desired, they should generally be written for the two hands. This equally applies to series of sixths. They are always—as with scales in thirds—practicable for a single hand, but only in descending; the thumb then sliding from one to the other of the upper notes, while the lower notes are played by the three fingers.

As an exception to what has been said above respecting the distance between the parts, these same scales in thirds are practicable for two hands, because, in the diatonic movement, the inconvenience of a string taken by one finger and retaken by another is much less great, since the intermediate note allows a little more time for vibration. Nevertheless, it is better either to write these series of thirds for two harps, by giving the higher part to one and the lower part to another; or, if there be but one harp, and much sound is wished to be obtained, by separating the parts an octave, and writing series of tenths.

If the object be to make heard a rapid ascending or descending arpeggio of greater extent than an octave, instead of writing it in two parts it should be dispersed by giving a fragment to one hand while the other changes its position, and so on, reciprocally. The passage would then appear thus :—

If doubled in the octave, it would be impracticable.

The following is impossible in a quick movement; but possible in a slow one :—

The shake can be executed on the harp, but its effect is only tolerable on the high notes. The *iteration* of the same note—unpleasant and difficult upon ancient harps, on account of the slight grating produced upon the string by the second finger, which strikes it after the first, and interrupts its vibration :—

is easy, and of good effect, upon modern harps; the double action of the pedals allowing the player to raise by a tone the next string to the one which gives the iterated sound, so that the iteration is thus produced on two strings in unison :—

Iteration in two or four parts (very useful sometimes in the orchestra) may likewise be obtained, and more simply, by employing two or more harps, and by writing *cross fires*, which present no difficulty in the execution, and produce precisely the desired effect:—

Result to the hearer :—

The effect of harps (setting aside the question of music intended to be heard near, as in a private room) is in proportion to their number. The notes, the chords, or the arpeggios which they then throw out amidst the orchestra and choir are of extreme splendour. Nothing can be more in keeping with ideas of poetic festivities, or religious rites, than the sound of a large body of harps ingeniously introduced. Alone, or in groups of two, three, or four, they have also a most happy effect, whether united to the orchestra, or serving to accompany voices and solo instruments. Of all known qualities of tone, it is singular that the *timbre* of horns, trombones, and brass instruments generally, mingles best with theirs. The lower strings (exclusive of the soft and dull strings which are lowest), with their sound so veiled, mysterious, and beautiful, have scarcely ever been employed but for bass accompaniments of the left hand; and the more the pity. It is true that harp-players do not care to play long pieces among octaves so far removed from the body of the performer that he must lean forward, with his arms at full length, maintaining an awkward posture for more or less time; but this reason can have had little weight with composers. The fact is, they have not thought to avail themselves of the especial quality in tone just indicated.

Example of a beautiful and soft sonority of the bass strings:—

The strings of the last upper octave have a delicate crystalline sound, of voluptuous freshness, which renders them fit for the expression of graceful fairy-like ideas, and for giving murmuring utterance to the sweetest secrets of smiling melodies; on condition, however, that they are not attacked with violence by the performer; as then they yield a dry hard sound, similar to that of broken glass,—disagreeable and snapping.

The *harmonics* of the harp—particularly of many harps in unison—are still more magical. Solo-players frequently employ them in the pedal-points and cadences of their fantansies, variations, and concertos. But nothing comes near the sonority of these mysterious notes when united to chords from flutes and clarinets playing in the medium. It is really strange, that only once,—and that not more than three years ago,—the affinity of these qualities, and the poetry of their association, should have been demonstrated.*

The best, and almost the only, harmonics for the harp, are those obtained by touching with the lower and fleshy part of the palm of the hand the centre of the string, while playing with the thumb and two first fingers of the same hand; thus producing the high octave of the usual sound. Harmonics may be produced by both hands.

It is even possible to produce two or three at a time, with one hand; but then, it is prudent to let the other have but one note to play.

* See example (No. 2) of the harmonics on the violin employed in combination with those on the harp.

All the strings of the harp are not fit for harmonics: only the two octaves above the last should be employed for this purpose; they being the sole ones of which the strings are sufficiently long for division by touching in the centre, and sufficiently tightened for neatly producing harmonics.

In case the quickness of the movement and the character of the instrumentation demands a speedy transition of a harp part from one key into another, very remote from that which precedes it (from E♭ into E♮, for instance), it cannot be effected upon the same instrument; there must then be a harp tuned in the *sharpened* key, to succeed immediately the one playing in the *flattened* key. If the transition be not sudden, and there be but one harp-player available, the composer must let the performer have a sufficient number of rests for time to apply the requisite modulatory pedals. When the harps are numerous,—treated as integral parts of the orchestra, and not merely used to accompany a vocal or instrumental solo,—they are generally divided into firsts and seconds, with distinct written parts for each; which greatly adds to the richness of their effect. A still greater number of different harp-parts might doubtless be excellently employed; and indeed, they become indispensable, as has just been seen, when the object is to render possible, without interruption to their playing, a sudden change of key.

The Theban bas-reliefs, where an elaborate representation of antique harps may be found, prove that they had no pedals; and that, consequently, they were incapable of modulation.

Those, not less antique, employed in our own days by the Welsh and Irish bards, have several rows of strings and, without doubt, this arrangement places modulations and the chromatic style more or less within their power.

I have specified above, in speaking of *iteration*, the essential advantage possessed by modern harps, of placing two strings in unison, by means of the double-action pedals :— one of these C♭'s being produced by the C♭ string, and the other by the B♭ string raised a semitone; or one of these E♭'s being produced by the E♭ string, and the other by the D♭ string raised *two* semitones. It is hardly to be believed what resources great harp-players are now able to derive from these double notes,—which they have named *synonimes*. Mr. Parish Alvars, the most extraordinary player, perhaps, that has ever been heard on this instrument, executes passages and arpeggios which at first sight appear utterly impossible, the whole difficulty of which, nevertheless, consists only in an ingenious use of the pedals. He plays, for instance, with wonderful rapidity, passages like the following:—

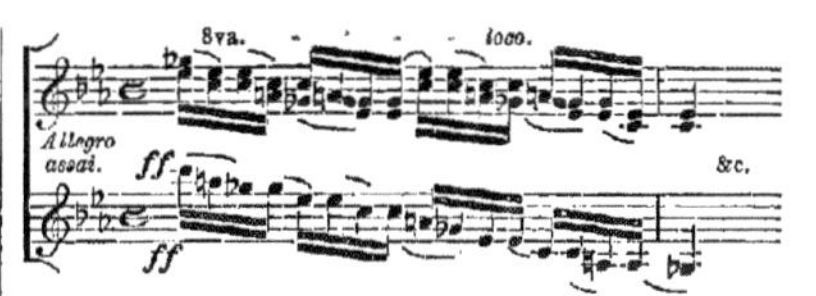

It will be understood how easy such a passage is on learning that the player has only to slide three fingers from top to bottom along the harp-strings, without fingering, and as fast as he likes; since, by means of *synonimes*, the instrument is self-tuned exclusively in series of minor thirds, producing the chord of the *diminished seventh*; and that, instead of having for the scale,—

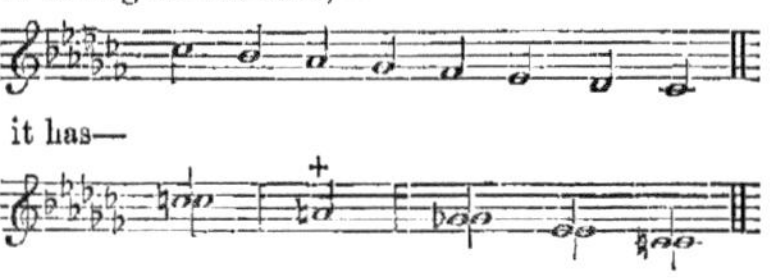

it has—

The A♮, it must be remarked, cannot be double, and therefore has no repercussion. In fact, it is not possible to have four *synonimes* at once, since there are only seven notes in the scale, and four synonimes would require eight strings. Moreover, be it observed, that the A♮ can only be obtained upon *one* string (the A♭ string), and does not exist upon the next string (the G♭ string); this latter being only raised by the two actions of the pedal two semitones, which bring it to A♭. The same remark applies also to two other strings,—C♭ and F♭.

There are therefore still wanting on the harp three synonimes, D♮, G♮, and A♮; but this defect—for it is a serious one—will be obviated when the manufactures contrive (as Mr. Parish Alvars proposes) to construct for the pedals of the three notes, C♭, F♭, and G♭, a triple action which will permit them to be raised three semitones.

Mr. Erard should not allow such a defect to remain in this instrument; it would be worthy so skilful a manufacturer's ingenuity to be the first to remove it.

It is evident that, if all the synonime strings be not used at once, there will be chords left other than those of the *diminished seventh*; and the various combinations that each affords, when an exact account is taken of the action of the pedals on the strings, will be still more numerous when the triple action of the pedals, C♭, F♭, and G♭, shall have furnished the three synonimes of which the harp at present is deficient.

The Guitar.

The guitar is an instrument suited for accompanying the voice, and for figuring in certain quiet compositions, as also for executing, singly, pieces more or less complicated in several parts, which possess a true charm when performed by really good players.

The guitar has six strings, tuned in fourths and thirds, as thus :—

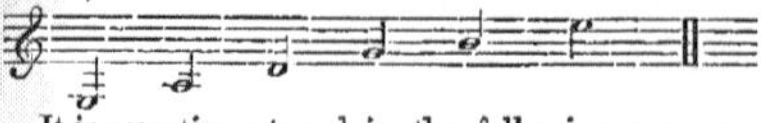

It is sometimes tuned in the following manner; especially for pieces written in the key of E :—

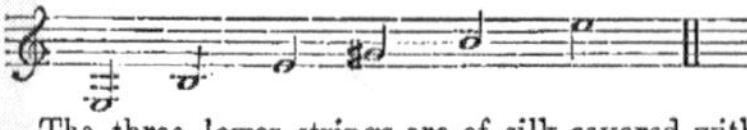

The three lower strings are of silk covered with silver wire; and the three others, of catgut. The guitar is a transposing instrument of three octaves and a fifth in compass; and written for with the G clef, an octave above the real sound :—

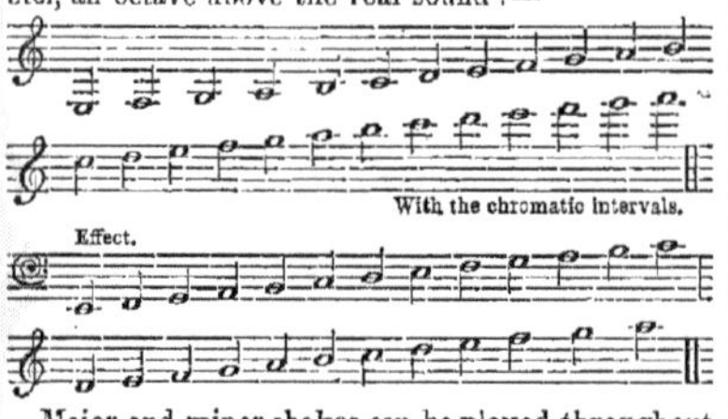

Major and minor shakes can be played throughout the extent of this scale.

It is almost impossible to write well for the guitar without being a player on the instrument. The majority of composers who employ it, are, however, far from knowing its powers; and therefore they frequently give it things to play of excessive difficulty, little sonority, and small effect.

I shall endeavour, notwithstanding, to point out the proper method of writing simple accompaniments for it.

In the usual position of the right hand, the little finger resting upon the body of the instrument, the thumb is used for playing the three lower strings, ; the forefinger plays the G, ; the middle finger, the B, ; and the third finger, the first string, or E, ; whence it arises that, in playing chords of more than four notes, the thumb is obliged to slide over one or two of the lower strings, while the three fingers directly strike the three high strings. In chords of four notes, each finger strikes only the string appropriated to it; the fingers change strings only when there is occasion to strike low chords like these :—

The guitar being especially an instrument of harmony, it is very important to know the chords and likewise the arpeggios which it can execute.

Here is a certain number in different keys. We will begin with the easiest—those which are played without the use of Barrage (marked Barré), a procedure by which the forefinger of the left hand placed across the neck of the instrument, upon two, three, or four strings, serves as a temporary *fret*. (The *fret* is the little piece across the neck, on which the strings rest, and which decides the proper length to be put in vibration.)

The flat keys are incomparably more difficult than the preceding; and all require Barrage The most easy chords are the following :—

In all chords, the employment of the first and the third of the lower strings *without the second* should be avoided; because the thumb would then be obliged to skip over this second string in order to go from the first to the third :—

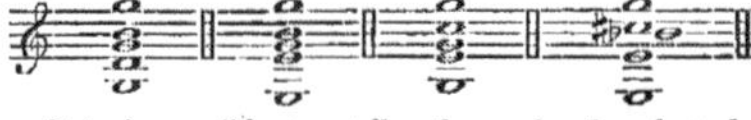

It is impossible to strike these chords; but, by adding the second string to them, they become easy :

Chords of the dominant seventh also should not be written in the usual position of three thirds above each other, as—

They are next to impossible; this one is difficult, but still, practicable, on account of the G, which is played on an open string. The following is very easy, and at the same time sonorous:— on account of the E on the open string.

The three following chords are easy, and link well together, in all keys:—

Likewise in F♯, in G, in A♭, &c.:—

Of course, these chords may sometimes have more than four notes, in keys which permit their having a low open string; in A♮, for instance, in E♮, in G, in F; in short, wherever one of these three notes may be introduced as the bass:—

This succession, which requires Barrage (marked Barré) of four strings, is equally practicable on the two lower thirds of the neck of the guitar:—

and then, ascending by semitones to

which is the extreme point of height where this fingering can be employed.

The following arpeggios have an excellent effect on the guitar:—

In this last arpeggio the two bound high notes are played by catching the first string with the little finger of the left hand.

Arpeggios from high to low are rather troublesome but quite feasible:—

The same reversed are, on the contrary, very easy.

On account of the retrograde movement of the thumb on the two low notes, the following are much more difficult, and less advantageous:—

Scales bound by twos and twos, with the reiteration of a note, are elegant, and tolerably sonorous; particularly in the brilliant keys of the instrument:—

Scales in thirds, although difficult at their extremities, may be used in a moderately quick movement:—

This applies equally to series of sixths and octaves.

Reiterated notes, two, three, four, and even six or eight times repeated, are easily done; prolonged reiterations (*roulements*) on the same note are rarely good excepting on the first string, or at the utmost on the three high strings:—

The notes marked with a + are played with the thumb; the others with the first and second finger in succession.

For reiterations (*roulements*), the thumb should be made to succeed the first and second fingers on the same string:—

Harmonics are easily obtained from the guitar, and upon many occasions felicitous use may be made of them. The best are those produced by touching the octave, the fifth, the fourth, and the third, major, of the open strings.

As was explained in the chapters on instruments played with a bow, the touched octave brings out that same octave:—

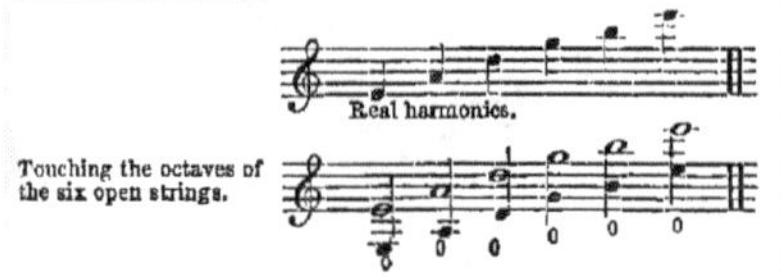

These latter harmonics are the least sonorous, and are obtained with difficulty. It should be understood that this expression of *real harmonics* is relative to the diapason belonging to the guitar, and not to the ordinary diapason; for, strictly speaking, these *real harmonics* are heard an octave below, like all the other sounds on this instrument.

On each string, moreover, chromatic and diatonic scales in artificial harmonics can be produced. For this purpose, it is necessary to press the fingers of the left hand on the notes desired to be heard an octave higher, then to touch the *middle* of the string with the right forefinger, and to play behind the forefinger with the thumb of the same hand:—

I repeat that, without being able to play the guitar, one can hardly write for it pieces in several parts, containing passages demanding all the resources of the instrument. In order to have an idea of what the best performers are able to produce in this way, the compositions of such celebrated guitar-players as Zanni de Ferranti, Huerta, Sor, &c., should be studied.

Since the introduction of the pianoforte into all houses where the least taste for music exists, the guitar has been little used, save in Spain and Italy. Some performers have studied it, and still study it, as a solo instrument, in such a way as to derive from it effects no less original than delightful. Composers employ it but little, either in the church, theatre, or concert room. Its feeble sonority, which does not allow its union with other instruments, or with many voices possessed even of ordinary brilliancy, is doubtless the cause of this. Nevertheless, its melancholy and dreamy character might more frequently be made available; it has a real charm of its own, and there would be no impossibility in so writing for it as to make this manifest. The guitar—unlike the majority of instruments—loses by being employed in numbers. The sound of twelve guitars playing in unison is almost absurd.

The Mandolin.

The mandolin has almost fallen into disuse at present; and this is a pity, for its quality of tone—thin and nasal though it be—has something piquant and original about it which might occasionally be made of effective use.

There are several kinds of mandolins; the best known has four double strings; that is to say, four times two strings in unison, and tuned in fifths, like the violin.

It is written for on the G clef:—

The E strings are of catgut; the A strings, of steel; the D strings, of copper; and the G strings, of catgut covered with silver wire.

The compass of the mandolin is about three octaves:—

With the chromatic intervals.

It is an instrument more for melody than for harmony; though its strings, being put in vibration with a quill or plectrum, which the player holds in the left hand, may certainly allow chords of four notes to be heard, such as these—

which are obtained by passing the quill rapidly over the four double notes; but the effect of these groups of simultaneous notes is rather poor, and the mandolin has its real character and effect only in such melodious accompaniments as the one written by Mozart in the second act of *Don Giovanni*:—

The mandolin is at present so neglected, that, in theatres where *Don Giovanni* is played, there is always a difficulty in performing this serenade piece. Although a few days' study would enable a guitar-player, or even an ordinary violin-player, to acquire sufficient knowledge of the mandolin for the purpose, so little respect is entertained for the intentions of the great masters, whenever it is a question of breaking through old habits, that almost everywhere, even at the Opera (the last place in the world where such liberties should be taken), they venture to play the mandolin part of *Don Giovanni* on violins pizzicati, or on guitars. The timbre of these instruments has not the keen delicacy of that for which they are substituted; and Mozart knew quite well what he was about in choosing the mandolin for accompanying the amorous lay of his hero.

STRINGED INSTRUMENTS WITH KEYS.

The Pianoforte.

The pianoforte is an instrument with a key-board and metallic strings, put in vibration by hammers. Its present compass is six octaves and seven-eighths. It is written on two different clefs at once: the F clef is appropriated to the left hand; and the G clef, to the right hand. Sometimes,—according to the degree of height or depth of the passages assigned to the two hands,—the clefs are interchanged :—

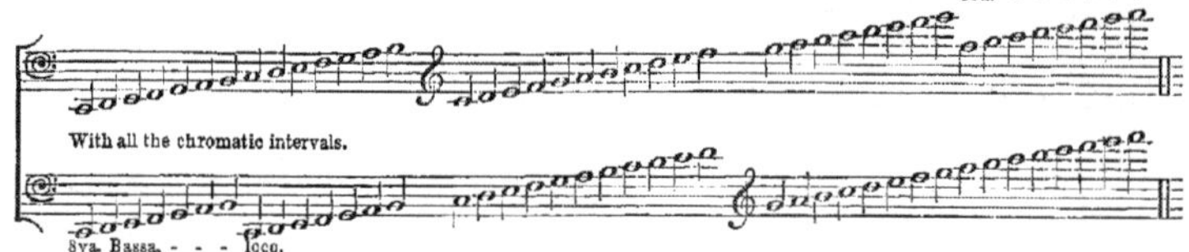

The shake is practicable on all the notes of the scale. The player may strike or arpeggio in any way, and with both hands, a chord of four or even five notes; but, at the same time, the harmony should be as close as possible :—

Chords embracing an interval of a tenth may be played, by omitting the third, and even the octave, for greater facility, as thus :—

Four, and even five real parts may be written for the pianoforte, by taking care not to place between the extreme parts of each hand a distance greater than an octave or a ninth at most; unless indeed the pedal which raises the dampers, by prolonging the sounds without the player's finger remaining on the key-board, allows of augmenting the distance between the parts.

Here is an example in four parts, the pedal not used :—

And here is another, employing the pedal :—

This sign ⊕ indicates that the dampers must be replaced by quitting the pedal. It is mostly used when the harmony changes, in order to prevent the vibration of the notes of the last chord from continuing on to the following chord. As regards this excessive prolongation of the sound of each note, care should be taken, in employing the principal pedal, to avoid as much as possible appoggiaturas with accidentals [*altérées*], and passing notes in the middle of the instrument; because these notes, being sustained like the others, and thereby becoming introduced into the harmony—to which nevertheless they do not belong—produce intolerable discords. In the upper extremity of the key-board, where the very short strings do not maintain their sound so long, these melodic ornaments are practicable.

The hands are sometimes made to cross—either in obliging the right hand to pass over the left, or in causing the left to pass over the right :—

The number of such combinations among the various parts playable on the pianoforte is very considerable. It would, indeed, be impossible to instance them all here, and only by studying the compositions of the great performers—those of Liszt especially,—can a just idea be formed of the excellence to which the art of pianoforte-playing has nowadays attained.

It will there be seen that the limits of possibility on this instrument are unknown; and that every day they are farther removed by the new prodigies which performers achieve.

For the pianoforte, as for the harp, it is better in certain cases—in arpeggios, for example—not to bring the hands too near each other. An arpeggio like the following would be rather inconvenient :—

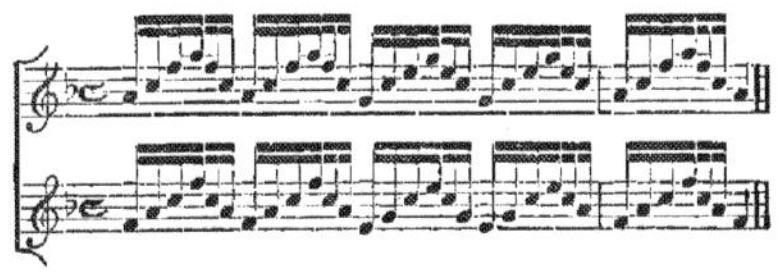

It would be incomparably better to write it thus :—

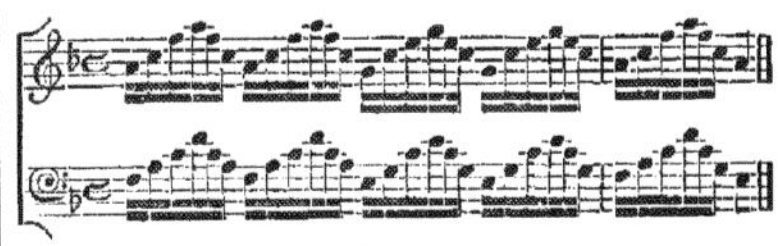

Diatonic and chromatic scales in thirds, for both hands, are, however, easy :—

These scales in two parts are practicable by one hand alone, although difficult in a quick movement. Moreover, in keys where there are few sharps and flats, the two hands may be written for in series of sixth-thirds in three parts:—

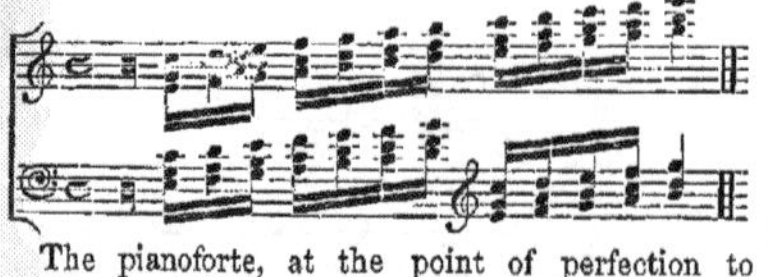

The pianoforte, at the point of perfection to which our skilful manufacturers have brought it nowadays, may be considered in a double point of view: as an orchestral instrument, or as forming a complete small orchestra in itself. On only one occasion has it been deemed well to employ the pianoforte in the orchestra under the same conditions as other instruments; that is to say, letting it bring to the ensemble its own peculiar resources,—which nothing can replace. Certain passages in Beethoven's concertos ought, nevertheless, to have drawn the attention of composers to this point. Doubtless they have all admired the marvellous effect produced in his grand concerto in E♭, by the slow beatings [*batteries*] of the two hands on the piano in the high octave during the air for the flute, clarinet, and bassoon, and upon the *contretemps* of the stringed instruments. Thus attended, the sonority of the pianoforte is of the most seductive kind; it is full of calm and freshness, and is a type of grace itself:—

No. 19.

Concerto in E♭.—BEETHOVEN.

8ves. loco.
Ped. Sempre piu dim.
Morendo.

pp
pp
Pizz.
Pizz.
Pizz. p
Pizz. p
Pizz. p
pp
Ped.
Fagot. Corni.

The part taken by the pianoforte, on the unique occasion alluded to, is quite different. The author, in a chorus of airy spirits, has employed the instrument *à quatre mains*, in accompanying the voices. The lower pair of hands execute rapid ascending arpeggios in triplets, to which respond, at the second half of the bar, another (descending) arpeggio in three parts executed by a piccolo flute, a flute, and a clarinet, upon which trembles a double shake in octaves by the upper pair of pianoforte hands. No other known instrument could produce this sort of harmonious quivering, which the pianoforte delivers without difficulty, and which the sylph-like character of the piece here renders desirable :—

8ves.
8ves.
8ves.
- - ran - - - da Mi-ran - - da, Mi-ran - - - - da,
- - ran - - - da, Mi-ran - - da, Mi-ran - - - - da,
- - ran - - - da, Mi-ran - - - da,
- - ran - - - da, Mi-ran - - - da,
- - ran - - - da, Mi-ran - - - da,
- - ran - - - da, Mi-ran - - - da,
- - ran - - - da, Mi-ran - - - da,
- - ran - - - da, Mi ran - - - da,
- - ran - - - da, Mi-ran - - - da,
- - ran - - - da, Mi ron - - - da,

8ves.
now, now comes thy pre - des - tin'd hus - - - band.
vien' chi t'è de - sti - na - to spo - - - so.

Whenever, on the contrary, the pianoforte is made to go beyond soft effects, and attempt a forcible competition with the orchestra, it vanishes entirely. It should accompany, or be accompanied; unless, like harps, employed in large numbers. This would not be unadvisable, I feel persuaded; but there would always be—on account of the large space they occupy—much difficulty in assembling a dozen grand pianos in a moderate sized orchestra.

Considered as a small orchestra in itself, the pianoforte has its own appropriate instrumentation, which forms a portion of the pianist's art. It is his duty, on many occasions, to judge if it be requisite to render certain parts prominent, whilst others are left in shadow; and if he ought to play conspicuously an intermediate passage, by giving lightness to the upper ornaments, and less force to the bass. It is for him to decide the occasion for changing fingers, or the eligibility of using the thumb only, for such and such melody. He knows, in writing for his instrument, when the harmony should be spread or brought close; the various degrees of distance that arpeggios should have, and the different sonority thence resulting. He should know, above all, how to use the pedals judiciously. On this subject, it ought to be observed that the great pianoforte composers have never failed to mark with as much care as appropriateness the places where the principal pedal should be taken and quitted. Yet many performers—both great and small—persist in neglecting these indications, and keep the dampers constantly raised, utterly forgetting that the harmonies must necessarily be prolonged one into the other, in a manner the most discordant. This is a deplorable abuse of an excellent thing; it is noise and confusion substituted for sonority. It is, besides, the natural consequence of that intolerable tendency in performers—great and small—singers and instrumentalists—to rank foremost whatever they imagine conduces to their own personal interest. They think little of the respect which is invariably due from executant to composer, and of the tacit but absolute compact, made by the former to the audience, that he will faithfully transmit the latter's idea to them, whether he honour moderate talent by acting as its interpreter, or deliver the immortal thought of a man of genius. In both cases, the performer who thus allows himself—following the caprice of the moment—to go contrary to the intentions of the composer, should reflect that the author of the work, whatever it may be, has probably devoted a hundred times more consideration to the place and duration of certain effects, to the indication of particular movements, to the design of his melody and rhythm, and to the choice of his chords and instruments, than he has given, before thus interfering. There cannot be too strong a protest made against the senseless privilege too often claimed by instrumentalists, singers, and directors of orchestras. Such a mania is more than ridiculous; it will lead, unless care be taken, to the introduction of innumerable and unjustifiable irregularities into the Art, and to results the most disastrous. It rests with composers and critics to combine in never tolerating it.

A pedal much less used than that which raises the dampers—of which, nevertheless, Beethoven and some others have availed themselves with delicious results—is the soft pedal (one-string pedal). It is not only of excellent effect, contrasted with the usual sound of the pianoforte, and with the pomp of sonority produced by the principal pedal, but it is of indisputable utility in accompanying singing, when a character of softness and gentleness is to be given to the execution. It is indicated by these words:—"soft pedal;" or, in Italian, "*una corda.*" Its action consists in preventing the hammers from reaching two of the three strings strung in unison for each note. Then only the third string vibrates; whence results a diminution of sound by two thirds, and a very remarkable difference of character.

Wind Instruments.

Before studying individually each member of this large family, we will fix as clearly as possible the musical vocabulary indicating the different degrees of height or depth of certain instruments, the transpositions to which these differences lead, the established mode of writing for them, and the denominations which have been applied to them.

We will first indicate a line of demarcation between those instruments of which the sound is produced as shown by the musical signs, and those of which the sound issues above or below the written note. From this classification the following lists result:—

TABLE.

NON-TRANSPOSING INSTRUMENTS; FROM WHICH THE SOUND ISSUES AS IT IS WRITTEN.	TRANSPOSING INSTRUMENTS; OF WHICH THE SOUND IS DIFFERENT FROM THE WRITTEN NOTE.
The Violin.	
Viola.	
Viole d'amour.	
Violoncello	The Double-Bass.
Usual Flute	All other Flutes than the usual one.
Hautboy	The Corno Inglese.
Clarinet in C	All Clarinets excepting the Clarinet in C.
Bassoon	Basson-quinte.
Russian Bassoon	Double-Bassoon.
Horn in high C	All Horns excepting the Horn in high C.

NON-TRANSPOSING INSTRUMENTS	TRANSPOSING INSTRUMENTS
Cornet à Piston in C	All Cornets à Piston excepting that in C.
Trumpet in C	All Trumpets excepting the Trumpet in C.
Alto Trombone, Tenor Trombone, Bass Trombone	Cornets without Pistons; Alto Trombones with Valve
Ophicleide in C	All Ophicleides excepting that in C.
Bombardon	The Serpent
Bass-Tuba	
Harp	The Guitar.
Pianoforte.	
Organ	
Voices { when written on their respective clefs, and not all equally on the G clef }	Tenors and Basses { when written on the G clef, their sounds then issuing an octave below the written note }
Kettle-Drums	
Bells	
Ancient Cymbals	
Sets of Bells	
Glockenspiel	Keyed Instrument with steel bars
Keyed Harmonica.	

It will be seen by this table that if all the non-transposing instruments said to be in C, emit their sounds as they are written, those, like the violin, hautboy, and flute, which have no designation of key, are in the same condition They are therefore, in the composer's eye, similar to instruments in C Now, the denomination of some wind instruments, based on the natural sound of their tube, has led to the most singular and most absurd consequences, it has caused the art of writing for transposing instruments to become a very complicated task, rendering the musical vocabulary perfectly illogical This is the place to show a better way, and to establish some kind of order where we find so little existing

Peformers sometimes say—speaking of the tenor trombone—the trombone in *B*♭, in speaking of the alto trombone, the trombone in *E*♭, and still more frequently, in speaking of the usual flute, the flute in *D*

These designations are correct in the sense that the tubes of the two trombones, with the slide closed, give out, the one the notes of the chord of *B*♭, the other those of the chord of *E*♭, while the usual flute, with its holes stopped and its keys closed, gives out the note *D*. But as performers pay no regard to this resonance of the tube, as they produce really the written notes, as the *C* of a tenor trombone is a *C* and not a *B*♭ as that of the alto trombone is still a *C* and not an *E*♭, as that of the flute is also a *C* and not a *D*, it evidently follows that these instruments are not, or are no longer in the list of *transposing* instruments, that they consequently belong to that of the *non-transposing* instruments, and that they are supposed to be in *C*, like hautboys, clarinets, horns, cornets and trumpets in *C*; while no designation of key should be applied to them, other, at least, than that of *C*. This established, it will be seen of what importance it is not to call the usual flute, flute in *D*. The other flutes, higher than this one, having been designated according to the difference existing between their pitch and that of the usual flute, it has become the fashion—instead of saying simply, tierce flute, ninth flute, which at least offers no confusion in the terms—to call these instruments, flute in *F*, flute in *E*♭ And to what does this lead? In a score, the small clarinet in *E*♭, of which the *C* really makes *E*♭, can execute the same part as a third flute so-called in *F*, and these two instruments, bearing the names of different keys, are nevertheless in unison The denomination of one or other must be false, and it is absurd to adopt solely for *flutes* a mode of appellation and of designation of keys, different from that in use for *all other instruments*.

Hence the principle which I propose, and which renders impossible all misunderstanding —the key of *C* is the point of comparison which should be taken in specifying the keys of transposing instruments. The natural sound of the tube of non-transposing wind instruments can never be taken into consideration

All non-transposing instruments, or transposing only in the octave—of which consequently the written *C* gives *C*—are considered as being in C.

Accordingly, if an instrument of the same kind is tuned above or below the pitch of the typical instrument, this difference will be designated according to the relation which exists between it and the key of *C* Consequently, the violin, the flute, and the hautboy which plays in unison with the clarinet in *C*, the trumpet in *C*, the horn in *C*, *are in C*, and if a violin, a flute, or a hautboy be employed, tuned a tone higher than the usual instruments of this name, this violin, this flute, this hautboy, then playing in unison with clarinets in *D*, and trumpets in *D*, *are in D*

Whence I conclude that the old mode of designating flutes should be abolished that the tierce flute should no longer be called flute in *F*, but flute in *E*♭, since its *C* makes *E*♭, and that ninth flutes and minor second flutes should no longer be called flutes in *E*♭, but large or small flute in *D*♭, since their *C* makes *D*♭. and so on with all the other keys

Reed Instruments.

The family of double reed instruments should be distinguished from that of single reed instruments. The former is composed of five members :—the hautboy, the corno inglese, the bassoon, the basson-quinte, and the double-bassoon.

The Hautboy.

Its compass is two octaves and a sixth. It is written on the G clef :—

The last two notes should be used with much reserve ; the F particularly is hazardous, when it presents itself abruptly. Some hautboys have the low B♭, ; but this note, not being generally acquired on the instrument, is better avoided. Boëhm's system obviates the difficulties of fingering still belonging to the hautboy in its present state, and met with in rapid passages from the middle C♯ to the note above :—

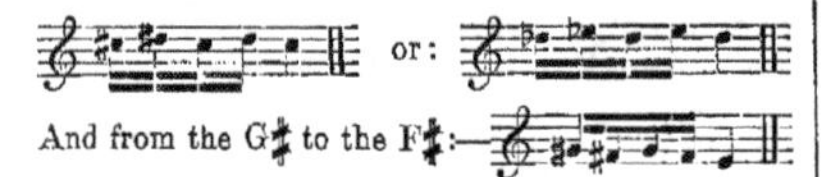

And from the G♯ to the F♯:—

The shakes formed of these different intervals, and of some others also, are impossible, or excessively difficult, and produce a bad effect, as will be seen from the following table :—

Hautboys, like all other instruments, are much more at their ease in keys where there are few sharps or flats. They should hardly be made to play out of this limit :—

The sounds that exceed it, either below or above, being weak or thin, hard or shrill, are all of rather a bad quality. Rapid passages, chromatic or diatonic, can be tolerably well executed on the hautboy ; but they only produce an ungraceful and almost ridiculous effect. The same is the case with arpeggios.

The opportunity for such passages can be but very rare ; and, indeed, we confess to not having yet met with them. That which tempts solo-performers to use them in their fantasias or airs with variations goes but a little way to prove the contrary. The hautboy is especially a melodic instrument : it has a pastoral character, full of tenderness—nay, I would even say, of timidity.

It is nevertheless always written for, in the *tutti* parts, without paying attention to the expression of its *timbre*, because there it is lost, and the peculiarity of that expression cannot be distinguished. It is the same—let it be at once understood—with most other wind instruments. The only exception lies where the sonority is excessive, or the quality of tone markedly distinctive. It is impossible — without trampling under foot both Art and good sense—to employ such exceptional instruments as simple instruments of harmony. Among them may be ranked trombones, ophicleides, double-bassoons, and —in many instances—trumpets and cornets. Candour, artless grace, soft joy, or the grief of a fragile being, suits the hautboy's accents ; it expresses them admirably in its cantabile.

A certain degree of agitation is also within its powers of expression ; but care should be taken not to urge it into utterances of passion or violent outbursts of anger, menace, or heroism ; for then its small acid-sweet voice becomes ineffectual, and absolutely grotesque. Some great masters—Mozart among others—have not escaped this error. In their scores passages are to be found, the impassioned meaning and martial accent of which contrast strangely with the sound of the hautboy that executes them ; and thence result, not only effects missed, but startling disparities between stage and orchestra, melody and instrumentation. The theme of a march, however manly, grand, or noble, loses its manliness, its grandeur, and its nobility if hautboys deliver it. It has a chance of preserving something of its character if given to flutes, and loses scarcely anything by being assigned to clarinets. Where—in order to give more weight and body to the harmony, and more force to the group of wind instruments employed—hautboys are absolutely needful in a piece such as I have just described, they should at least be written for in such a way that their quality of tone (not suited to this particular style) is completely covered by the other instruments, and so blends with the mass as no longer to be recognized. The lower sounds of the hautboys, ungraceful when displayed, may agree with certain wild and lamenting harmonies, united to the low notes of the clarinets, and to the low D, E, F, and G of the flutes and corni inglesi.

Gluck and Beethoven understood marvellously well the use of this valuable instrument. To it they both owe the profound emotions excited by several of their finest pages. I have only to quote, from Gluck, the hautboy solo of Agamemnon's air in *Iphigenia in Aulide*: "Peuvent-ils," &c. ("Can the harsh Fates"). These complaints of an innocent voice, these continued supplications ever more and more appealing,—what instrument could they suit so well as a hautboy? And the celebrated burden of the air of *Iphigenia in Tauride*: "O malhereuse Iphigénie!" And again, that childlike cry of the orchestra, when Alceste, in the midst of her enthusiasm and heroic self-devotion, struck by the recollection of her young sons, suddenly interrupts the phrase of the theme: "Eh, pourrai-je vivre sans toi?" to respond to this touching instrumental appeal, with the heart-rending exclamation; "O mes enfans!" And then, the discord of the minor second in Armida's air on the words: "Sauvez moi de l'amour" ("Save my weak heart from love")! All this is sublime: not only in dramatic thought, in profound expression, in grandeur and beauty of melody; but also in the instrumentation, and the admirable choice of the hautboys from amidst a throng of instruments, either inadequate, or incapable of producing such impressions:—

No. 21.

daughter! Is it thus they com-mand? I ne-ver will o-bey their in-human decree! I
chè-re peu-vent ils l'or-don-ner je n'o-bé-i-rai point à cet ordre in-humain. Je
Col. Vni.
Hautboy Solo.
ne-ver will o-bey their in-hu-man de-cree. I hear in each
n'o-bé-i-rai point à cet ordre in-hu-main, J'en-tends re-ten-
Fagot.
Pizz.
throb of my breast the plain-tive cry of outrag'd Na-ture, How she
-tir dans mon sein le cri plain-tif de la na-tu-re el-le

speaks to my heart, and her voice is more migh - ty
parle à mon cœur, et sa voix - - est plus su - re
than or - a - cles pro - nounced by Fates, than or - a - cles pro - nounced by
que les o - ra - cles du des - tin, que les o - ra - cles du des -
Fl. ed Ob:
Fates. I ne - ver will obey their in - hu - man decree, I ne - ver will obey their in-
- tin. Je n'o - bé - i - rai point à cet ordre in - humain, Je n'o - bé - i - rai point a cet
arco.

Col Vni.
hu - man decree.
ordre in - hu - main
No. 22.
Armide.—GLUCK.
Moderato.
1st Violins.
Unis.
2nd Violins.
Hautboys.
Violas.
Horns in F.
Bassoons.
ARMIDA.
Double-basses.
O come, O come, HATRED un - dy - ing, come forth from
Venez, ve - nez, Haine im - pla - ca - ble sor - tez du

out the hor-rid Hell - - pit, where, fo - men - ted by thee, e - -
gouffre é - pou-van - ta - ble où vous fai - - tes re - gner une
- ter - - - ual con - - tests rage. O come, O come, Hatred un - -
é - - ter - nella hor - reur, ve - nez, ve - nez, haine in-pla -
Col Basso.
- - dy - - - ing, come forth from out the ho - rid hell - - -
- - ca - - - ble sor - tez du gouffre é - pou - van - ta - - - -

p
- pit, save my weak heart from Love, save my weak heart from Love,
- ble sau-vez-moi de l'a-mour, sau-vez-moi de l'a-mour.
Col Basso.
Naught can so well de-fend me 'gainst a too too
Rien n'est si re-dou-ta-ble contre un en-ne-
f
charm-ing op-po-nent! Give me back my dis-dain, rouse my
-mi trop ai-ma-ble ren-dez-moi mon cour-roux ral-lu-

p
f
p
ire . . . . . once a - gain. O come, O come,
- mez . . . . . ma fu - reur ve - nez, ve - nez,
HA - TRED un - dy - ing, come forth from out the hor - rid hell pit,
haine im - pla - ca - ble sor - tez du gouffre é - pou - van - ta - ble
where, fo - ment - ed by thee, e - ter - nal contests rage.
où vous fai - tes ré - gner une é - ternelle hor - reur.

Beethoven has demanded more from the joyous accent of the hautboys: witness the solo in the scherzo of the Pastoral Symphony; that in the scherzo of the Choral Symphony; that in the first movement of the Symphony in *B*♭, &c. But he has no less felicitously succeeded in assigning them sad or forlorn passages. This may be seen in the minor solo of the second return of the first movement of the Symphony in A; in the episodical andante of the finale to the Eroica Symphony; and, above all, in the air of *Fidelio*, where Florestan, starving with hunger, believes himself,—in his delirious agony,—surrounded by his weeping family, and mingles his tears of anguish with the broken sobs of the hautboy.

No. 24.

Symphony in A.—BEETHOVEN.
Poco sostenuto.
Flutes.
Hautboys
Clarinets in A.
Horns in A.
Bassoons.
Violins.
Violas.
Violoncellos.
Double-basses
1mo Solo.
1mo Solo.
1mo Solo.
p
p
p
p
Pizz.
pp
pp
pp
pp

No. 25.

Eroica Symphony.—BEETHOVEN.

Kettle-drums in E♭.

sf p pp Pizz.

Flute. Solo.

cres. p pp

No. 26.

Fidelio.—BEETHOVEN.

cres.
cres.
cres.
heart is re - liev'd, what calmness pre - vails o'er my senses! an an - gel de-
- - père en mon cœur Quel cal-me sou - dain je res-pi - re mon â - me, mon
cres.
cres.
p
cres.
p
cres.
p
cres.
p
cres.
p
- scendeth to watch o'er my woes, and bright - en the pros - pect of ear - ly de-liv'rance.
â - me re-nait au bon - heur quel ê - tre di - vin à mes maux vient sou - ri - re.
p
p

dim.
cres.
My wife, my Le - o - no - ra, Le - o - no - ra. She smiles thro' the
E - pou - se que j'a - do - re El - le - no - re. c'est toi c'est
Cres. a poco a poco.
f
Dol.
darkness she beck' - neth me for - ward. My an - - - gel! I come!
toi oui l'a - mour vient m'ouvrir . . . m'ou - vrir . . . ce sé - jour.
Cres. a poco a poco.

The Corno Inglese.

This instrument is, so to speak, the alto of the hautboy, the compass of which it nearly equals. It is written on the G clef, like a hautboy in F below; and, consequently, a fifth above its real sound.

Its scale—

produces for the hearer this :—

Many corni inglesi possess also the low B♭.

If the orchestra play in *C*, the corno inglese ought to be written in *G*; if it play in *D*, the corno inglese should be written in *A*; &c.

What has just been said upon the difficulties of fingering for the hautboy, in certain groups of sharpened or flattened notes, applies also to the corno inglese; rapid passages upon it have a still worse effect; its quality of tone, less piercing, more veiled, and deeper than that of the hautboy, does not lend itself so well as the latter to the gaiety of rustic strains. Nor can it give utterance to anguished complainings; accents of keen grief are almost beyond its powers. It has a melancholy, dreamy, and rather noble voice, the tone of which possesses a vague, remote quality that renders it superior to all others in exciting regret, and reviving images and sentiments of the past, when the composer desires to touch the secret chords of tender memories. M. Halévy has, with extreme felicity, employed two corni inglesi in the ritornello of Eleazar's air, in the fourth act of *The Jewess*.

pp
ppp

In the Adagio of one of my own symphonies, the corno inglese, after having repeated in the bass octave the phrases of a hautboy—as the voice of a youth might reply to that of a young girl in a pastoral dialogue—reiterates fragments of them (at the close of the movement) with a dull accompaniment of four kettle-drums, during the silence of all the rest of the orchestra. The feelings of absence, of forgetfulness, of sorrowful loneliness, which arise in the bosoms of the audience on hearing this forsaken melody would lack half their power if played by any other instrument than the corno inglese.

No. 28.

The mixture of the low sounds of the corno inglese with the bass notes of the clarinets and horns, during a tremolo of double-basses, gives a sonority as peculiar as it is novel, and well suited to colour, with its menacing impression, ideas in which fear and solicitude predominate. This effect was unknown either to Mozart, Weber, or Beethoven. A magnificent example of it is to be found in the duet in the fourth act of the *Huguenots*; and I think M. Meyerbeer is the first who caused it to be heard on the stage.

No. 29.

a duo.

- veal'd ; yes, thou lov'st . . . me. Hence shall . . . .

dit oui tu m'ai - - - mes. dans ma

Imitate the singer.

shine a bril - liant star o'er my course.

nuit quelle é - toi - le a bril - lé.

In compositions where the prevailing impression is that of melancholy, the frequent use of the corno inglese, hidden in the midst of the great mass of instruments, is quite suitable. Then, only one hautboy part need be written; replacing the second by that of the corno inglese. Gluck has employed this instrument in his Italian operas *Telemaco* and *Orpheo;* but without manifest intention, and without much resultant effect. He never introduced it in his French scores. Neither Mozart, Beethoven, nor Weber have used it; wherefore, I know not.

The Bassoon.

The bassoon is the bass of the hautboy; it has a compass of more than three octaves; and it is written thus, upon two clefs:—

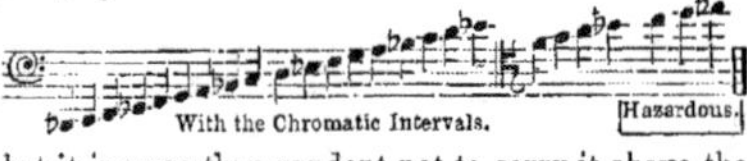

but it is more than prudent not to carry it above the last B♭. The keys with which it is now-a-days provided allow it to give the two low notes, which formerly were out of its reach. Its fingering is the same as that of the flute.

There are many shakes quite impossible for the bassoon, at the two extremes of its scale.

All others above F♯ are either bad or impossible.

This instrument leaves much to desire on the score of precision of intonation; and would gain, perhaps, more than any other wind instrument from being constructed according to Boëhm's system.

The bassoon is of the greatest use in the orchestra on numerous occasions. Its sonority is not very great, and its quality of tone, absolutely devoid of brilliancy or nobleness, has a tendency towards the grotesque—which should be always kept in mind when bringing it into prominence. Its low notes form excellent basses to the whole group of wooden wind instruments. The bassoon is ordinarily written for in two parts; but large orchestras being always provided with four bassoons, it can then be without inconvenience writtten for in four real parts; or, still better, in three—the lowest part being doubled an octave below, to strengthen the bass. The character of its high notes is somewhat painful and suffering—I would say even miserable—but they can sometimes be introduced into either a slow melody, or passages of accompaniment, with most surprising effect. Thus the odd little cluckings heard in the scherzo of Beethoven's C minor Symphony, towards the close of the decrescendo, are solely produced by the somewhat forced sound of the high A♭, and the G of the bassoons in unison:—

No. 30.

Symphony in C minor.—BEETHOVEN.

When M. Meyerbeer, in his resurrection of the Nuns, wished to find a pale, cold, cadaverous sound, he, on the contrary, obtained it from the weak middle notes of the bassoon :—

No. 31.

Rapid passages of bound notes may be successfully employed; they come out well when they are written in the favorite keys of the instrument, such as *D*, *G*, *C*, *F*, *B♭*, *E♭*, *A*, and their relative minors. The following passages produce an excellent effect in the second act of the *Huguenots* :—

No. 32.

Andante.
Sordini.
The Huguenots.—MEYERBEER.
8ve.
Violins.
ppp
Sordini.
Violas.
Pizz.
Flute.
Clarinet in B♭.
Imo. Solo.
Col Vno. 2ndo.
Bassoons.
Col Vlles.
2 Horns in E♭.
p
1 Horn in B♭, (low.)
Kettle-drums in C♭ and B♭.
2 Harps.
Chorus of young girls.
Young maidens fair, in this green
Jeunes beau-tés sous ce feuil
Young maidens fair,
Jeunes beautés,
Violoncellos.
Very soft, legato.
Double basses.
Andante.

The Basson-quinte.

The basson-quinte is a diminutive of the preceding; and its pitch is a fifth higher. It has about the same compass; and, like it, is written upon two clefs,—but transposing :—

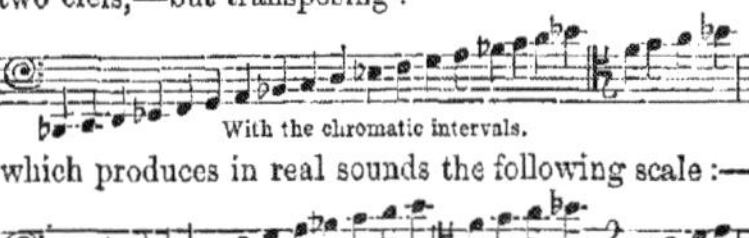

With the chromatic intervals.

which produces in real sounds the following scale :—

With the chromatic intervals.

The basson-quinte occupies the same position above the bassoon as does the corno inglese below the hautboy. The corno inglese should be written a fifth above the real sound, and the basson-quinte a fifth below; therefore the basson-quinte will play in *F* when the bassoons play in *C*, and in *G* when they are in *D*, &c. There is no such instrument in the generality of orchestras, where the corno inglese replaces it advantageously in its two upper octaves. Its quality of tone has less feeling, but more force, than that of the corno inglese, and would be of excellent effect in military music. It is a great pity, and very detrimental to wind instrument bands, where masses of large and small bassoons might soften the harshness of its sound, that the basson-quinte should be entirely excluded from them.

The Double-Bassoon.

This instrument is to the bassoon, what the double-bass is to the violoncello. That is to say, its sound is an octave lower than the written note. It has seldom more than this compass :—

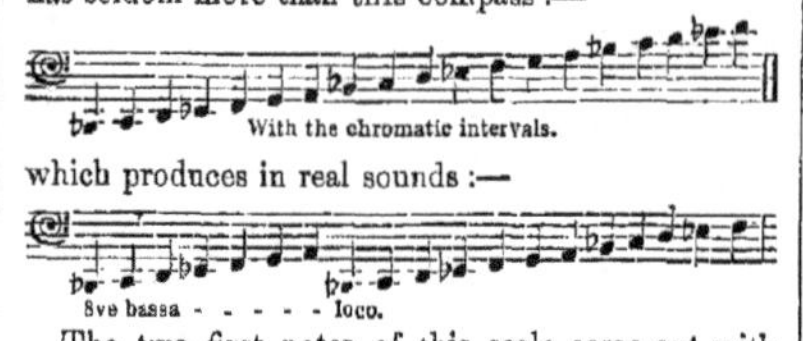

which produces in real sounds :—

The two first notes of this scale come out with difficulty; and are very ineffective, on account of their extreme depth.

It is needless to add that this very ponderous instrument is only suitable for grand effects of harmony, and to basses of a moderate degree of speed. Beethoven has used it in the finale of his Symphony in C minor; and in that of his Choral Symphony. It is very valuable for large wind instrument bands; nevertheless, few players care to learn it. Occasionally an attempt is made to replace it by the ophicleide, the sound of which has not the same depth, since it is in unison with the usual bassoon, and not on the octave below. Moreover, its quality of tone has no analogy in point of character with that of the double-bassoon. I think therefore it is better, in the majority of cases, to do without the double bassoon part than to give it to an ophicleide.

Clarinets.

Simple reed instruments, such as the clarinet, and the corno di bassetto, form a family whose connection with that of the hautboy is not so near as might be thought. That which distinguishes it especially, is the nature of its sound. The middle notes of the clarinet are more limpid, more full, more pure than those of *double reed* instruments, the sound of which is never exempt from a certain tartness or harshness, more or less concealed by the player's skill. The high sounds of the last octave, commencing with the C above the stave, partake only a little of the tartness of the hautboy's loud sounds; while in character the lower sounds approach, by the roughness of their vibrations, those of certain notes on the bassoon.

The clarinet is written on the G clef; and its compass in three octaves and a half, or more :—

Four registers are reckoned on the clarinet :—the low, the chalumeau, the medium, and the high.

The first comprises this part of the scale :—

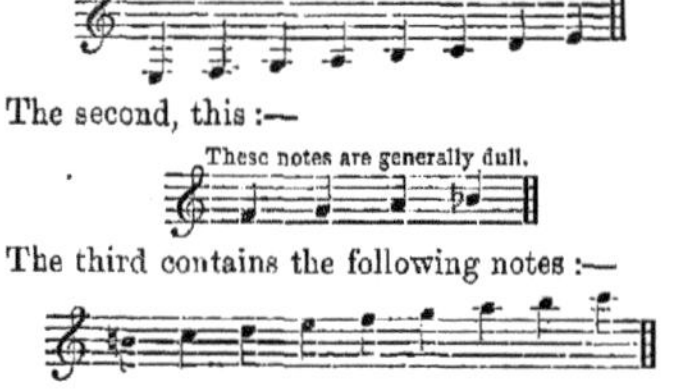

The second, this :—

The third contains the following notes :—

And the fourth is found in the remainder of the scale up to the highest D :—

A considerable number of diatonic successions, arpeggios and shakes, formerly impracticable, are no longer so, thanks to the ingenious mechanism of keys added to the instrument. They will become even easy when the system of Sax is adopted by all the manufacturers. It is however prudent—these improvements not being yet generally adopted—not to write such passages as the following, unless the movement be very slow :—

The number of major and minor shakes practicable on the clarinet is considerable. Those which are not to be played with surety are designated in the subjoined scale :—

The favorite keys of the clarinet are the keys of *C*, *F*, *G*, principally; and then those of *B♭*, *E♭*, *A♭*, *D♮* major, and their relative minors. As there exist clarinets in different keys, their use makes it needless for the performer to play in keys containing many sharps and flats; as *A♮*, *E♮*, *B♮*, *D♭*, *G♭* major, and their relative minors.

There are four clarinets in general use at present:

The *small clarinet in E♭*; to which it is not well to give a compass beyond three octaves and two notes :—

It is a minor third above the clarinet in C, and is written for by transposing. Thus, to have the following passage—

it must be written—

Of the *clarinet in C*, and the *clarinets in B♭* and *in A*, the two latter have a compass equal to the clarinet in *C*; but, the one sounding a major second and the other a minor third lower, their parts should be written in keys so much higher.

These expressions, "good," "bad," "passable," do not here apply to the difficulty of execution of the phrases themselves; but merely to that of the key in which they are written. Moreover, it should be said that the rather difficult keys,—such as A♮ major, and E♮ major,—are not to be entirely shunned, for simple phrases and for a slow movement.

It will be seen that, independently of the particular character of their quality of tone—of which we are about to speak,—these different clarinets are very useful as affording facility of execution. It is to be regretted that there are not more still. For instance, those in the keys of *B*♮, and of *D*, which are rarely to be found, would on numerous occasions offer great resources to composers.

The clarinet in D is little used, and unduly neglected, for its quality of tone is pure, besides having remarkable power of penetration; and on many occasions excellent effect might be produced by it.

The small clarinet in *F* (high), formerly employed in military music, has been almost abandoned for that in *E*♭, which is found, and with reason, to be less screamy, and quite sufficient for the keys ordinarily used in wind instrument pieces. Clarinets have proportionately less purity, sweetness, and clearness, as their key is more and more removed above that of *B*♭, which is one of the finest on the instrument. The clarinet in *C* is harder than that in *B*♭, and its voice has much less charm. The small clarinet in *E*♭ has piercing tones, which it is very easy to render mean, beginning from the *A* above the stave. Accordingly it has been employed, in a modern symphony, in order to parody, degrade, and blackguardize (if I may be pardoned the expression) a melody; the dramatic intention of the work requiring this strange transformation. The small clarinet in *F* has a still more marked tendency of the same kind. In proportion as the instrument becomes lower, it produces, on the contrary, sounds more veiled and more melancholy.

Generally speaking, performers should use only the instruments indicated by the author. Each of these instruments having a particular character, it is at least probable that the composer has chosen one rather than the other from preference for such and such a quality of tone, and not from caprice. To persist—as some performers do—in playing (by transposing) on the clarinet in *B*♭, is therefore, with a few exceptions, faithlessness of execution. And this faithlessness becomes more manifest and more culpable when, for instance, the clarinet in *A* is employed by the composer, who may have written for it only to have the low *E*, which gives the *C*♯:—

Clarinets in A. Real sound:

What, in such a case, would the player of the clarinet in *B*♭ do, whose low *E* gives only the *D*?—

Clarinet in B♭. Real sound:

He would transpose the note in the octave! and thus destroy the effect, intended by the author!—which is intolerable!

It has been said that the clarinet has four registers; each of these registers has also a distinct quality of tone. That of the high register is somewhat tearing, and should be used only in the fortissimo of the orchestra (some very high notes may nevertheless be sustained *piano*, when the effect of the sound has been properly prepared); or in the bold passages of a brilliant solo. Those of the chalumeau and medium registers are suited to melodies, to arpeggios, and to smooth passages; and the low register is appropriate—particularly in the holding notes—to those *coldly threatening* effects, those dark accents of *motionless rage* which Weber so ingeniously invented. If it be desired to employ with salient effect the piercing cries of the extreme upper notes, and if a too sudden advent of the dangerous note be dreaded on the performer's account, the introduction of the clarinet should be hidden beneath a loud chord from the whole of the orchestra, which—ceasing the moment the clarinet sound has had time to settle firmly and become clear—leaves it then fully displayed without danger:—

The occasions for appropriately inserting these extremely high holding notes are very rare.

The character of the sounds of the medium register, imbued with a kind of loftiness tempering a noble tenderness, render them favorable for the expression of sentiments and ideas the most poetic. Frivolous gaiety, and even perhaps artless joy, seem alone unsuited to them. The clarinet is little appropriate to the *Idyl*; it is an *epic* instrument, like horns, trumpets, and trombones. Its voice is that of heroic love: and if masses of brass instruments, in grand military symphonies, awaken the idea of a warlike troop covered with glittering armour, marching to glory or death, numerous unisons of clarinets, heard at the same time, seem to represent loving women, with their proud eyes and deep affection, whom the sound of arms exalts; who sing while fighting, and who crown the victors, or die with the defeated. I have never been able to hear military music from afar, without being profoundly moved by that feminine quality of tone in the clarinets, and struck by images of this nature, just as after the perusal of ancient epic poems. This beautiful soprano instrument, so ringing, so rich in penetrating accents, when employed in masses,—gains, as a solo, in delicacy, fleeting *nuances*, and mysterious tenderness, what it loses in force and powerful brilliancy. Nothing is so virginal, so pure, as the tint imparted to certain melodies by the tone of a clarinet played in the *medium* by a skilful performer.

It is the one of all the wind instruments which can best breathe forth, swell, diminish, and die away its sound. Thence the precious faculty of producing *distance*, echo, an echo of *echo*, and a *twilight* sound. What more admirable example could I quote of the application of some of these *nuances*, than the dreamy phrase of the clarinet, accompanied by a tremolo of stringed instruments, in the midst of the Allegro of the overture to *Freyschütz!* Does it not depict the lonely maiden, the forester's fair betrothed, who, raising her eyes to heaven, mingles her tender lament with the noise of the dark woods agitated by the storm?—O Weber!!

No. 33.

Solo 1mo., con passione.
tenuto.
Violoncello.
Doublebass.

Pizz.
Col. Imo.
Pizz.
Pizz.
Arco. Dol.
Arco.
p
Arco.
Arco.

I take leave again to quote, from my Monodrame, the effect—if not similar, yet analogous—of a clarinet air, the fragments of which, interrupted by rests, are also accompanied by a tremolo of a portion of the stringed instruments, while the double-basses play pizzicato an occasional low note, producing beneath the harmony a heavy pulsation, and a harp introduces bits of scarcely-heard arpeggios. But in this case, in order to give to the sound of the clarinet an accent as vague and remote as possible, I have caused the instrument to be enveloped in a leather bag, which serves as a "mute." The mournful murmur, and half-stifled sound of the solo, repeating a melody previously heard in another movement, has always forcibly struck the hearers. This shadow of music gives birth to sorrowful dejection, and provokes tears, more than the most dolorous accents. It excites melancholy as much as the trembling harmonies of the Æolian Harp.

* The instrument should be wrapped in a bag of cloth or leather.

a Tempo.
Rall. poco.
a Tempo.
mf
pp
ppp
rf
p
divisi.
Double string.
Pizz.
poco f
ten.
sf
rall
Almost nothing.
pp
f
mf

Beethoven, bearing in mind the melancholy and noble character of the melody in *A* major of the immortal Andante in his 7th Symphony, and in order the better to render all that this phrase contains at the same time of passionate regret, has not failed to consign it to the clarinet. Gluck, for the ritornello of Alceste's air, "Ah, malgré moi, &c.," had at first written a flute; but, perceiving doubtless that the quality of tone of this instrument was too weak, and lacked the nobleness necessary to the delivery of a theme imbued with so much desolation and mournful grandeur, gave it to the clarinet. The clarinets again play, simultaneously with the voice, that other air of Alceste, replete with sorrowful resignation, "Ah, divinités implacables."

An effect of another kind results from three slow notes of the clarinets in thirds in the air of Œdipus, "Votre cœur devint mon asile." It is after the conclusion of the theme, that Polynice, before beginning his air, turns towards the daughter of Theseus, and adds, as he looks at her, "Je connus, &c." These two clarinets in thirds, descending softly previous to the commencement of the voice part, at the moment when the two lovers interchange a tender regard, have an excellent dramatic meaning, and produce an exquisite musical result. The two instrumental voices are here an emblem of love and purity. Listening to them, one almost sees Eryphile modestly casting down her eyes. It is admirable!—

Substitute two hautboys for the two clarinets, and the effect will be destroyed.

This delicious orchestral effect is wanting, however, in the printed score of Sacchini's chef d'œuvre; but I have too often remarked it in the representation, not to feel certain of my memory.

Neither Sacchini, nor Gluck, nor any of the great masters of that time availed themselves of the low notes of the instrument. I cannot guess the reason. Mozart appears to be the first who brought them into use for accompaniments of a serious character, such as that of the trio of masks, in *Don Giovanni*. It was reserved for Weber to discover all that is terrible in the quality of tone of these low sounds, when employed in sustaining sinister harmonies. It is better, in such a case, to write them in two parts, than to place the clarinets in unison or in octave. The more numerous the notes of the harmony, the more striking will be the effect. If there be three clarinets at disposal for the chord, *C♯, E, B♭*, for instance, this diminished seventh well worked, well introduced and instrumented in that way, would have a fearful aspect, which might be further rendered gloomy, by adding a low double G given to a bass-clarinet:—

The Alto Clarinet

Is no other than a clarinet in *F (low)* or in *E♭ (low)*; and consequently is a fifth below the clarinets in *C* or in *B♭*, of which it has the whole compass. It is written therefore, in transposing, either a fifth, or a sixth major above the real sound.

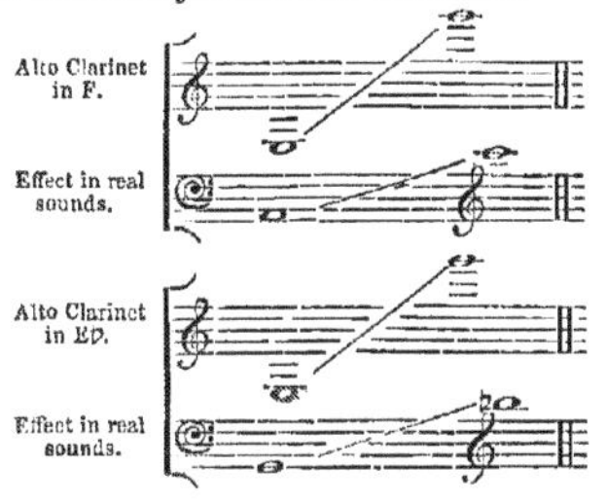

It is a very beautiful instrument, and one regrets not to find it in all well-constituted orchestras.

The Bass Clarinet,

Lower still than the preceding, is an octave below the clarinet in *B♭*; there is another in *C*, however (an octave below the clarinet in *C*); but that in *B♭* is much more usual. As it is always the same instrument,—constructed on larger dimensions,—as the ordinary clarinet, its compass remains much the same. Its reed is a little weaker and more covered than that of the other clarinets. The bass clarinet is evidently not destined to replace in the upper notes the high clarinets; but, certainly, to extend their compass below. Nevertheless, very beautiful effects result from doubling, in the octave below, the high notes of the *B♭* clarinet, by a bass clarinet. It is written, like other clarinets, on the G clef:—

The best notes are the lowest ones; but, owing to the slowness of the vibrations, they should not be made to follow each other too rapidly. M. Meyerbeer has caused the bass clarinet to utter an eloquent monologue in the trio of the fifth act of *The Huguenots*:—

No. 35. *Les Huguenots.*—MEYERBEER.

According to the manner of writing for it, and the talent of the performer, this instrument may borrow the wild quality of tone which distinguishes the bass notes of the ordinary clarinet, or the calm, solemn, and sacerdotal accent belonging to certain registers of the organ. It is therefore of frequent and fine application; and moreover, if four or five be employed in unison, it gives a rich and excellent sonority to the wind instruments of the orchestral bass.

The Corno di Bassetto

Would no otherwise differ from the alto clarinet in *F* (*low*) than by the little brass bell mouth which prolongs its lower extremity, were it not that it has the faculty of descending chromatically as far the *C*, a third below the lowest note of the clarinet:—

The notes which extend above this compass are very hazardous; nor is there any good reason for employing them, since the high clarinets yield them without difficulty, and with much more purity.

Like those of the bass-clarinet, the low notes of the corno di bassetto are the finest and the most marked in character. It should be observed, however, that all those below the E,—

can only be emitted *slowly*, and by *detaching* them one from another. A passage like the following would not be practicable:—

Mozart has used this fine instrument in two parts for darkening the colour of his harmonies in his *Requiem*; and has assigned to it some important solos in his opera, *La Clemenza di Tito*.

Improvements in Clarinets.

The manufacture of these instruments, which remained for so long almost in its infancy, is now-a-days in a state of progress that cannot fail to bring the most valuable results. Already great advance has been made by M. Adolphe Sax, the skilful and accomplished Parisian manufacturer. By slightly elongating the tube of the clarinet towards the bell, he has caused it to gain an additional semitone below; and consequently it can now produce the E♭ or D♯. The B♭ of the medium, which was bad on the old clarinet, is one of the best notes on the modern instrument. The following shakes:—

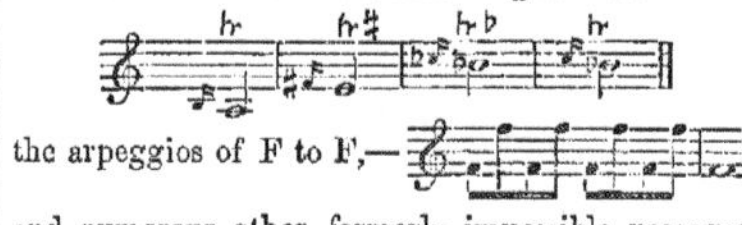

the arpeggios of F to F,— and numerous other formerly impossible passages, have now become easy and of good effect. It is well known that the notes of the high register are the dread of composers and performers, who dare to use them very seldom, and only with extreme precaution. Thanks to a little key placed close to the mouth-piece of the clarinet, M. Sax has rendered these sounds as pure, as smooth, and almost as easy, as those of the medium. Thus the double B♭, which composers hardly ventured to write, comes out from the clarinets of M. Sax without urging, or preparation, or effort, on the part of the performer; it may be played *pianissimo* without the least danger, and it is at least as sweet as that of the flute. As a remedy against the obstacles arising from the too great dryness or too great moisture necessarily induced by the use of wooden mouth-pieces, according as the instrument may have remained some days without being played, or, on the contrary, have been too long used, M. Sax has given to the clarinet a mouth-piece of gilt metal, which enhances the brilliancy of its tone, and is free from the drawbacks to which wooden mouth-pieces are subject. This clarinet has more compass, more equalness, more facility, and more precision than the old one; while the fingering remains the same, excepting that it is in some respects simplified.

M. Adolphe Sax's new *bass clarinet* is still more improved. It has 22 keys. That which especially distinguishes it from the old one is its perfect precision of intonation, an equalized temperament throughout the chromatic scale, and a greater intensity of tone.

As its tube is very long, the bell of the instrument, the performer standing upright, nearly touches the ground; hence an unfortunate smothering of the sound, had not the skilful fabricator thought of remedying this by means of a concave metallic reflector, which, placed beneath the bell, prevents the sound from being lost, directs it at will, and considerably augments its volume.

The bass-clarinets of M. Sax are in B♭.

Wind Instruments without Reeds.

The Flute.

This instrument, which for a long time remained imperfect in very many respects, is now,—thanks to the skill of certain manufucturers, and to the system of fabrication pursued by Boëhm, according to the discovery of Gordon,—as complete, as true, and of as equal a sonority as could be desired.

All wood wind instruments, moreover, will soon be in the same condition. One can understand that their truth of intonation could not be irreproachable under the old system—far from it; since their holes were always pierced according to the natural stretch of the performer's fingers, and not according to the rational division of the sound-tube—a division based upon the laws of resonance, and decided by the focus of vibration. Gordon, and after him, Boëhm, began by piercing the holes of their wind instruments at the exact points of the tube indicated by the physical principle of resonance, without paying regard to the facility, or even the possibility of placing the fingers of the hand upon them; assured as they were of being able to accomplish this at last in one way or other.

The instrument once pierced and rendered true by this proceeding, they invented a mechanism of keys and rings placed in certain spots were the performer's fingers could easily reach them, and serving to open and close those holes which were beyond the command of the fingers. By this means the old fingering necessarily became changed; and the performers had to commence new methods of practice: but this difficulty soon being surmounted, and the new instruments offering such ample compensation, we have no doubt that in a few years, the example spreading ever more and more, wooden wind instruments, constructed on Gordon's and Boëhm's system, will have entirely superseded the old ones.

The flute, a few years ago, had only the following compass:—

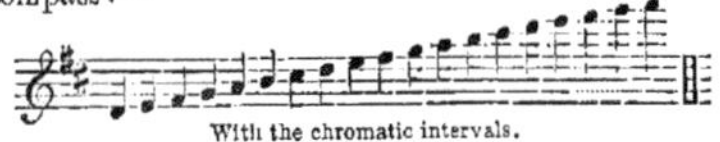

With the chromatic intervals.

There have been successively added to this scale two semitones below, and three above, which gives three complete octaves:—

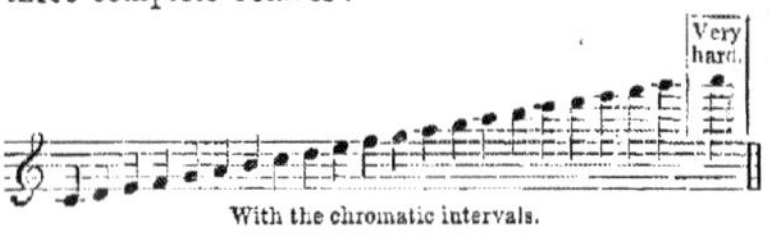

With the chromatic intervals.

However, as all performers have not the C key, that is to say, the little metalic valves which give to the flute the low *C*♯ and *C*♮, it is better, in the majority of cases, to abstain from these two notes in writing for the orchestra. The two last high sounds *B*♮, *C*, should not be employed pianissimo, on account of a certain difficulty which attends their emission, and their rather harsh sounds.

The *B*♭, on the contrary, [music], comes out without trouble; and may be sustained as piano as desired, without the least danger. The number of notes on which shakes may be made were rather restricted in the old flute; but, thanks to the keys added to the modern one, the major and minor shake is practicable upon a large portion of its chromatic scale:—

With flutes constructed upon Boëhm's method, shakes are practicable on the notes of the very extreme upper part of the scale; and from the *D♭* below up to the highest *C*; moreover, they are incomparably more true of intonation.

The flute is the most *agile* of all the wind instruments; it is equally suited to rapid passages (diatonic or chromatic) slurred or detached, to arpeggios, and even to very extended passages like this :—

Also, to iterated notes, like those played staccato on the violin; which are obtained by *double-tonguing*:—

The keys of *D, G, C, F, A, E♮, B♭, E♭*, and their relative minors, are the favorite keys of the flute; the others are greatly more difficult. A flute of Boëhm's, on the contrary, can be played in *D♭* almost as easily as in *D♮*.

The sound of this instrument is sweet in the medium, rather piercing in the high notes, and very characteristic in the low ones. The quality of tone of the medium, and of that of the high portion, has not a very special or decided expression. It may be employed in melodies, or accents of varied character; but without equalling either the artless gaiety of the hautboy, or the noble tenderness of the clarinet. It should seem then that the flute is an instrument well-nigh devoid of expression, but which may be introduced anywhere and everywhere, on account of its facility in executing groups of rapid notes, and in sustaining high sounds useful in the orchestra for adding fullness to the upper harmonies. Generally speaking, this is true; nevertheless, on studying the instrument carefully, there may be discovered an expression peculiar to it, and an aptitude for rendering certain sentiments, in which no other instrument can compete with it. If, for instance, it were requisite to give to a sad air an accent of desolation, but of humility and resignation at the same time, the feeble sounds of the flute's medium, in the keys of *C* minor and *D* minor especially, would certainly produce the desired effect. One master only, seems to me to have known how to avail himself of this pale colouring; and he is Gluck. On listening to the melodramatic movement in *D* minor, which he has placed in the Elysian fields scene of *Orfeo*, it will be at once seen that a flute only could fittingly utter this melody. A hautboy would have been too puerile, and its voice would not have seemed sufficiently pure; the corno inglese is too low; a clarinet would doubtless have answered better; but certain sounds would have been too powerful—none of its softest notes could have reduced themselves to the feeble, faint, veiled sound of the *F* natural of the medium, and of the first *B♭* above the lines, which imparts so much sadness to the flute in this key of *D* minor, where these notes frequently occur. In short, neither the violin, the viola, nor the violoncello, used in solo or in masses, would serve to express this very sublime lament of a suffering and despairing departed spirit. It required precisely the instrument selected by the author. And Gluck's melody is conceived in such a way that the flute lends itself to all the uneasy writhings of this eternal grief, still imbued with the passions of earthly life. It is at first a voice scarcely audible, which seems to fear being overheard; then it laments softly, rising into the accent of reproach, then into that of profound woe, the cry of a heart torn by incurable wounds, then falling little by little into complaint, regret, and the sorrowing murmur of a resigned soul. What a poet!

No. 36. *Orfeo.*—GLUCK.

Sempre Legato.

An effect remarkable for its sweetness is that of two flutes playing, in the medium, successions of thirds in *E♭* or in *A♭*—both being keys extremely favorable to the velvet sounds of this instrument. Beautiful examples of this are to be found in the chorus of Priests in the first act of *Œdipus:* "O vous, que l'innocence même," and in the cavatina of the duet in the *Vestale:* "Les Dieux prendront pitié." The notes, *B♭*, *A♭*, *G*, *F*, and *E♭*, in flutes, have, thus grouped, something of the sonorousness of the harmonica. Thirds of hautboys, corni inglesi, or clarinets, do not resemble them.

The low sounds of the flute are seldom, or else ill, employed by the majority of composers. Weber, in numerous passages of the *Freyschutz*, and, before him, Gluck, in the religious march in *Alceste*, have nevertheless shown what may be done with it in harmonies imbued with seriousness and thought. These bass notes,—as I have already said,—mingle admirably with the low sounds of corni inglesi and clarinets; they give the softened shade of a dark colouring:—

No. 37.

Another instance of this occurs in the example quoted from Weber's *Freyschutz* (page 35). There is something ineffably dreamy in these low holding notes of the two flutes, as, during her melancholy prayer, Agatha contemplates the summits of the trees silvered by the rays of the night planet.

In general the modern masters keep their flutes too constantly in the high range; they seem afraid that these instruments will not be sufficiently distinguished amidst the mass of the orchestra. It hence results that they predominate, instead of blending with the whole; and thus the instrumentation becomes hard and piercing rather than sonorous and harmonious.

Flutes form a family of themselves—like hautboys and clarinets—and are quite as numerous. The large flute—of which mention has just been made—is the most used. For ordinary orchestras no more than two parts for the large flute are written; nevertheless soft chords held on by three flutes would often have an excellent effect. A charming result is produced by the association of a single flute above, with four violins sustaining a high harmony in five parts. Notwithstanding the prevailing custom—for which there is reason, however—of always giving to the first flute the highest notes of the harmony, there are many occasions in which a contrary plan might be pursued with success.

The Piccolo Flute.

It is an octave higher than the preceding :—

It has the same compass, always excepting the double high C, which comes out with great difficulty, and with a sound almost insufferable; so that it should never be written. The B♮, is of exceeding hardness, and can only be employed in a *fortissimo* of the whole orchestra. It is almost useless, by contrary reason, to write the notes of the lower octave, since they would be scarcely heard, and, unless for an effect to be produced by the peculiarity of their feeble tone, it is better to replace them by their corresponding sounds in the second octave of the large flute.

Piccolo flutes are strangely abused now-a-days—as is the case with all instruments whose vibrations thrill, pierce, or flash forth. In pieces of a joyous character, the sounds of the second octave,—

may be very suitable, in all their gradations; while the upper notes,—

are excellent (fortissimo) for violent and tearing effects: in a storm, for instance, or in a scene of fierce or infernal character. Thus, the piccolo flute figures incomparably in the fourth movement of Beethoven's Pastoral Symphony—now alone and displayed, above the low tremolo of violas and basses, imitating the whistlings of a tempest whose full force is not yet unchained—now on the higher notes still, together with the entire mass of the orchestra. Gluck, in the tempest of *Iphigenia in Tauride*, has shown how to make the high sounds of the piccolo flutes in unison grate still more roughly, by writing them in a succession of sixths, a fourth above the first violins. The sound of the piccolo flutes issuing out in the upper octave produces therefore a succession of elevenths with the first violins, the harshness of which is here of the very best effect.

No. 38. *Pastoral Symphony.*—BEETHOVEN.

8ve.
loco.
cres.
With the large flutes, an octave below.
cres.
cres.
p
cres.
f
sf
cres.
f
sf
p
cres.
cres.
8ve.
Sempre più f
Horns in F.
f
Sempre più f
f

8ve.
sf
ff
Trumpets in E♭.
Trombone Alto.
Trombone Tenor.
Drums in F.
tr

No. 39.

Iphigenia in Tauride.—GLUCK

In the chorus of Scythians in the same opera (*Iphigenia in Tauride*), the two piccolo flutes double in the octave the little grouped passages of the violins; these whistling notes, mingled with the ravings of the savage troop, with the measured and incessant din of the cymbals and tambourine, make one shiver. (See Ex. 64.)

Everyone has remarked the diabolic sneer of the two piccolo flutes in thirds, in the drinking song of the *Freyschutz*. It is one of Weber's happiest orchestral inventions :—

Spontini, in his magnificent bacchanalian strain in the *Danaïdes* (since become an orgy chorus in *Nurmahal*) first conceived the idea of uniting a short piercing cry of the piccolo flutes to a stroke of the cymbals. The singular sympathy discovered between these very dissimilar instruments had not been thought of before. The effect cuts and rends instantaneously, like the stab of a poignard. This effect is very characteristic—even when employing only the two instruments mentioned; but its force is augmented by an abrupt stroke of the kettle-drums, joined to a brief chord of all the other instruments.

These different examples, and others that I could cite, appear to me admirable in every respect. Beethoven, Gluck, Weber, and Spontini have thus made ingenious use—no less original than rational—of the piccolo flute. But when I hear the instrument employed in doubling in triple octave the air of a baritone, or casting its squeaking voice into the midst of a religious harmony, or strengthening and sharpening—for the sake of noise only—the high part of the orchestra from beginning to end of the act of an opera, I cannot help feeling this mode of instrumentation to be a platitude and stupidity worthy, generally speaking, of the melodic style to which it is applied.

The piccolo flute may have a very happy effect in soft passages; and it is mere prejudice to think that it should only be played loudly. Sometimes it serves to continue the high scale of the large flute, by succeeding the latter at the moment when it reaches high notes beyond its command. The passing from one instrument to the other may then be easily managed by the composer in such a way as to make it appear that there is only one flute of extraordinary compass.

A charming instance of this device occurs in a phrase played *pianissimo* on a low holding note of the stringed instruments, in the first act of Auber's opera, *Le Dieu et la Bayadère*.

In military music advantageous use is made of three other flutes, which might be very serviceable in ordinary orchestras; these are :—

Firstly, *The tierce flute* (said to be in *F*), of which the C makes *E*♭, and which should—from all that has been said in commencing this chapter—be classed among transposing instruments in *E*♭. It is exactly a minor third above the ordinary flute—from which it differs only in that particular, and in its more crystalline quality of tone.

Secondly, *The minor ninth piccolo flute* (said to be in *E*♭), the C of which makes D♭; and which accordingly may be classed among the transposing instruments in *D*♭. It is a semitone higher than the *octave piccolo flute*; and it should be similarly treated :—

Thirdly, *The tenth piccolo flute* (said to be in F), of which the C makes *E*♭; and which we will call *tenth piccolo flute in E*♭. It is an octave above the minor third flute, and a tenth above the ordinary flute :—

It should not be made to go above the high [music], and even this note is excessively piercing, and comes out with difficulty.

Some orchestras also possess a large *minor second flute*, of which the C makes D♭, which should be called flute in *D*♭, and of which the diapason is only a semitone higher than that of the ordinary flute

All these flutes, which concur in increasing the high compass of the instrument, and of which the qualities of tone are variously characterised, are useful, moreover, in rendering the execution more easy, and in preserving to the flute its sonorousness, by allowing it to play in one of its brilliant keys, while the orchestra is written in one of its duller keys. It is evidently much more advantageous, for a piece in *E*♭ for instance, to prefer the *ninth minor piccolo flute in D*♭, to the *octave piccolo flute*, because the former of these plays in the key of *D*, which is much easier and more full-sounding.

It is a pity that the *Flûte d'amour* should have been allowed to fall into disuse; its diapason was a minor third below the ordinary flute (in *A*, therefore).

This completes the low-compassed family of the instrument (which might be made, however, as numerous a family as that of the clarinets, if needful); and its soft smooth quality of tone might be of excellent effect, either for contrasting with the quality of high flutes or hautboys or for giving greater body and depth of colour to those harmonies—already so peculiar—which result from the bass notes of flutes, corni inglesi, and clarinets.

Wind Instruments with Key-boards

*The Organ**

Is an instrument with a key-board and pipes of wood and of metal, made to vibrate by means of the wind sent through them from bellows.

The number, greater or less, of series of pipes of different kinds and different dimensions possessed by an organ, gives it a proportional variety of *stops*, by means of which the organist can change the quality of tone, the power of sound, and the compass of the instrument.

The mechanism by means of which, on drawing out a little piece of wood, the organist makes such and such a stop speak, is called a register.

[* What is here said upon the organ refers to Continental organs, and therefore applies but partially to the organ in this country.—*Translator.*]

The compass of the instrument is indefinite; it varies with its dimension,—which is ordinarily designated by the length in feet of the pipe forming the lowest note of the key-board. Thus they say: an organ of thirty-two feet, of sixteen, of eight, or of four feet.

An instrument which possesses, with the lowest stop—called *open flute of thirty-two feet*—an open flute of *sixteen feet*, an open flute of *eight feet*, a Prestant, or open flute of *four feet*, and the Principal which sounds the octave above the preceding, has the immense compass of eight octaves:—

Compass of 32 feet

Compass of 16 feet

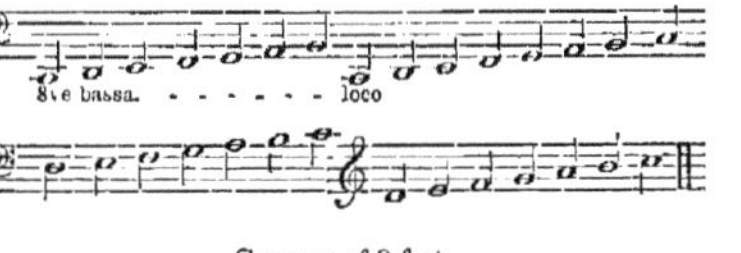

Compass of 8 feet

Compass of the Prestant of 4 feet

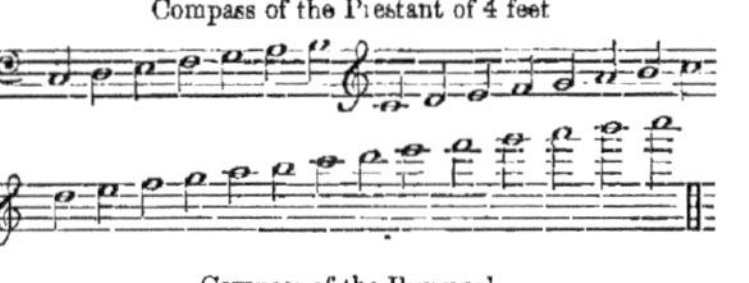

Compass of the Principal.

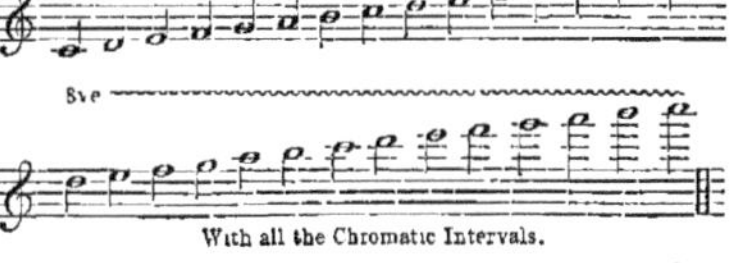

With all the Chromatic Intervals.

These five stops—as may be seen—have each four octaves; but many others among those of which we shall presently speak, have only three, or even two.

At the present time, organ-builders give five notes higher to their key-boards. The compass above is thus extended, chromatically, up to F, [music]

A large organ generally possesses five key-boards one above another

The first—nearest to the organist—is the choir-organ key-board (*le clavier du Positif*).

The second, that of the *great organ*.

The third is the bombarde key-board.

The fourth, the recitative key-board.

The fifth, the echo key-board.

There is, moreover, a sixth key-board placed in such a manner as to be put in action by the feet of the performer; and for this reason it is called the pedal key-board. This is dedicated to the lowest notes of the organ. It has only the two octaves at the lower end, and often even lacks certain notes of these. Many of the stops—the eight-feet stops, for instance—occurring at the same time on the three key-boards of the great organ, the choir-organ, and the pedal, may be doubled or tripled.

The stops of the organ are divided into *mouth* stops, and reed stops; thus named, the first, from a sort of open mouth at one of the extremities, serving for the formation of the sound, and the second, from a little tongue of brass placed also at the extremity, producing a peculiar quality of tone.

The *mouth* stops are divided into *foundation* or *octave* stops, and *mutation* stops. The foundation stops are open or closed; the closed stops—called bourdons—are an octave below the open pipes of the same size.

The mutation stops have this peculiarity,—that they give above each sound, its third, its fifth, its tenth, in such a way as to represent, by the action of several small pipes, the aliquot parts or harmonics of the large pipes. Organ manufacturers and organists agree in finding excellent the effect produced by this multiplied resonance, which, however, decidedly causes several different keys to be heard at once. They say, "it would be insufferable, if the higher sounds were distinguished; but *they are not heard*, the lowest sound absorbing them." It remains to be explained how that which is *not heard* can produce a good effect to the ear. At any rate, this singular proceeding will always tend to give the organ the harmonic resonance which is vainly sought to be avoided in horizontal grand pianofortes; and which, to my thinking, is one of the worst defects in sonority occasioned to this instrument by modern improvements.

Among the mutation stops are reckoned, the gros nazard, which sounds the fifth of the eight-feet open flute.

The grosse tierce, which sounds the fifth of the Prestant.

The onzième de nazard, which is in unison with the Principal.

The tierce, sounding the third above the Principal.

The *furniture*, or plein jeu, which consists of three ranks of pipes, and of seven ranks of aliquot pipes the one with the other.

The *cymbal*, which differs from the furniture stop, only by its pipes being less thick.

The *cornet*,—a very brilliant stop, of two octaves, and of five ranks of pipes; it only plays in the upper part. Large organs possess three cornet stops,—one on the choir-organ, another on the great organ, and a third on the recitative key-board.

Among the reed stops, we will only specify the following:—

First, the bombarde; a stop of great power, which is played on a separate key-board, or on the pedal. Its first pipe is sixteen-feet; and it is in unison with the open sixteen-feet.

Second, the *trumpet stop*; which sounds the unison of the eight-feet pipe, and consequently the high octave of the bombarde.

Third, the *clarion stop*; the high octave of the trumpet stop.

Fourth, the *Cremona stop*; the unison of the trumpet stop, but less brilliant; it is always placed in the choir-organ.

Fifth, the *vox humana stop*; which sounds the eight-feet pipe, and is placed in the great organ.

Sixth, the *hautboy stop*; which sounds in unison with the trumpet stop. It has usually the upper octaves only; but it is completed by means of the bassoon stop, which furnishes the two other octaves.

These different stops imitate tolerably well in their quality of tone the instruments whose names they bear. There are organs which possess many others, such as the *corno inglese stop*, the *trombone stop*, &c.

Every organ should have a draw-stop which serves for the principal sounds, which corresponds with the whole of the key-board, and which, for this reason, is called the *Principal.*

The fingering of the organ is the same as that of the pianoforte,—with this difference—that the emission of the sounds being less instantaneous, such rapid successions cannot be executed as on the pianoforte; the mechanism of the key-board, moreover, obliging the organist to press his fingers more upon each key. This instrument possesses the power of sustaining the sounds as long as may be desired: it is therefore more suited than any other to the *bound* style; that is to say, to that in which the harmony makes the most frequent use of suspensions and prolongations, and of oblique movement. In my opinion, however, this is no reason for invariably remaining within the limits of this style. Music for the organ is sometimes written upon three lines; the two upper ones for the hands, and the under one for the pedal key-board.

The organ seems able—like the pianoforte, and even better—to present itself in the instrumental heirarchy under two aspects:—as an instrument belonging to the orchestra, or as being in itself a complete and independent orchestra. It is doubtless possible to blend the organ with the divers constituent elements of the orchestra, and this has been many times done: but it is strangely derogatory to the majestic instrument to reduce it to a secondary place. Moreover, it should be felt that the smooth, equal, and uniform sonorousness of the organ, never entirely melts into the variously characterized sounds of the orchestra, and that there seems to exist between these two musical powers a secret antipathy. The Organ and the Orchestra are both Kings; or rather, one is Emperor, the other Pope; their mission is not the same; their interests are too vast, and too diverse, to be confounded together. Therefore, on almost all occasions when this singular connection is attempted, either the organ much predominates over the orchestra, or the orchestra, having been raised to an immoderate degree of influence, almost eclipses its adversary.

The soft stops of the organ seem alone suitable for accompanying the voice. In general, the organ is formed for absolute dominion; it is a jealous and intolerant instrument. In one case only, it seems to me, can the organ, without derogation, mingle with the choir and orchestra; but even then on condition of itself remaining in solemn isolation. For example, if a mass of voices placed in the choir of a church, at a great distance from the organ, interrupted its chaunts from time to time, that they might be repeated on the organ, in part, or entirely; if the same choir, in a rite of some sad character, were accompanied by a lament from the orchestra and from the organ, issuing thus from the two extreme points of the temple, the organ succeeding to the orchestra, like the mysterious echo of its lamentation,—this would be a mode of instrumentation susceptible of grand and sublime effects. But, even in this case, the organ would not really mingle with the other instruments; it would answer them, it would interrogate them: and the alliance between the two rival powers would be the more sincere, because neither the one nor the other would lose any of its dignity. Whenever I have heard the organ playing at the same time with the orchestra, it has seemed to me to produce a detestable effect, and to impair that of the orchestra instead of augmenting it. This is not the place for determining the manner in which the organ—considered as a complete orchestra in itself—should be individually treated. We have not undertaken the task of giving a series of systems of the different instruments; but merely a careful study of the best mode of making them conduce to musical effect in association. The knowledge of the organ, the art of choosing its different stops, and of contrasting them one with the other, constitutes the talent of the organist,—supposing him to be, according to custom, an extempore player. In the contrary case,—that is to say, considering him merely as a simple performer having to execute a written work,—he should scrupulously conform to the instructions of the composer; who is bound to know the special resources of the instrument he writes for, and to employ them judiciously. But these resources are so vast and numerous, that the composer will never be well acquainted with them,—as it appears to us,—unless he be himself an accomplished organist.

If, in a composition, the organ be combined with voices, and with other instruments, it should not be forgotten that its pitch is *lower* by a whole tone than the present pitch of the orchestra; and that, therefore, it should be treated as a transposing instrument in B♭. (The organ of St. Thomas at Leipzig, on the contrary, is a tone *higher* than the orchestra.)*

The organ possesses effects of sonority, soft, loud, and awe-striking; but it is not in its nature to deliver them in rapid succession. It cannot therefore, like the orchestra, suddenly pass from *Piano* to *Forte*, or from *Forte* to *Piano*. Improvements recently introduced into its construction enable it—by the successive employment of different *stops* in conjunction—to produce a sort of crescendo; and then bring in a *decrescendo* by withdrawing them in the same order. But the gradation and regradation obtained by this ingenious method do not admit of the intermediate shades which give so much force to these fluctuations of the orchestra. There is always felt—more or less—the operation of an inanimate mechanism. Erard's instrument, known under the name of the expressive organ ("l'orgue expressif") alone gives the possibility of really swelling and diminishing the sound; but it is not yet adopted in churches. Serious men—of otherwise excellent understanding—condemn its use, as destructive of the religious character and intention of the organ.

Without entering upon the great question, so often discussed, of the propriety of expression in sacred music—a question which simple good sense exempt from prejudice might resolve in a moment—we will take leave to point out to the partisans of unornate music, of plain-song, and of the *inexpressive organ* (as if the loud and soft stops of different qualities of tone did not already give to the organ variety and expression); we will just request them, we say, to observe that they are the first to exclaim with admiration, when the performance of a chorus, in a sacred work, shines by the delicacy of its graduated effects of crescendo, decrescendo, light and shade, swelled, sustained, or suppressed sounds,—in a word, by all those attributes which are wanting in the organ, and which Erard's invention will tend to supply. These persons are therefore evidently inconsistent with themselves; unless they pretend (as they are very capable of doing) that expressive gradations, perfectly appropriate, religious, and catholic, in the human voice, become suddenly, when applied to the organ, irreligious, heterodox, and impious. It is singular also,—let me be pardoned this digression,—that these critical conservatives of orthodoxy in the matter of religious music, who maintain, and with reason, that true religious sentiment directs inspiration (while prohibiting the expression of gradations in this sentiment), have never thought of blaming the use of quick fugues, which for ages have formed the staple of organ music in all schools. Is it that the themes of these fugues—some of which express nothing, while many others are of a fashion at least grotesque,—become grave and religious merely because they are treated in fugal style;—that is to say, in the form which tends to reproduce them oftenest and display them most constantly? Is it that these multiplied introductions of different parts, these imitations in canon, these scraps of twisted and tangled phrases, pursuing, flying, and rolling over one another, this "confusion worse confounded," where true melody is excluded, where the chords succeed each other so rapidly that their character can scarcely be discerned, this i[illegible]

* This is applicable only to ancient organs; modern organ-builders tune their instruments to the pitch of the orchestra.

sant subversion of all system, this appearance of disorder, these abrupt interruptions of one part by another, all these hideous musical pasquinades, excellent for depicting an orgy of savages, or a dance of demons—become transformed in passing through the pipes of an organ, and assume the serious, the grand, the calm accent, either suppliant or contemplative, of holy prayer, of meditation, or even of terror, religious awe and dread! There are organisations sufficiently monstrous to find all this true. At any rate, the critics I have just alluded to, without precisely affirming that quick organ fugues are imbued with religious feeling, have never blamed their inappropriateness and absurdity, probably because they found them in long-established use; because the most learned masters, following mere routine, have written large numbers of them; and lastly, because writers who treat of religious music, being ordinarily very much attached to christian dogmas, involuntarily consider everything that leads to alteration in ideas consecrated by time as dangerous and incompatible with the immutability of faith. For our parts,—and to return to our subject,—we confess to thinking that if Erard's invention were applied to the old organ, merely as a new stop, so that it might enable the organist to employ expressive sounds, if he thought proper, or at least so that it might swell and diminish certain sounds independently of others, it would be a real improvement, entirely to the advantage of the *true* religious style.

Brass Instruments with Mouth-pieces.

The Horn.

As this instrument possesses a large number of movable crooks, which render its pitch more or less low and more or less high,—its compass cannot be precisely stated, without at the same time knowing the kind of horn in question. It is, in fact, easier to produce high sounds than low sounds on horns of a low key; excepting, however, the keys of *A*, *B♭*, and *C* (low), when the extreme length of the tube renders the emission of high notes very difficult. It is easier, on the contrary, to give low notes than high notes, on horns whose keys are high. Moreover, certain horn-players, using a large mouthpiece, and being well-practised in giving low sounds, cannot bring forth the higher ones; while others, who use a narrow mouth-piece, and have accustomed themselves to give forth the high notes, cannot produce the lower ones.

There is then a particular compass for each key of the instrument, and likewise two others of a special character,. belonging to performers who play the high part (that of the first horn), and the low part (that of the second horn).

The horn is written on the G clef, and on the F clef; with this particularity established by custom, that the G clef is considered as being lower by an octave than it really is. The subjoined examples will make this understood.

All horns, with the exception of the horn in *C* above, are transposing instruments; that is to say, their written notes do not represent the real sounds.

They have two kinds of sounds, very different in character; *open* sounds, almost all of which are the natural resonance of the harmonic divisions of the instrument's tube, and come out without other assistance than that of the lips and breath of the player; and *closed* sounds, which are obtained by closing more or less the *bell* (the lower orifice of the horn) with the hand.

First, here is the table of *open* sounds on the different first and second horns:—

*This open F♯ cannot be so easily played as the G♮; but it comes out very well if it be preceded by a neighbouring note like G♮, or F♯, or A. It is a little too high.

The double G below, marked with the sign *, is easier in the higher keys; but is bad and uncertain in most other keys generally.

The family of horns is complete; there are horns in *all keys*, although it is generally thought otherwise. Those which appear to be wanting in the chromatic scale are obtained by means of a lengthening piece which lowers the instrument a semitone. Thus, although we have, in fact, formed of all pieces, only horns in *B♭* (low), in *C*, in *D*, in *E♭*, in *E♮*, in *F*, in *G*, in *A♭*, in *A♮* (high), in *B♭* (high), and in *C* (high); by adding lengthening pieces to the keys of *B♭* and *C* (low), *A♮* is obtained, and *B♮* (low); and, by the same means, the key of *D* is transformed into *D♭* (or *C♯*), the key of *G* into *G♭* (or *F♯*), and the key of *C* (high) into *B♮* (high) (or *C♭*); this last key is obtained by merely drawing the slide of the horn in *C* (high).

The *closed* sounds present, not only as compared with the open sounds, but even with themselves, marked differences of tone and sonorousness. These differences arise from the greater or smaller opening left in the *bell* by the hand of the performer. For certain notes the bell should be closed a *quarter*, a *third*, or one *half*; for others, it requires to be closed almost entirely. The narrower the opening left in the bell, the duller and rougher the note; and the more difficult are certainty and precision in the playing. There is therefore an important distinction to be made among the closed sounds; which will be designated by affixing the sign ½ to those which are the best notes and for which the bell must be only half closed.

The white notes are the open sounds,—the table of which is given above; and the black, represent the closed sounds.

Before going farther, and in order to be able to give the table of the complete compass of the horn, we will here mention that there are still some open notes, less known than the preceding, yet nevertheless very useful. They are, the high G♭, the intonation of which is always a little lower, and which only appears truly in tune when placed between two Fs,—

it can therefore never replace F♯; the low *A♭*, which is obtained by forcing a G, and by compressing the lips; and the low F♮, which comes out, on the contrary, by leaving the lips free. These two last notes are very valuable; the A♭, particularly, produces on many occasions an excellent effect in all the keys higher than the key of *D*. As to the F♮, it is of more uncertain emission; and there is more difficulty in sustaining it precisely in tune.

These low sounds can, strictly speaking, be played without preparation; but to this end they should not be preceded by notes too high: it is nevertheless much better, as a rule, to place them after a G:—

The passing from the A♭ to the F♮ is practicable in a moderate movement: —

Certain horn-players produce beneath these notes, the E♮, ; a detestable note, and almost unapproachable. I advise composers never to employ it, or the following five low notes, which rarely come out well in tune, which there is much trouble in fixing, and which should not be attempted,—at any rate, only on middle horns, such as the horns in *D*, *E*, and *F*; and in a *descending* progression:—

By uniting the compass of the first horn with that of the second, and by making the factitious open notes, or closed notes, succeed the natural open notes, the following immense chromatic scale results,—ascending from low to high:—

GENERAL COMPASS OF THE HORN.

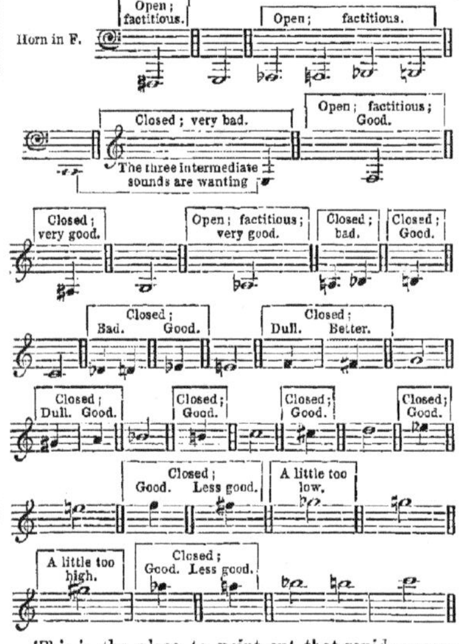

This is the place to point out that rapid successions are the more difficult on the horn according as its key is lower; its tube,—which is then of considerable length,—not being able to be put instantaneously in vibration. As for natural low notes, in almost all keys, they can only succeed each other in a moderate movement; it is, moreover, a general law, which should be observed in all instruments, that, since the low sounds are those which result from the smallest number of vibrations in a second, the sonorous body should have the requisite time for the production of its sound. Thus, the following passage, on a low horn, would be impracticable, and of bad effect:—

This one,—possible on a horn in *F*, and in the higher keys,—would also be very bad in the keys of *C* and of *B*♭ low:—

Care should be taken, as much as possible, in employing closed sounds, particularly in the orchestra, to intersperse them with open sounds; and not to skip from one closed note to another; or, at least, from a bad closed note to another equally bad. Thus, it would be absurd to write—

On the contrary, a passage like this—

is not deficient in sonority, and can easily be executed, because it contains but one bad closed note (the first A♭); while the same passage transposed would be ridiculous, and of excessive difficulty:—

From these three examples it appears that the best closed sounds—with the exception of the five following—

are to be found above the middle A♭; they form the series already indicated:—

Hence, the phrase in A♭ above cited, while good in one octave, becomes detestable when transposed an octave below, where it runs almost entirely upon the worst closed notes,—

moreover, it begins with an open note, the A♭, and a factitious note, which thus attacked rapidly, without preparation, is of extremely hazardous utterance.

The old masters limited themselves, in general, to the use of open sounds; which they wrote—it must be owned—very clumsily. Beethoven himself is exceedingly reserved in his use of closed sounds, when he does not treat the horns in *solo*. Examples of their employment are rather rare in his orchestral writing; and when he has recourse to them, it is almost always for a striking effect. Instance the closed sounds of the three horns in *E*♭, in the scherzo of the Eroica Symphony, and the low F♯ of the second horn in *D* in the scherzo of the Symphony in A:—

No. 40.

Sinfonia Eroica.—BEETHOVEN.

a duo.
cres.
cres.
Solo.
Dol. sempre legato.
Dol. sempre legato.
Solo.
Dol. sempre legato.

p
Cres.
Cres.
p
p
Cres.
p
f
Cres.
f
p
f
p
f
p
f
p

pp
sf
pp
f
p

No. 41.

Presto meno assai.
Symphony in A.—BEETHOVEN.
1mo. Solo.
Dol.
1mo. Solo.
2ndo. Solo.
Flute.
Hautboys.
Clarinets in A.
Horns in D.
Trumpet in D.
Bassoons.
Drums, A, F.
Violins.
Violas.
Violoncellos.
Double-bass.

cres.
cres.
cres.
cres.
cres.
cres.
ff
ff
ff
ff
ff
ff
tr
ff
ff
ff
cres.
ff
cres.
ff
cres.
ff

This system is doubtless greatly superior to the contrary method, adopted nowadays by the majority of French and Italian composers, which consists in writing for the horns exactly as for bassoons or clarinets, without taking into account the enormous difference existing between closed sounds and open sounds, as also between certain closed sounds and certain others, and without caring for the difficulty the player has in taking such and such a note after another note which does not lead to it naturally,—for the dubious correctness,—for the slight sonorousness or hoarse and strange character of the intonations produced by closing the two thirds or three fourths of the bell,—in short, without appearing to have a misgiving that a thorough knowledge of the instrument, together with taste and good sense, may have something to do with the use of the sounds which these pupil-masters thus introduce at all risks into the orchestra. Even the parsimony of the ancients is preferable to such ignorant and odious prodigality. When closed sounds are not w tt for a particular effect, those at least should be avoided of which the sonority is too weak and too much unlike the other sounds of the horn.

Of these, are, the D♮ and the D♭ below the stave, ; the A♮ and the low B♭, ; and the A♭ of the medium, ; which should never be employed as notes of filling up; but only in order to produce effects inherent to their dull, hoarse, and wild quality of tone. For a melodic design, the form of which imperiously demands the presence of this note, I would except only the middle A♭:—

The low B♭, is once introduced with excellent dramatic purpose, by Weber, in the scene of the *Freyschutz* where Gaspard invokes Zamiel; but this sound is so closed, and consequently so dull, that it is not heard. It could only be remarked by the whole orchestra suddenly ceasing at the moment of its utterance. Thus, the middle A♭, written by Meyerbeer in the Nun-scene of *Robert le Diable*, when Robert approaches the tomb to gather the enchanted branch, gains general attention only on account of the silence of almost all the other instruments; and yet this note is much more sonorous than the low B♭. In certain scenes of silent horror, a very great effect may result from these closed notes in several parts. Méhul is the only one, I believe, who has perceived this, in his opera of *Phrosine et Mélidore*.

Major and minor shakes are practicable on the horn; but in a small portion of the scale only. These are the best:—

Horns are generally written—whatever may be their key, and that of the orchestra—without sharps or flats at the clef. When the horn is treated as a reciting part, however, it is better, if the instrument be not in the same key as the orchestra, to indicate at the clef the sharps or flats required by the key; but it should always be so managed as that very few are employed. Thus, the horn in *F* is very well selected for the performance of a solo, when the orchestra is playing in *E♭*; first, because it is one of the best keys of the instrument, and next, because this combination does not necessitate for the horn part more than two flats (B and E) at the clef; one of which (the B) being, in the medium and in the high, an open note, does not diminish the sonorousness of the portion of its scale which would be most employed in such a case:—

It is true, that a horn in *E♭*, for a passage like this, would be quite as advantageous:—

But if the melody bring in frequently the fourth and sixth degree of this scale (*A♭* and *C*), the horn in *F* would be a great deal better than the horn in *E♭*; its two notes, [music] which produce [music] being much better than those of the horn in *E♭*, [music] representing the same sounds.

Orchestras formerly possessed but two horns; but at present composers always find them provided with four. With two horns—even by making use of the *closed sounds*, when needful to modulate rather far from the principal key,—the resources of the instrument would be very limited; but with four, on the contrary, even when it is desired to employ only the *open notes*, it is easy to manage by means of an *interchange of keys*.

A composer who takes four horns in the same key almost always gives proof of egregious want of judgment. It is incomparably better to employ two horns in one key and two in another; or the first and second horn in the same key, the third in another, and the fourth in another—which would be still more preferable; or, lastly, four horns in four different keys; which should be done especially when a large number of *open sounds* is wanted.

The orchestra playing, for instance, in *A♭*, these four horns might be, the first, in *A♭*; the second, in *E♮* (on account of its E producing G♯, which gives enharmonically the A♭); the third, in *F*, and the fourth, in *C*. Or, the first in *A♮*; the second, in *D♭*; the third, in *E♮*; the fourth, in low *B♮* (on account of its E producing D♯, which gives enharmonically E♭). The composer may also—according to the texture of the piece—combine the four keys in several other ways; it is for him to calculate the exigences of his harmonies, and to make the choice of his horns subservient to their need.

By this means there are very few chords in which four, three, or at least two open notes may not be introduced.

When many different keys are used at the same time, it is better to give the high keys to the first horns, and the low keys to the second horns.

Another precaution, which many composers unwisely neglect, is that of not making the performer, in the same piece, exchange a very high key for a very low key, and vice-versa. The horn player, for instance, finds it very awkward to pass suddenly from the key of *A* (high), to that of *B♭* (low); and by means of four horns—which are now to be found in all orchestras—there is never any necessity, when a change of key occurs, for skips so disproportioned.

The horn is a noble and melancholy instrument; yet the expression of its quality of tone, and its sonority, do not unfit it for figuring in any kind of piece. It blends easily with the general harmony; and the composer—even the least skilful—may, if he choose, either make it play an important part, or a useful but subordinate one. No master, in my opinion, has ever known how to avail himself of its powers more originally, more poetically, and at the same time more completely, than Weber. In his three finest works, *Oberon*, *Euryanthe*, and *Der Freyschutz*, he causes the horn to speak a language as admirable as it is novel—a language which Méhul and Beethoven alone seem to have comprehended before him, and of which Meyerbeer, better than any one, has maintained the purity. The horn is, of all orchestral instruments, that which Gluck wrote least well for; a simple inspection of one of his works suffices to lay bare his want of skill in this respect. We must however quote, as a stroke of genius, those three notes of the horn imitating the conch of Charon in the air from *Alceste*: "Charon now calls thee!" They are middle C's, given in unison by two horns in *D*; but the author having conceived the idea of causing the bells of each to be closed, it follows that the two instruments serve mutually as a sordine, and the sounds, interclashing, have a distant effect, and a cavernous *timbre* most strange and dramatic:—

I think, however, that Gluck would have obtained nearly the same result with the closed middle A♭ of two horns in *G♭*:—

Horns in G♭.

But perhaps, at that period, the performers were not so sure of taking such notes; and the author did well in using this singular means of giving gloom and remoteness to the most open sound of the horn in *D*.

Rossini, in the hunting-scene of the second act of *Guillaume Tell*, conceived the idea of causing a diatonic phrase to be executed by four *E♭* horns in unison. It is very original. When four horns are thus united, either in a sustained air, or in a rapid passage which requires the use of closed sounds and open sounds, it is far better (unless the idea be based on this very variety and inequality of sounds) to put them all in different keys; the open sounds on some, thus compensating the slight sonority of the corresponding closed sounds on others, preserve the balance, and give to the scale of the four combined horns a kind of homogeneousness. Thus, while the horn in *C* gives the E♭ (closed), if the horn in *E♭* gives the C (open), the horn in *F* the B♭ (open), and a horn in *B♭* the F (closed), there results from these four different qualities a very sonorous and beautiful E♭. It will be seen that nearly the same advantage attends all the other notes.

An advantageous proceeding—of which I know but one example—consists in making three or four horns in different keys succeed each other for the execution of a *solo* air. As each of them takes in the phrase those notes which correspond with its open sounds, there results,—if the melodic fragments be adroitly linked one to another,—a strain seemingly executed by a single horn, and having almost all its notes equal and open.

I have said that the horn is a noble and melancholy instrument, notwithstanding the *jocund hunting flourishes* so often quoted. In fact, the gaiety of these strains arises rather from the melody itself, than from the quality of tone of the horns. Hunting flourishes are only really *jocund* when played on *trumpets*—an instrument little musical, the strident tone of which, even in the open air, bears no resemblance to the chaste and reserved voice of the horn. By forcing in a particular way the emission of the air from the tube of a horn, it is brought, however, to resemble that of the trumpet.

The sound may sometimes be made brassy (*cuivré*) with excellent effect, even on closed notes. When there is need to force the open notes, composers generally require the performers—in order to give the sound all possible roughness—to elevate the bells of their instruments; and they then indicate the position of the horn by these words:—*Raise the Bells.* A magnificent example of the employment of this means is to be found in the final crash of the duet in Méhul's *Euphrosyne et Coradin:*—"Gardez vous de la jalousie." Under the influence of this fearful yell of the horns, Grétry one day answered somebody who asked him his opinion of the tempestuous piece:—"It is enough to split the roof of the theatre with the skulls of the audience!"

The Horn with three pistons; and the Horn with valves.

The horn with pistons can make all its notes open notes, by means of a particular mechanism of which the action consists in changing instantaneously the key of the horn. Thus the use of such and such a piston transforms the *F* horn into an *E* horn; or an *E♭* horn, into a *D* horn, &c.; whence it follows that the open notes of one key being added to those of other keys, the complete chromatic scale is obtained in open sounds. The use of the three pistons has moreover the effect of adding to the scale of the instrument *six semitones* below its lowest natural sound. Thus, in taking this C, as the extreme point of the compass of the horn below, the pistons give it the following notes in addition:—

It is the same with all the brass instruments,—trumpets, cornets, bugles, and trombones,—to which the mechanism of the pistons is applied.

The compass of the horn with three pistons, in a mixed key like the key of *E♭*, would therefore be this:—

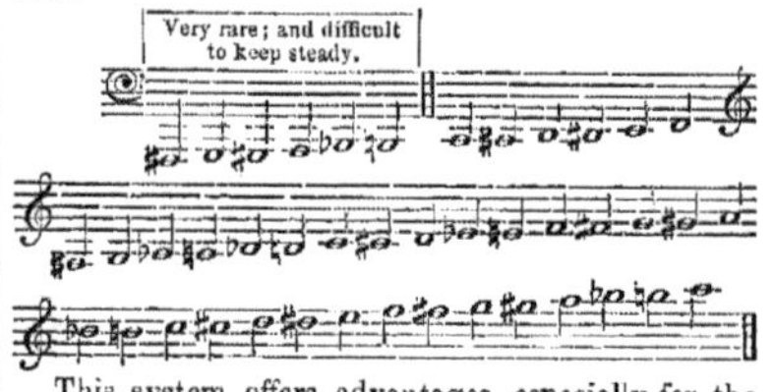

This system offers advantages, especially for the second horns, owing to the considerable blanks which it fills up between their natural low notes, commencing from the last low C ascending, ; but the *timbre* of the horn with pistons differs a little from that of the ordinary horn, which it cannot therefore entirely replace. I think it should be treated almost like an instrument apart, and as particularly fitted for giving good basses, vibrant and energetic, yet not possessing so much force as the low sounds of the tenor trombone, to which its own bear much resemblance. It can also render a melody well, especially one principally on the medium notes.

The best keys for the horn with pistons—the only ones indeed which leave nothing to desire on the score of correctness in tune—are the intermediate keys. Thus, the horns in *E♮*, *F*, *G*, and *A♭*, are much preferable to the others.

Many composers show themselves opposed to this new instrument, because, since its introduction into orchestras, certain horn-players, using the pistons for playing ordinary horn parts, find it more convenient to produce by this mechanism, as open notes, notes *intentionally* written as closed notes by the author. This is, in fact, a dangerous abuse; but it is for orchestral conductors to prevent its increase; and, moreover, it should not be lost sight of that the horn with pistons, in the hands of a clever player, can give all the closed sounds of the ordinary horn, and *yet more;* since it can execute the whole scale without employing a single open note. Since the use of the pistons, by changing the key of the instrument, gains the open notes of other keys, in addition to those of the principal key, it is clear that it must also secure the closed notes. Thus, the horn in *F* naturally gives this open C, which produces F; and, by means of the pistons, this open D, which produces G; but if the hand be employed in the bell, so as to lower these two notes one tone, the first becomes a B♭, producing E♭ closed, and the second a C, producing F, also closed.

It is for the composer to indicate, by the word "*closed*," and by the figures ½ or ⅔, showing how much the bell must be stopped, the notes which he does not wish produced *open*.

For a scale written like the following—

the performer will therefore take the proper pistons for the open scale of *C*:—

and the employment of the hand, stopping the two thirds of the bell upon each note, will make it into a scale of *B♭*, of which all the sounds will be the dullest and most closed that can be obtained on the horn. It is thus possible, on the horn with pistons, after having played a passage in open sounds, to repeat it in closed sounds, like a very distant echo.

The horn with valves differs from the preceeding only by the nature of its mechanism.

This difference is all in its favor on the score of flexibility and quality of tone. The sounds of the horn with valves do not materially differ from those of the ordinary horn. This instrument is already in general use throughout Germany, and, without doubt, will soon become so everywhere.

The Trumpet.

Its compass is nearly the same as that of the horn, of which it possesses (in the upper octave) all the natural open notes; it is written on the G clef:—

Some performers succeed tolerably well in producing certain closed notes on the trumpet, by introducing,—as on the horn—the hand into the bell; but the effect of these notes is so bad, and their intonation so uncertain, that an immense majority of composers have wisely abstained, and still abstain, from using them. From this proscription should be excepted, and considered as an open note, the high F, It comes out by aid of the lips only, but its intonation is always too sharp. It should only be written as a passing note placed between a G and an E,—

and care must be taken neither to come upon it unprepared nor to sustain it.

The medium B♭, on the contrary, is always a little too flat.

It is well to avoid the employment of the low C, on trumpets lower than the trumpet in F. this note is weak, of common quality in tone, without being appropriate for any characteristic effect; and it can easily be replaced by a sound of the horn, incomparably better in all respects.

The three extreme high notes—

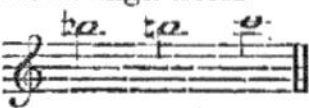

while very hazardous on trumpets in *low A*, *B♭*, and *C*, are impracticable in higher keys. The C might, however, be reached, even in the key of *E♭*, if it were thus brought in, loud:—

Such a passage,—which the greater number of German and English players would face without hesitation,—would be, however, very dangerous in France, where there exists generally, in the use of brass instruments, much difficulty in going high.

There are trumpets of many kinds, in *B♭*, in *C*, in *D*, in *E♭*, in *E♮*, in *F*, and in *G*; very rarely in high *A♭*. By means of the lengthening piece, of which mention was made in speaking of horns, and which lowers the instrument a half tone, trumpets are produced in *A*, in *E♮*, in *D♭* (or *C♯*), in *G♭* (or *F♯*). By means of a double lengthening piece which lowers the trumpet a whole tone, the key of low *A♭* is even obtained; but this key is the worst of all. The finest quality of tone, on the contrary, is that of the trumpet in *D♭*; an instrument full of brilliancy, and of remarkably precise intonation; but which is seldom employed, because the majority of composers are ignorant of its existence.

After what I have said above of the notes of the two extremes of the trumpet scale, it is easy to conclude that the compass of this instrument is not the same in all keys. The low trumpets—like all other instruments of this kind—should avoid the lowest note; while the high trumpets cannot reach the most acute sounds.

Here is a table of the different keys:—

The low double C marked with this sign *, and which must be written on the F clef, is of excellent sonority in the three high keys; on many occasions admirable use may be made of it.

Trumpets in high *A♭* are seldom found but in military bands; their sound is very brilliant, but their compass is still less than that of trumpets in *G*, since they cannot go above the fourth C:—

Adolphe Sax now makes small octave trumpets and tenth trumpets (in high *C*, and in high *E♭*,) of excellent sound. They should be found in all orchestras, and in all military bands.

The shake is hardly practicable in general on the trumpet, and I think it should be abstained from in the orchestra.

The following three shakes, however, come out tolerably well :—

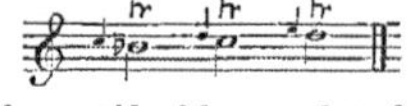

What I have said with regard to different keys on the horn, and of the way of using them by means of interchange, is applicable in all respects to the trumpet. It should be added, though, that the opportunity of writing for it in different keys does not often present itself. The greater part of our orchestras only provide a composer with two trumpets and two cornets-à-pistons, instead of four trumpets. It is better, in this case, to leave the two trumpets both in one key, as the cornets-à-pistons can give all the intervals, and as their quality of tone is not so dissimilar from that of the trumpets but that they can resemble them well in the whole combination, and thus suffice to complete the harmony.

In general, there is no need of employing trumpets in two different keys, excepting when, in the minor mode, it is desired to empower them to produce simultaneously the third and fifth degree of the scale. In *G*♯ minor, for instance, if it be necessary to cause one trumpet to sound successively the two notes, G♯, B, while the other sounds, at a third above or a sixth below, the other two notes, B, D♯, a trumpet must be taken in *E*♮ (of which the E and the G produce G♯, B), and a trumpet in *B*♮ (of which the C and the E give the B and the D♯); this is what has been done by M. Meyerbeer in the grand scene of the fourth act of the *Huguenots*.

Notwithstanding the routine generally pursued, charming *piano* effects are to be obtained from trumpets. Gluck was one of the first to prove it by his long holding-note of the two trumpets, united pianissimo on the dominant, in the andante of the introduction to *Iphigenia in Tauride;* and since then, Beethoven (especially in the andante of his Symphony in A) and Weber have obtained great advantage therefrom.

No. 43. *Iphigenia in Tauride.*—GLUCK.

No. 44.

Allegretto.
Symphony in A.—BEETHOVEN.
Flutes.
Hautboys.
Trumpets in D.
Bassoons.
Drums, D, A.
Violins.
Viola.
Violoncello.
Double-bass.
cres.
Dim.
pp

In order that these notes may be produced with certainty, they should, in general, be taken in the medium, and not succeed each other too rapidly

The five following may be taken and sustained pianissimo —

The B♭ of the medium being too flat, this defect of precision should be corrected as much as possible by the force of emitting the sound It cannot be included among the soft notes The C above, does not offer the same risk · it may be sustained and taken softly at least on the four lower keys *A♮ B♭, B♮*, and *C* In the key of *D*, I think that a clever player can even give to this C, when sustaining it, much softness; but it is prudent to *conceal its entrance* by a *forte* in the rest of the orchestra

The quality of tone of the trumpet is noble and brilliant; it comports with warlike ideas, with cries of fury and of vengeance, as with songs of triumph, it lends itself to the expression of all energetic, lofty, and grand sentiments, and to the majority of tragic accents It may even figure in a jocund piece provided the joy assume a character of impulse or of pomp and grandeur.

Notwithstanding the real loftiness and distinguished nature of its quality in tone, there are few instruments that have been more degraded than the trumpet Down to Beethoven and Weber, every composer—not excepting Mozart—persisted in either confining it to the unworthy function of filling-up, or in causing it to sound two or three commonplace rhythmical formulæ, as vapid and ridiculous as they are incompatible, very often, with the character of the pieces in which they occur This detestable practice is at last abandoned All composers, nowadays, of any merit and style, accord to their melodic designs, their form of accompaniment, and the trumpet's powers of sound, all the latitude, variety, and independence which the nature of the instrument allows It has needed almost a century for the attainment of this end

Trumpets with pistons and with cylinders have the advantage of being able, like the horns with pistons, to give all the intervals of the chromatic scale They have lost nothing of the quality of the ordinary trumpet by the super-addition of these facilities, and their correctness of intonation is satisfactory The trumpets with cylinders are the best they will soon come into general use

Keyed trumpets, still employed in some Italian orchestras, cannot be compared to them in this respect

The general compass of trumpets with pistons and with cylinders is this —

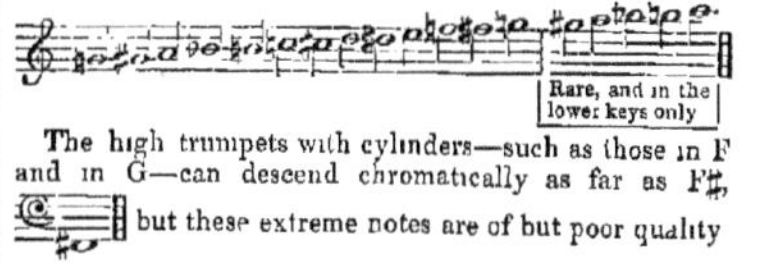

The high trumpets with cylinders—such as those in F and in G—can descend chromatically as far as F♯, but these extreme notes are of but poor quality

Major and minor shakes feasible on the trumpet with cylinders are the same as those of the cornet with three pistons (See, farther on, the table of shakes for this instrument)

Valved trumpets,—called so on account of a movable valve similar to that of the trombone, and worked by the right hand,—are adapted to produce the truest intervals Their sound is precisely the same as that of simple trumpets, and their compass is this —

The Cornet with three pistons, and with cylinders

Its compass is about two octaves and two or three notes. The mechanism of the pistons with which it is furnished allows of its giving all the chromatic degrees as far as the low F♯, nevertheless this note and the two or three that precede it in descending,—such as A, A♭, G, are hardly practicable save on high cornets It is possible on these high cornets, to get out the double C below, , the first note of the natural resonance of the trumpet, as will presently be seen but it is a note of very hazardous utterance, of very bad quality, and of very dubious utility

There are cornets in *C*, in *B♭*, in *A*, in *A♭*, in *G*, in *F*, in *E♮*, in *E♭*, and in *D*. By means of the lengthening-piece, mentioned in speaking of horns and trumpets, which lowers the instrument half a tone, it is doubtless possible to obtain the keys of *B♮*, *F♯*, and even *D♭*, but the facility of modulating, given by the pistons, renders these changes of key almost useless Besides the low keys,—such as those of *G*, *F*, *E*, and *D*,—are generally of indifferent quality, and wanting in correctness of intonation. The best cornets—those, I, think, which should be almost exclusively used—are the cornets in *G*, and especially in *A♭*, A♮, and *B♭* The highest of all, the cornet in *C*, is rather hard to play, while its intonation is not beyond reproach.

Subjoined is the compass we may assign to the different keys of the cornet-à-piston; certain players, however, obtain some very dangerous notes, both above and below, but these shall not be reckoned. Its music is written on the G clef. The natural resonance of its tube—shorter than that of trumpets—gives the following notes:—

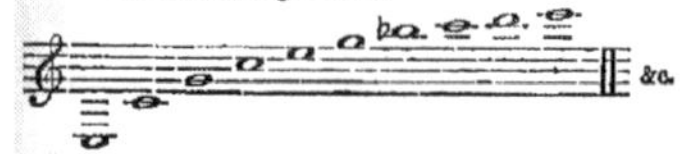

The chromatic compass given by the pistons, in the different keys is as follows:—

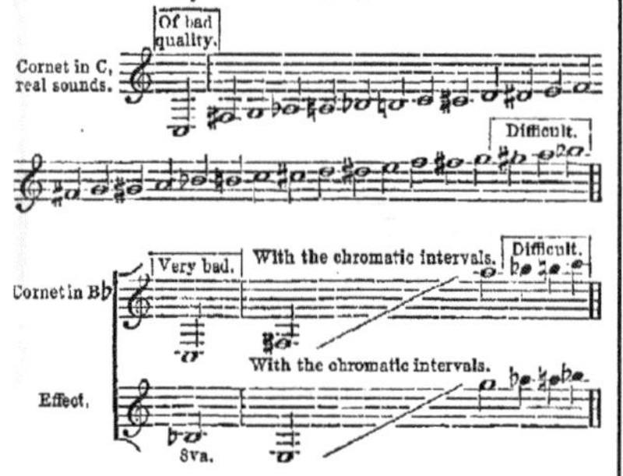

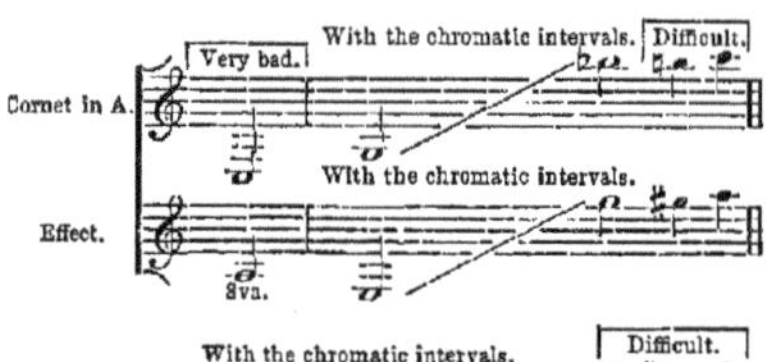

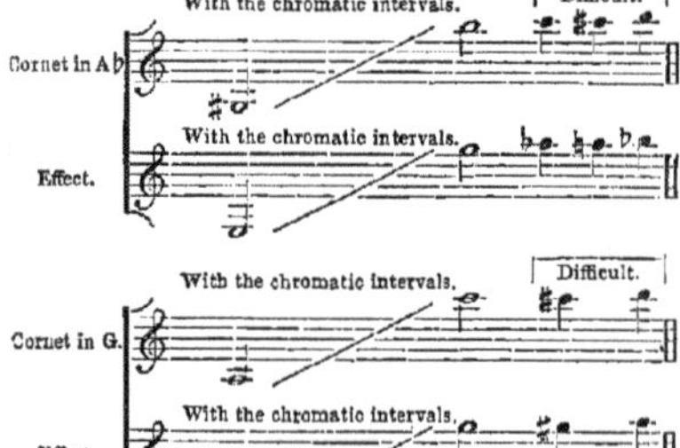

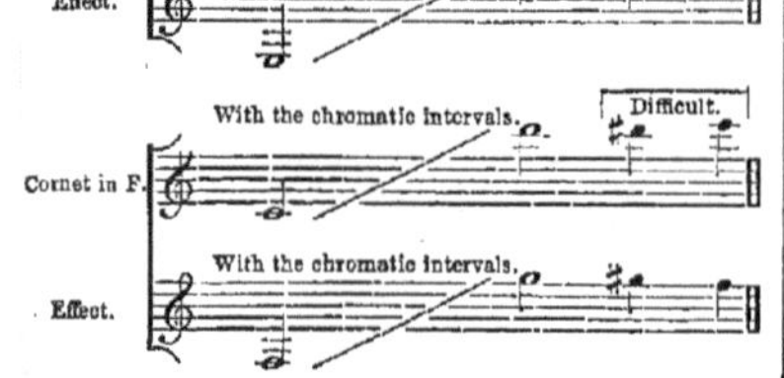

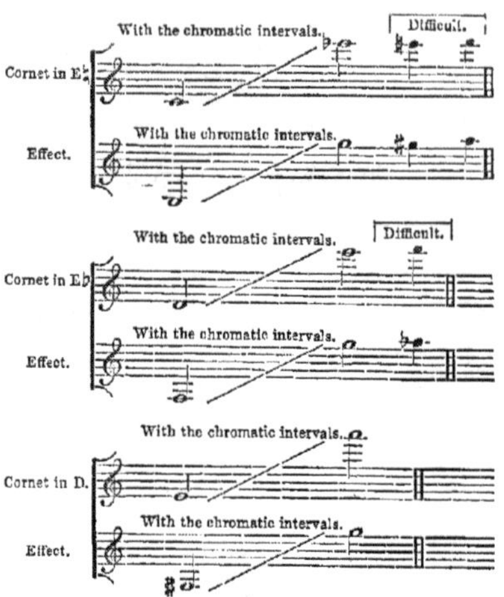

An opportunity occurs here for pointing out with regard to the last high notes of these examples,—which all produce the same G, —that they are of much less hazardous emission, and of much better sonority in the high keys than in the low ones. Thus the high B♭ of the cornet in *A*, the high A of the cornet in *B♭*, and the high G of the cornet in *C*, are incomparably better and more easy to play than the high F of the cornet in *D*, or than the high E of the cornet in *E♭*, And yet all these notes sound the same G, Moreover, this observation applies equally to all brass instruments.

The greater number of major and minor shakes are practicable and of good effect on the following part of the compass of the high cornets-à-pistons,—such as those in *A*, *B♭*, and *C*.

We now proceed to the relations established between the pitches of the various keys of horns, trumpets, and cornets.

The first low sound of the cornet in *C*,—as already seen,—is an octave above that of the trumpet in *C*; just as the first low sound of this trumpet is an octave above that of the horn in (low) *C*. The natural notes of the horn (those which result from the resonance of the tube) thus reproduce themselves an octave above, and in the same order, in the trumpet; while those of the trumpet also all reproduce themselves an octave above, and in the same order, in the cornet, if the player's lips had the necessary force to bring out the highest ones; which is not the case.

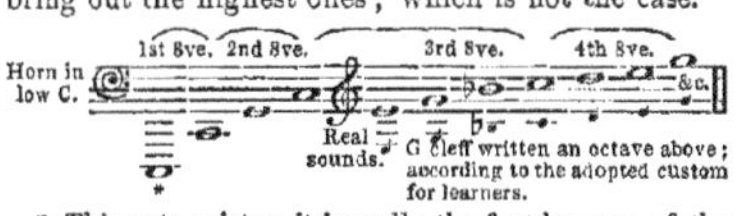

* This note exists: it is really the first low one of the horn; but in all the low keys it is so detestable, and even so indistinct, that we have abstained from giving it a place in the scale of the sounds of the horn in (low) *C*; and for even greater reason, in that of the key of (low) *B♭*.

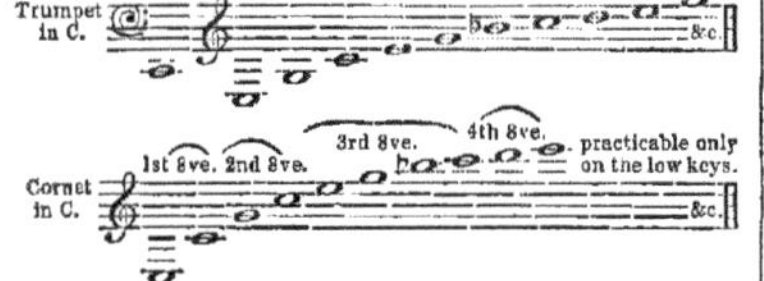

It will be seen by the above,—and it is highly important to be remembered,—that the portion of the scale of a brass instrument in which it can naturally produce (without pistons) these three notes only—

is always its second octave going from low to high. Therefore, cornets-à-pistons have their favorite notes; especially in this second octave. By considering the cornets in A, in B♭, and in C, as trumpets an octave above the trumpets in A, in B♭, and in C, they might be so written for; but this has been judiciously avoided, and cornets are actually written for in their place on the musical scale, by making their lowest sound proceed from an octave above the lowest sound of the trumpet. The best notes of these cornets are within the compass, and in the vicinity, of their second octave:

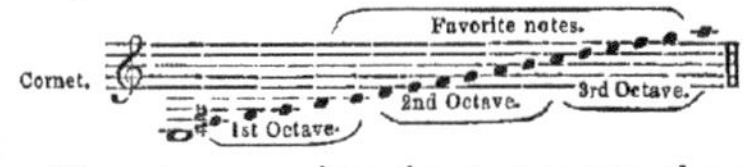

If cornets were written for as trumpets, these notes would always be below the stave, and would involve the constant employment of ledger lines. Thus:—

This inconvenient method of writing for cornets-à-pistons is nevertheless adopted in Prussian military music; and of this it is well to be aware.

There remains to consider (the key of C being taken as the point of departure, in horns, trumpets, and cornets), that the changing keys of the cornet proceed by elongation, and therefore, *by becoming lower and lower*: this is why, in displaying their scale, we have commenced with the highest keys; whereas, those of trumpets and horns (with the exception of three,—those in B♮, in B♭, and in low A, which are lower than the key of C) proceed by shortening, and consequently by becoming higher and higher.

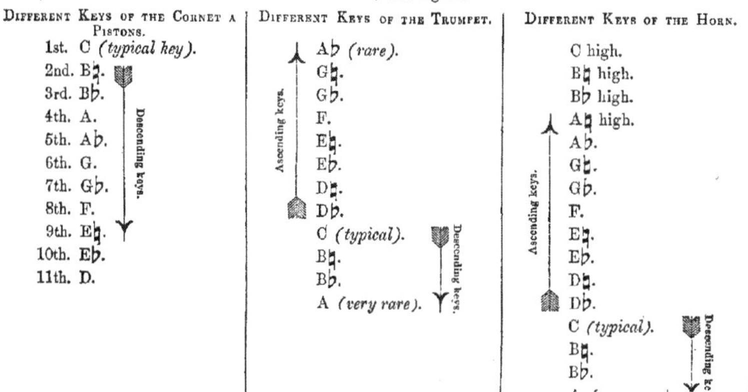

Different Keys of the Cornet a Pistons.

1st. C *(typical key)*.
2nd. B♮.
3rd. B♭.
4th. A.
5th. A♭.
6th. G.
7th. G♭.
8th. F.
9th. E♮.
10th. E♭.
11th. D.

(Descending keys.)

Different Keys of the Trumpet.

A♭ *(rare)*.
G♮.
G♭.
F.
E♮.
E♭.
D♮.
D♭.
(Ascending keys.)
C *(typical)*.
B♮.
B♭.
A *(very rare)*.
(Descending keys.)

Different Keys of the Horn.

C high.
B♮ high.
B♭ high.
A♮ high.
A♭.
G♮.
G♭.
F.
E♮.
E♭.
D♮.
D♭.
(Ascending keys.)
C *(typical)*.
B♮.
B♭.
(Descending ke[ys.])

Let us now observe what affinities exist between horns, trumpets, and cornets; and the respective position they occupy in the scale of sounds.

I will here add that trumpets with pistons, or with cylinders, having—as I have just said—their best notes within the compass, and in the vicinity, of their third octave *(which is found in unison with that of the second of the cornet)*, passages written for cornets-à-pistons in *A*, in *B*, and in *C*, within this compass :—

will necessarily be executable on trumpets in *A*, in *B*, and in *C*, without causing any change. This allows of replacing, without disadvantage, cornets by trumpets with cylinders, in orchestras like German ones, which have no cornets.

Cornets in *A*, in *B*, and in *C*, have,—minutely analysed—less compasss than trumpets in *A*, in *B*, and in *C*; since they can scarcely reach above the A real,

Trumpets, on the contrary, have, in the first place, several more notes below—however poor they may be; and, moreover, produce, more easily than cornets, this same A. in the keys of *D* :—

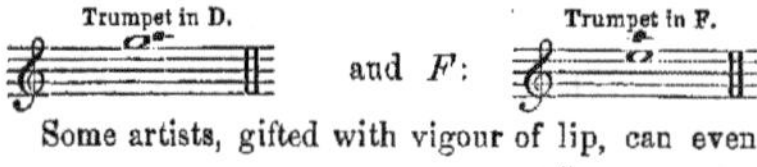

Some artists, gifted with vigour of lip, can even sound the E of the trumpet in *G*, which produces B, and the G of the trumpet in *F*, which produces C, ; but merely in passing, and if these notes be adroitly led up to.

But performers capable of reaching these extreme notes are rare, and they should not, in writing, be too much counted upon.

Trumpets, having a narrow tube, a small mouthpiece and a bell of little extent, attack the high notes with more facility. The tube of cornets, on the contrary, being rather thick, and almost conical, their bell and their mouthpiece, also, being rather larger, the mastery of low notes becomes more easy to them than that of high notes, and their tone acquires the peculiar quality which distinguishes that of trumpets. This is the cause of difference.

Before proceeding to the examination of the expressive character of the cornet-à-pistons it is not unneedful to repeat here what I have said, in speaking of the horn with pistons, respecting the action of the three cylinders, or pistons, adapted to brass instruments generally. Not only do these three cylinders give to instruments the chromatic scale (above their first octave), thereby supplying all the gaps which separate their natural notes from each other, but they also add six chromatic notes below the two lowest sounds. Thus, for cornets :—

For trumpets :—

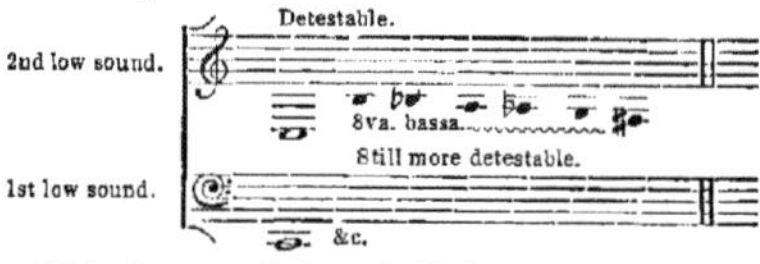

This first low C is so indistinct and difficult to sustain that the notes added below it for the pistons become,—as may be imagined,—absolutely impracticable. It is the same for the horns.

Although the cornet possesses all the degrees of the chromatic scale, the choice of key in changing is not immaterial. It is always better to take that which offers the means of employing the most natural notes,—it is scarcely necessary here to repeat that the natural notes are those which come out without the aid of the pistons, by the sole effect of the resonance of the tube of the instrument; such as,—

—and which bears few or no sharps or flats at the signature. When the orchestra is playing in *E*♮, for instance,—as the cornet in *E*♮ is one of the least good,—the cornet in *A*♮ should be used, which would then play in *G* :—

If the orchestra be in *D*, the cornet in *A*♮ should still be used; it would then play in *F*:—

If the orchestra be in *E*♭, the cornet in *B*♭ should be taken, playing with one flat at the signature,—consequently in *F*; and so on with the rest.

The cornet-à-pistons is very much the fashion in France at present, particularly in a certain musical world where elevation and purity of style are not considered essential qualities; and it has thus become the indispensable solo instrument for quadrilles, galops, airs with variations, and other second-rate compositions. The frequency with which nowadays we hear melodies devoid of all originality and distinction executed on this instrument in the ball-room, together with the character of its *timbre*, which has neither the nobleness of the horn, nor the loftiness of the trumpet, renders the use of the cornet-à-pistons in exalted melodies a matter of great difficulty. It may figure there with advantage, however; but very rarely, and on condition of playing only phrases of large construction and of indisputable dignity. Thus, the ritornello of the trio in *Robert le Diable*, "O my son," &c., agrees well with the cornet-à-pistons:—

No. 45.

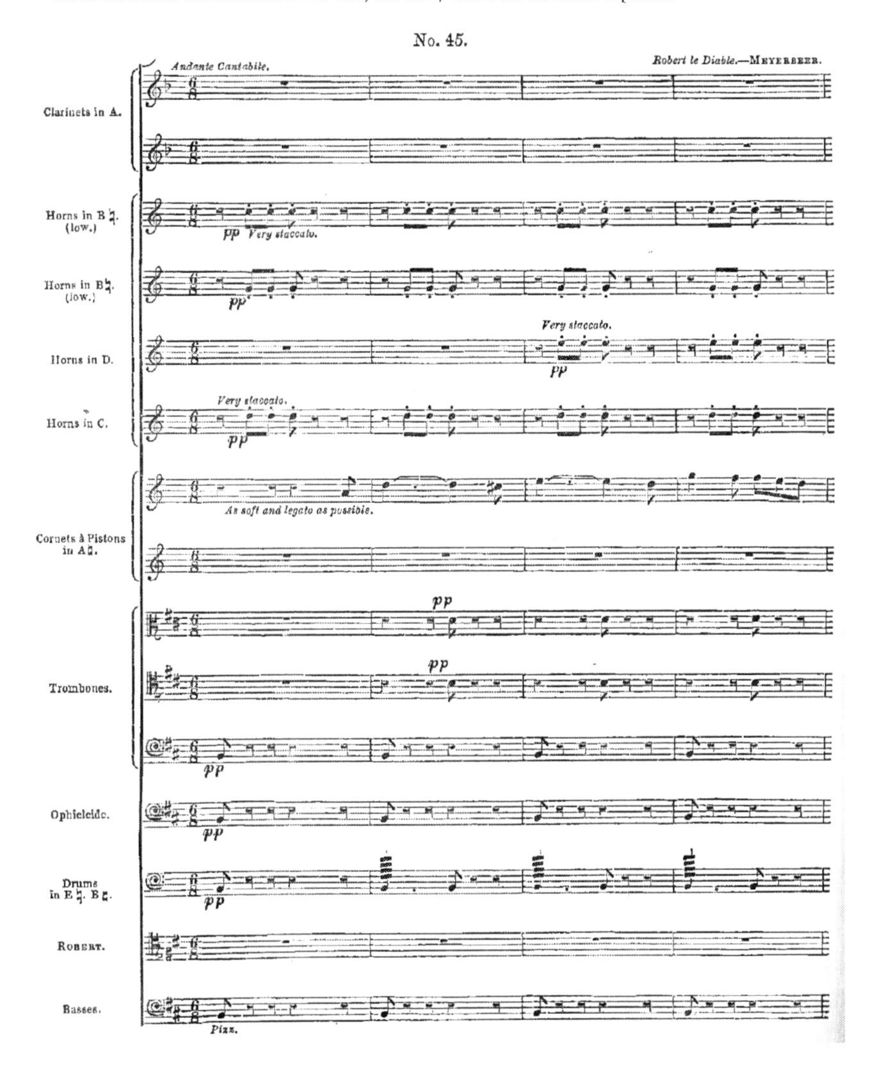

Joyous melodies will always have to fear from this instrument a loss of a portion of their nobleness, if they have any, or, if they have none—an additional triviality. A phrase which might appear tolerable, played on violins, or on wooden wind instruments, would become poor and detestably vulgar if brought out by the biting, noisy, shameless sounds of the cornet-à-pistons. This danger is obviated if the phrase be of such a nature that it can be played at the same time by one or more trombones; the grand tone of which then covers and ennobles that of the cornet. Employed in harmony, the cornet blends very well with the general mass of brass instruments; it serves to complete the chords of the trumpets, and to contribute to the orchestra those diatonic or chromatic groupes of notes which, on account of their rapidity, suit neither the trombones nor the horns. Cornets-à-pistons are generally written for in two parts, each often in a different key.

Trombones.

There are four kinds of trombones, each of which bears the name of the human voice to which it has the nearest resemblance in quality of tone and compass. The *Soprano* Trombone,—the smallest and highest of them all,—exists still in some parts of Germany, but is unknown in France; it has scarcely ever been used in the scores of the great masters; which is no reason, however, why it should not figure there sooner or later, as it is by no means certain that trumpets with pistons—even the highest—can advantageously supply its place. Gluck alone, in his Italian score of *Orfeo*, has written for the soprano trombone under the name of *Cornetto.* He has made it double the soprano voices of the chorus, while the alto, tenor, and bass trombones double the other voices.

These three last-named trombones are the only ones in general use. It should also be stated, however, that the alto trombone does not exist in all French orchestras, while the bass trombone is almost unknown among them; being in nearly every case confounded with the third tenor trombone, which plays the lowest part, and for this reason is, very improperly, called the bass trombone, though materially differing from it.

Trombones are instruments with slides, of which the double tube can be lengthened or shortened instantaneously, by a simple movement of the player's arm. It may be conceived that these variations of the length of the tube completely change the key of the instrument,—which is the case. Whence it follows that trombones, possessing, like all brass instruments, the notes resulting from the natural resonance of the tube *in all positions*, have a complete chromatic scale, interrupted only at one point below, as will be presently seen.

The Alto Trombone.

This trombone has a compass of more than two octaves and a half; it is written for on the C clef, third line:—

Its quality of tone is rather shrill, compared with that of the deeper trombones. Its lower notes sound somewhat badly, which is one good reason for avoiding them in general, as well as because these same notes are excellent on the tenor trombone, from which the alto trombone, in the orchestra, is scarcely ever separated. The high sounds, such as B, C, D, E, F, on the contrary, may be very useful; and on their account it is to be regretted that the alto trombone is at present almost banished from our French orchestras. When its slide is closed, the following notes may be obtained by means merely of the lips. They are emitted in the same order as those from the natural resonance of brass horns, trumpets, and cornets, in *E♭*:—

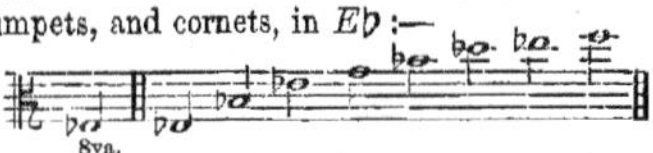

Hence the name of small trombone, or alto trombone in *E♭*, which players give it; but which it is generally useless to adopt in scores; because, sounding the notes *as they are written*, it does not come under the head of transposing instruments,—for which alone, as we have said, these various designations of key are necessary.

The Tenor Trombone.

This is, without doubt, the best of them all. It has a full and powerful sonority; it can execute passages the rapidity of which renders them impracticable on the bass trombone; and its quality of tone is good throughout the whole extent of its scale. It is ordinarily written for on the C clef, fourth line; but as it happens in certain orchestras that the three trombone parts, under three different names, are played on three tenor trombones, it follows that they are then written for: one on the C clef, third line (like the alto), the second on the C clef, fourth line (like the tenor), and the third on the F clef (like the bass. Its slide being closed, it produces naturally the following notes, which are those of the resonance of all brass tubes in *B♭*; that is to say, tubes which,—sounded in their totality,—give for first low sound, a B♭:—

Hence the instrument is sometimes called the trombone in *B♭*. It is therefore a fourth below the alto trombone; and its compass is this:—

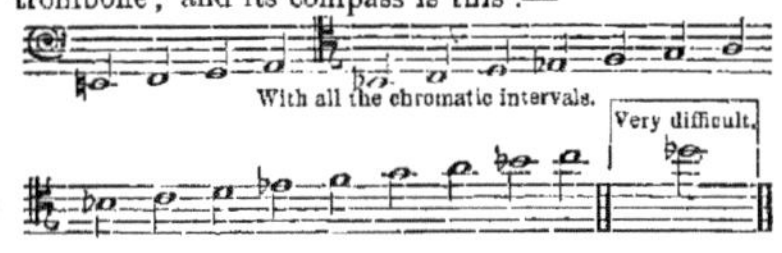

It will be observed that the low E♭, is wanting in the tenor trombone; and this note constantly gives rise to a host of errors in scores the most learnedly written. Thus, one of our living composers—whose skill in the art of instrumentation is eminent—has commenced an opera of his with several low E♭s for the tenor trombone. It is the ophicleide which plays them, while the trombone only doubles them an octave above, and the author perhaps never perceived that his low E♭ was not given by the instrument for which he wrote it.

The Bass Trombone.

Is only rare on account of the fatigue experienced in playing it, even by the most robust performers. It is the largest—and consequently the lowest—of them all. When employed, it should have sufficiently long rests given to it, that the player may repose; and it should moreover be used with extreme discretion and well-reflected intention.

With the slide closed, it gives the notes,—

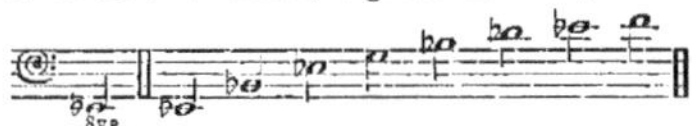

on which account it is called the great trombone, or the bass trombone in *E♭*.

It is consequently an octave lower than the alto trombone, and a fifth below the tenor trombone. It is written for on the F clef:—

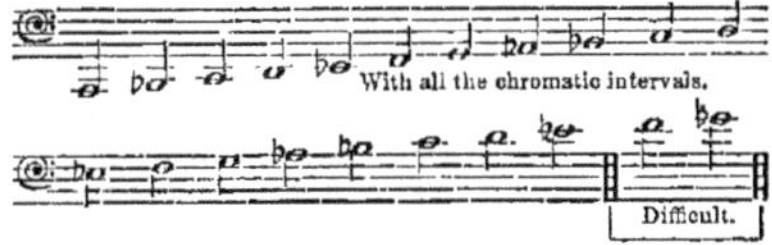

The sound of the bass trombone is majestic, formidable, and terrible; and to it belongs, of right, the lowest part in all masses of brass instruments. Nevertheless, we have the misfortune, in Paris, of being utterly deprived of it; it is not taught at the Conservatoire, and no trombone-player has yet been willing to acquire its familiar practice. Whence it follows, that the majority of modern German scores, and even of ancient French and Italian scores, written for orchestras which possess, or did possess, this instrument, must be more or less deranged when they are performed in Paris. Thus, in Weber's *Freyschütz*, there are some low D♮s beneath the stave, in the accompaniment of the huntsmen's chorus; and farther on, where the hermit enters, there are some low E♭s, These notes are of necessity carried into the octave above, because the three players in the Opera orchestra use only the tenor trombone, which has them not. It is the same with the sustained low C♮s, in the chorus of Gluck's *Alceste:* "Pleure, O patrie." Here, the effect of the double C's is extremely important, which makes their transposition truly deplorable.

The bass trombone cannot lend itself to rapid movements with the celerity which marks others of the same family; the length and size of its tube necessitate rather more time for vibration; and it will readily be imagined that its slide—manœuvred by the aid of a handle which supplements, in certain positions, the length of the arm—does not admit of great agility. Hence the real impossibility for German artists who use the bass trombone to execute a crowd of passages in modern French scores, which our own trombone-players render as well as they can on the tenor trombone. The imperfection in the execution of these passages—notwithstanding the talent of some of our artists—evidently proves that they are too rapid even for the tenor trombone; and that trombones in general are not fit for rendering such sequences. It proves at the very least—assuming that composers are guilty of only a little exaggeration on the point of difficulty—that those instruments should always be used which they indicate, and no others. Unfortunately, many masters—although very well knowing that in most of our orchestras there are only tenor trombones—persist in writing in their scores, *Alto Trombone, Tenor Trombone*, and *Bass Trombone*, instead of stating 1st, 2nd, and 3rd tenor trombone. Consequently, in order to be able to execute their operas abroad as they perform them in Paris, it would be requisite, without paying regard to the printed indications, to employ the instruments used in Paris. To sanction generally such a latitude in the interpretation of a composer's wishes would be to open a door to all sorts of incorrectness, and to all sorts of abuses? And is it not just to make those authors who are so neglectful in supervising their works suffer a little, rather than to let those run the chance of seeing theirs mutilated who write with unfailing care, and with a profound knowledge of instrumental resources?

All trombones—commencing from points more or less low—have the same compass; which, as we have seen, is two octaves and a sixth. But this is not all. Besides this extensive scale, they also possess—at the extreme depth, and commencing from the first low sound of A (natural resonance of the tube),—four notes, enormous and magnificent on the tenor trombone, of indifferent sonority on the alto trombone, and terrible on the bass trombone when they can be got out. They are called pedals; doubtless on account of their resemblance in quality of tone to that of the very low notes on the organ, which are so named. It is rather difficult to use them well, and they are even unknown to many trombone-players. These notes are,

for the alto trombone;

for the tenor trombone; and the bass trombone would have these :—

if all performers had the power of bringing them out. Supposing, however, that the bass trombone possesses the first only of these pedal notes, the double E♭, it would be of great value for certain effects which are unattainable without it; since no other instrument in the orchestra, with the exception of the bass-tuba and the double-bassoon, attains this extraordinary depth. These notes—on all the trombones—are isolated from the others by a gap of an augmented fourth, which separates the first natural low note from the last (descending) of the scale produced by the employment of the slide :—

On account of this gap it is indispensable, in certain cases, to designate the keys of the trombones employed; for it changes place in the scale of sounds, according to the length of the tube or the key of the instrument; and consequently, one or more pedals of a certain key may fail upon a trombone in another key. For example, if the composer who has written these pedal notes—

have not taken care to indicate that he desired a trombone in *B♭*, it may be that there is in the orchestra where his work is to be executed, a true bass trombone in *E♭*, which lacks the A♭ and the low G; or a bass trombone in *F*, which lacks the four notes, B♭, A, A♭, and G (these instruments are very prevalent in Germany); or, lastly, a bass trombone in *G* (there are some of these in England), which equally lacks B♭, A, and A♭. It will be better comprehended by the following :—

If the pedals of the alto trombone were not of so bad a quality, they might be employed,—in orchestras which have no bass trombone,—to fill up the space existing between the E♮, of the tenor trombone and its first pedal, , but unfortunately they are so shrill and so thin that they cannot be counted on as a substitute for the fine low tones of the tenor trombone. The bass trombone—with the powerful notes of the lower extremity of its scale,—

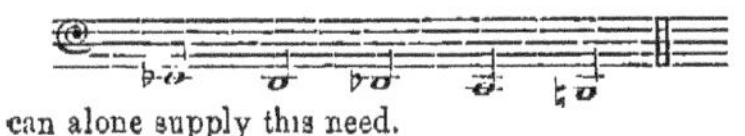

can alone supply this need.

Fortunately, the clever maker, Sax (of Paris), has surmounted the difficulty by means of a single piston affixed to the body of the tenor trombone, which piston the performer moves with his left thumb, maintaining the entire liberty of his right arm for manipulating the slide, and which, supplying the gap, now gives to the tenor trombone in *B♭* this immense compass —

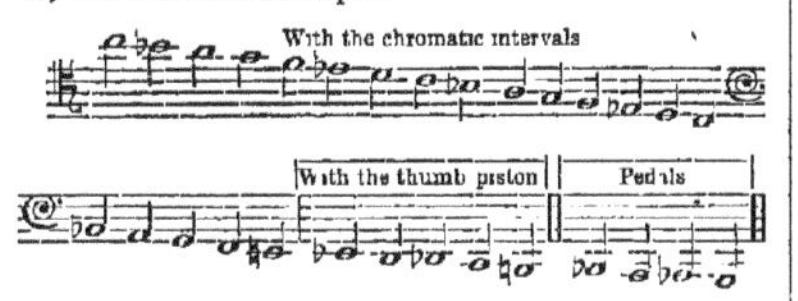

The vibrations of the pedal notes are slow and require much wind, in order, therefore, to make them come out well it is necessary to give them a sufficiently long duration, to make them succeed each other slowly, and to intersperse them with rests which give the player time to take breath. Care should be taken also that the part in which they occur should be written generally so low as to allow the lips of the trombone-player to become gradually habituated to the production of very low tones. The best manner of taking the pedals on the tenor trombone, for instance, is to make on the first a leap of a fifth or an octave, going from the F or the B♭ upwards; then, after having allowed for taking breath, to pass, descending chromatically, to the A or to the G♯ (the G♮ is more difficult, of extreme roughness and of very perilous utterance). It is thus, at least, that in a modern Requiem Mass, the author has brought in these three notes, and although, at the first rehearsal of his work, out of the eight trombone players who had to sound them, five or six exclaimed that the notes were not possible, the eight B♭s, the eight As, and the eight G♯s did not the less come out quite full and quite true,—given by artists who, never having tried to produce them, did not believe in their existence. The sonority of the three pedal notes seemed much finer than even that of notes far less low, and frequently employed —

This effect occurs, in the work I have just quoted, beneath a harmony of flutes in three parts, during an absence of voices and of all the other instruments. The sound of the flutes, separated from that of the trombones by an immense interval, seems thus to be the extreme high harmonic resonance of these pedals, whose slow movement and profound voice tends to redouble the solemnity of the pauses by which the choir is interrupted, at the verse —" hostias et preces tibi laudis offerimus"

No. 46.

Andante non troppo.
Lento.
Requiem.—Berlioz.
Three Flutes.
Eight Tenor Trombones.
Violins.
Violas.
1st Tenors.
2nd Tenors.
1st Basses.
2nd Basses.
Violoncello.
Double Bass.
Quorum ho-di-e
me-mo-ri-am
fa - - - - - - ci-
- - mus.
cres.
poco f
Unis.
pizz.

I have elsewhere employed the pedals of the tenor trombone, but with quite another intention. The object was to give some low harmonies of extreme roughness, and of strange *timbre.* I believe I have obtained them by means of this fifth on two tenor trombones, [music]; and, farther on, by a diminished seventh between an ophicleide and a pedal A of the tenor trombone :—

Another particular, ignored by the majority of composers—yet nevertheless very important to be known—is the difficulty, and even, in certain cases, the impossibility, for trombones to give in succession, and with any rapidity, the following notes :—

The passing from one of these notes to the other, demanding an enormous change in the position of the slide of the instrument, and consequently, a considerable stretch of the performer's arm, cannot be effected except in a very moderate movement. A celebrated master having written this rapid succession, B, A♯, B, several times repeated, the trombone-players of the Théâtre-Italien undertook its performance by playing it like the Russian horn-players, each of whom gives a single note; one took the B♮, and the other the A♯, to the great amusement of their colleagues, who especially laughed at the pains the second trombone was at to edge in his A♯ contra-tempo.

It is also—and for the same reason—rather difficult to play with speed this passage on the tenor trombone :—

It is better to write it reversed; this succession of the notes, [music] requiring no change of position.

The shake is practicable on trombones, but only on the notes of their upper octave; and composers should abstain from writing it for the bass trombone, on account of extreme difficulty. The tenor and alto trombones, in the hands of skilled performers, may shake on the following notes :—

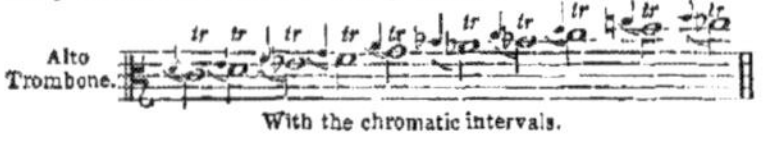

With the chromatic intervals.

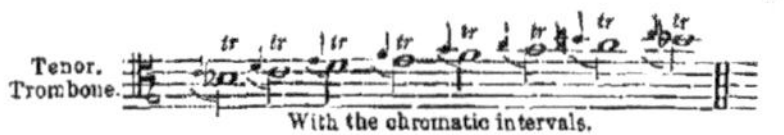

With the chromatic intervals.

It will be perceived that all these shakes are major; the minor shakes are impracticable.

The trombone is, in my opinion, the true chief of that species of wind instruments which I have designated epic instruments. It possesses, in an eminent degree, both nobleness and grandeur; it has all the deep and powerful accents of high musical poetry,—from the religious accent, calm and imposing, to the wild clamours of the orgy. It depends on the composer to make it by turn chant like a choir of priests, threaten, lament, ring a funeral knell, raise a hymn of glory, break forth into frantic cries, or sound its dread flourish to awaken the dead or to doom the living.

Means have nevertheless been found—some thirty years since—to degrade the trombone, by reducing it to a servile doubling, as useless as grotesque, of the double-bass part. This plan is now almost abandoned. But there may be seen in a host of scores, otherwise very beautiful, the basses doubled almost constantly, in unison, by a single trombone. I know nothing less harmonious or more vulgar than this mode of instrumentation. The sound of the trombone is so markedly characterised that it should never be heard but for the production of some special effect; its duty, therefore, is not to strengthen the double-basses, with the sound of which, moreover, its *timbre* has no sort of sympathy. Besides, it should be understood that a single trombone in an orchestra seems always more or less out of place. The instrument needs harmony, or at least, unison with the other members of its family, in order that its various attributes may be completely manifested. Beethoven has sometimes employed it in pairs, like the trumpets; but the time-honored custom of writing for trombones in three parts appears to me preferable.

It is difficult to determine with precision the degree of rapidity to which trombones can attain in passages; nevertheless, the following may be said on this point: in a bar of four-time, and in the movement *Allegro moderato*, for instance, a passage of simple quavers (eight notes in a bar) is feasible on the bass trombone :—

The other trombones—alto and tenor—being a little more agile, will execute without much difficulty, passages of quavers in triplets (twelve notes in a bar) :

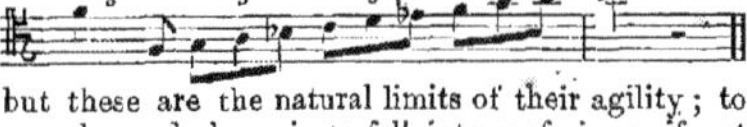

but these are the natural limits of their agility; to pass beyond them, is to fall into confusion,—if not to attempt impossibility.

The character of the *timbre* of trombones varies according to the degree of loudness with which their sound is emitted. In a *fortissimo* it is menacing and formidable; particularly if the three trombones be in unison, or at least, if two of them be in unison, the third being an octave below the two others. Instance the terrific scale in *D* minor, upon which Gluck has founded the chorus of Furies in the second act of his *Iphigenia in Tauride.* Such also—but still more sublime—is the immense shout of the three united trombones, answering, like the wrathful voice of the infernal gods, to Alceste's summons :—" Ombre! larve! compagne di morte!" in that prodigious air the original idea of which Gluck allowed to be perverted by the French translator; but which, as it is, has dwelt in the memory of all the world, with its unlucky first verse :—"Divinités du Styx! ministres de la mort!" Let us here remark moreover that towards the close of the first movement of this piece. when the trombones divided into three parts respond —imitating the rhythm of the air in the phrase : " Je n'invoquerai point votre pitié cruelle!"—let us here observe, I say, that by the very effect of this division, the *timbre* of the trombone instantly assumes something of an ironical, hoarse, frightfully joyous quality—very different from the grand fury of the preceding unisons :—

Adagio.
Tempo 1mo.
pp
Ye pow'rs of as - pect dread; I no lon - ger in - voke your too un - feel - ing pi - ty,
Mi - nis - tres de la mort je n'in - vo - que - rai point, vo - tre pi - tié cru - el - le
I no longer invoke, I no longer invoke your too unfeel - ing pi - - - -
Je n'in - voquerai point, je n'invoquerai point vo - tre pi - tié cru - el - - - -

- ty, your too unfeel -ing pi - - ty,
- le, vo - tre pi-tié cru -el - - le,
Andante un poco.
while saving a tender hus - band from his un-hap - py fate. Can one
J'en - le - ve un tendre é - poux- à son fu-nes - te sort mais je
Andante un poco.

moment of weak hes - i - ta-tion make me shrink from my du-ty ? E'en grim Death . . shall not stay me.
vous a - ban-donne une é - pou-se mais je vous a - bandon-ne une é - pou - - - se fi - dè - le
Animato.
Lento.
Ye gods that dwell in night, ye gods that dwell in night, ye pow'rs of as - pect
Di-vi - ni - tés du Stix, di - vi - ni - tés du Stix, Mi - nis - tres de la
Fag.
Fag.
Animato.
Lento.

Animato.—Tempo 1mo.
dread; to die for my be-lov'd one, for my be - lov'd one shall cancel all re - gret, my beating heart shall know his
mort mou rir pour ce qu'on, ai - me, pour ce qu'on ai - me est un trop doux ef - fort, une ver- tu si na - tu -
Tempo 1mo.
Prestissimo.
safety, his safety gain'd by me; 'tis this sweet thought ex - alts ev'n the death that I meet for his sake.
- - rel - le, si na - tu - rel - - - le mon cœur est a - ni - mé du plus no - ble plus noble trans - port.
Prestissimo

The thought of his dan - ger im - pels me,
je sens u - ne for - ce nou - vel - le,
I hasten to pro - vide for his
je vais ou mon a - mour m'ap -
Col Basso.
safe - ty,
- pel - le
The thought of his dan - ger im - pels me,
je sens u - ne for - ce nou - vel - le,
I hasten to pro -
je vais ou mon a -

- vide for his safety, my heart is free from dread. and I tri - - - - umph in death.
- - mour m'ap - pel - le mon cœur . . . . est a - ni mé du plus no - - - - - ble transport.
No. 48.
Iphigenia in Tauride.—GLUCK.
Animated.
Violins.
Violas.
Bassoons.
Trombones.
Chorus.
Basses.
Re- venge of - fend-ed na - ture, re - venge of - fend-ed man, and the out - rage to
Ven - geons et la na - tu - - re, ven-geons et la na - ture, et les Dieux en cour -
Re-venge of - fend-ed na - - ture, re-venge of-fended man, and the
Ven-geons et la na - tu - - re, ven-geons et la na - ture, et les
Re-venge, re-venge, of - fend-ed
Ven-geons, ven-geons, et la na -
Re - - venge of - fend-ed na - ture, re - venge of - fend-ed man, and the out - rage to
Ven - - geons et la na - tu - - re, ven-geons et la na - tu - re, ven-geons et la na -
Animated.

Hautboys.
Clarinets in C.
Col Oboi.
Heav'n, and the out - rage to Heav'n tortures new should be made, tortures new should be
- roux, et les Dieux en cour - roux in - ven - tons des tour - mens, in - ven - tons des tour -
man, and the out - rage to Heaven; tortures new should be made, tortures new should be
Dieux et les Dieux en cour - roux; in - ven - tons des tour - mens, in - ven - tons des tour -
man, and the out - rage to Heav'n; tortures new should be made, tortures new should be
- ture, et les Dieux en cour - roux; in - ven - tons des tour - mens, in - ven - tons des tour -
Heav'n, and the out - rage to Heav'n; tortures new should be made, tortures new should be
- ture, et les Dieux en cour - roux; in - ven - tons des tour - mens, in - ven - tons des tour -

In simple *forte*, trombones, in three-part harmony, in the medium particularly, have an expression of heroic pomp, of majesty, of loftiness, which the prosaic commonplace of a vulgar melody could alone impair or destroy They then acquire—with enormously increased grandeur—the expression of trumpets; they *no* longer menace, they proclaim; they chaunt, instead of roar. It should be remarked, however, that in such a case the sound of the bass trombone predominates more or less over the two others; particularly if the first be an alto trombone.

No. 49.

Allegro non troppo e pomposo.
Symphonie Funèbre et Triomphale.—Berlioz.
1st & 2nd Horns in E♭.
3rd & 4th Horns in G.
5th & 6th Horns in D.
1st & 2nd Trumpets in B♭.
3rd & 4th Trumpets in B♭.
1st & 2nd Cornets à Pistons in B♭.
1st Alto or Tenor Trombones, & 2nd Tenor Trombones.
3rd Tenor Trombones.
Bass Trombone, non obligato.
1st Drums unmuffled.
2nd Drums.
Kettle-drums, B♭, F.
Change to F.
cres. a poco.
La moitié des 2es Tambours.
Cres poco a poco.

Piccolo in D♭.
ff
Tierce Flutes in E♭.
ff 8ves.
Small Clarinet in E♭.
ff With the 3rd Flute, an 8ve lower.
1st & 2nd Clarinet in B♭.
ff
Hautboys.
cres.
cres.
ff
Ophicleides in C.
cres.
Ophicleides in B♭.
mf cres.
Bass Clarinets in B♭.
1st and 2nd Bassoons.
Double-bassoon non obligato.
mf cres.
With the Bassoons.
1st Violins.
2nd Violins.
Violas.
Violoncello and double-bass.
1st drums unmuffled, and 2nd drums, a duo.
p All the 2nd drums.
Pavillon Chinois.
Cymbals and Long Drum.
cres. molto.

8ves.
8ves.

In *mezzo-forte* in the medium, either in unison or harmony, and in a slow movement, trombones assume a religious character. Mozart, in the choruses of the *Priests of Isis* (*Die Zauberflöte*), has produced admirable examples :—

No. 50.

Zauberflöte.—MOZART.

the hor - - - rid gloom The friend-ly ray of rea - son to thinking man a -
e il fos - - - co or - ror d'a - mi - co sole al rag - gio già il forte il saggio un
- - no-ther life dis - co - vers. Dress me O-siri's al - tar for his ser - - - - vice.
al - tra vita im - pa - - ra pronto e per lui sull' a - ra il sa - cro ri - - - - to.

The *pianissimo* of trombones, applied to harmonies belonging to the minor mode, is gloomy, lugubrious, I had almost said hideous. If, particularly, the chords be brief, and broken by rests, it has the effect of strange monsters giving utterance, in dim shadow, to howls of ill-suppressed rage. Never, to my thinking, has a better dramatic effect been obtained from this special quality of trombones than by Spontini, in his matchless funeral march of the *Vestale:*—"Périsse la Vestale impie," &c.; and by Beethoven, in the immortal duet of the second act of *Fidelio,* sung by Leonora and the jailer, while digging the grave of the prisoner about to die.

No. 51.

ob - - - ject of hate to the Gods. Her pun - - ish -
- - jet de la hai - ne des Dieux, que son tré -
ob - - - ject of hate to the Gods. Her pun - - ish -
- - jet de la hai - ne des Dieux, que son tré -
ob - - - ject of hate to the Gods. Her pun - - ish -
- - jet de la hai - ne des Dieux, que son tré -
Col Basso.
- - ment may atone, her dis - grace-ful of - fence.
- - pas ex - - pi - e son for - fait o - - di - eux.
- - ment may atone, her dis - grace-ful of - fence.
- - pas ex - - pi - e son for - fait o - - di - eux.
- - ment may atone, her dis - grace-ful of - fence.
- - pas ex - - pi - e son for - fait o - - di - eux.

The custom, adopted nowadays by some masters, of forming a quatuor with three trombones and an ophicleide, confiding to the last the true bass, is not altogether blameless. The *timbre* of trombones, so penetrating, so dominant, is far from being the same as that of the ophicleide, and I think it is much better to simply double the lowest part by this instrument, or, at least, to give a correct bass to the trombones, by writing their three several parts as if they were to be heard alone.

Gluck, Beethoven, Mozart, Weber, Spontini, and some others, have comprehended all the importance of the trombone's duties, they have with perfect intelligence applied the various characteristics of this noble instrument to depicting human passion, and to illustrating the sounds of Nature, and they have, in consequence, maintained its power, its dignity, and its poetry. But to constrain it—as the herd of composers now do—to howl out in a *credo* brutal phrases less worthy of a sacred edifice than of a tavern, to sound as for the entry of Alexander into Babylon, when there is nothing more forthcoming than the pirouette of a dancer, to strum chords of the tonic and the dominant in a light song that a guitar would suffice to accompany, to mingle its olympian voice with the trumpery melody of a vaudeville duet, or with the frivolous noise of a quadrille, to prepare, in the *tutti* of a concerto, the triumphal advent of a hautboy or a flute,—is to impoverish, to degrade a magnificent individuality, to make a hero into a slave and a buffoon, to tarnish the orchestra, to render impotent and futile all rational progress in instrumental work, to ruin the past, present and future of Art, to commit a voluntary act of vandalism, or to give token of an absence of feeling for expression amounting to stupidity.

The Alto Trombone with Pistons; or with Cylinders.

There are alto trombones in $E\flat$ and in F; and it is absolutely requisite to denote for which of these keys the composition is written, since the habit has obtained of treating this trombone as a transposing instrument. It has no slide; and is in some sort, only a cornet-à-pistons in $E\flat$ or in F, with rather more sonority than the regular cornets.

The compass of the alto trombone with pistons is nearly the same as that of the ordinary alto trombone. It is written for on the G clef, transposing as with the cornet-à-pistons.

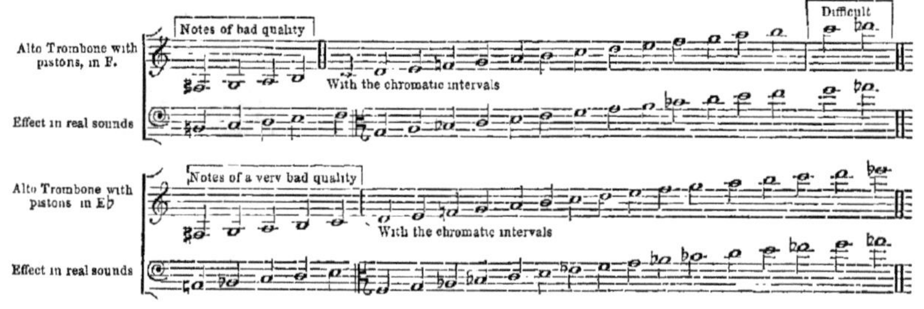

The trombone with pistons, being deprived of the aid of the slide, cannot produce the low notes, called pedals, of the other trombones.

The shakes of the alto trombone with a slide, made by the performer with the lips only, are practicable on the trombone with pistons. Some of them may be made also with the pistons, but it should be observed that the minor shakes are the only ones which produce a good effect, and which can be done rapidly. These are the best —

Example of shakes produced by the pistons.

The system of pistons adapted to the trombone gives it much agility, but causes it to lose somewhat in correctness of intonation. It may easily be conceived that the movable slide, obeying instantaneously the slightest impulse, converts—if the performer possess a good ear—the ordinary trombone into the most correct of all wind instruments; and that the trombone with pistons, deprived of the slide, becomes thereby one of those instruments with fixed intonations, to which the lips can give but very slender modifications. Solo themes are frequently written for the alto trombone with pistons. Well phrased, a melody thus played may have great charm; but it is erroneous to believe that—if confided to a fine artist—it would have less on the trombone with slides. M. Dieppo has many times triumphantly proved this. Besides, I repeat it, unless the execution of rapid passages be the point in view, the main advantage of greater correctness is far preferable, and should have its due weight with composers in forming their decision. In Germany there are some tenor trombones with cylinders which descend as low as the B♭, , but notwithstanding this advantage, I hold the trombones with slides to be greatly preferable.

The Bugle, or Clarion.

We conclude the discussion of wind instruments with a few words on the bugle family.

The simple bugle, or clarion, is written for on the G clef, like the trumpet; it possesses, in all, eight notes,—

but the last, the high C, is only practicable on the deepest bugle; while the low one is of a very bad quality of tone. There are bugles in three keys: *B♭*, *C*, and *E♭*; and they are seldom to be found in any other. The flourishes played upon them, lying always exclusively on the three notes of the common chord, are necessarily so monotonous as to be almost wearisome. The *timbre* of this instrument is rather ungracious; it generally wants nobleness; and it is difficult to play well in tune. As it can execute no diatonic succession, shakes are of course impossible.

Bugles appear to me to rank no higher in the hierarchy of brass instruments than fifes among wooden instruments. Both the one and the other can hardly serve for more than leading recruits to drill; while, to my idea, such music should never be heard by our soldiers, young or old, since there is no need to accustom them to the ignoble. As the sound of the bugle is very loud, it is not impossible that an opportunity may occur for employing it in the orchestra, to give additional violence to some terrible cry of trombones, trumpets, or horns united. This is probably all that can be expected from it.

The bugle, a much shorter instrument than the trumpet, possesses only the notes of the three lower octaves of this latter:—

but on account of the small length of its tube, these notes come out an octave higher. Hence they are written—

Thus the bugle, or clarion, in *C*, is a non-transposing instrument: while the bugles in *B♭* and in *E♭*, on the contrary, are written in transposition as trumpets in *B♭* and in *E♭* are written.

The Keyed Bugle.

In cavalry music, and even in certain Italian orchestras, bugles with seven keys are found, which traverse chromatically a compass of more than two octaves, running from B♮ beneath the stave, up to the C above:—

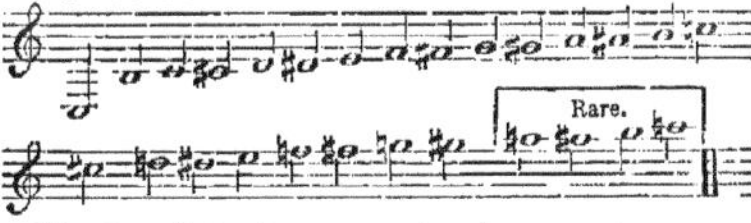

The keyed bugle can make the shake upon all the notes of the scale, with the exception of this:—

It does not want for agility, many artists play it in a remarkable way; but its quality does not differ from that of the simple bugle or clarion.

The Bugle with Pistons; or with Cylinders.

It has a lower compass than the preceding: but this is a slender advantage, for its bass notes are of very bad quality, and moreover come out easily only upon the small bugle in *E♭*; the compass of which, consequently, is this:—

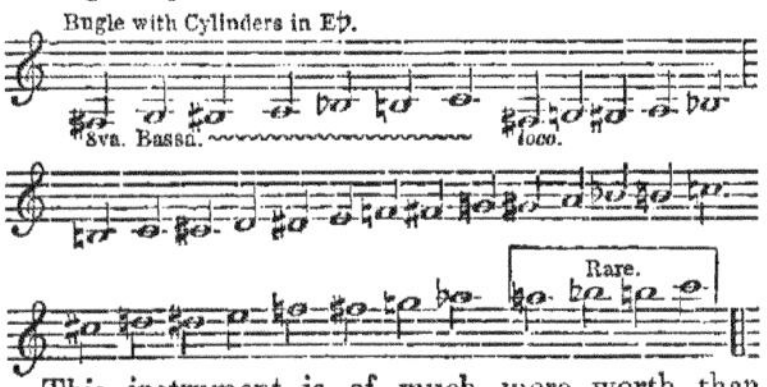

This instrument is of much more worth than the keyed bugle; it produces a good effect in certain melodies of slow, or at least moderate movement; its *timbre* presents, for lively or gay phrases, the same inconvenience which we pointed out in the cornets à pistons, that of lacking distinction; nevertheless, this may be favorably modified by the talent of the performer. Beginning from middle E, all the major and minor shakes are good upon the bugle with pistons, excepting this:—

The Bass Ophicleide.

Ophicleides are the altos and basses of the bugle. The bass ophicleide offers great resources for maintaining the low part of masses of harmony; and it is also the most used. It is written for on the F clef; and its compass is three octaves and one note:—

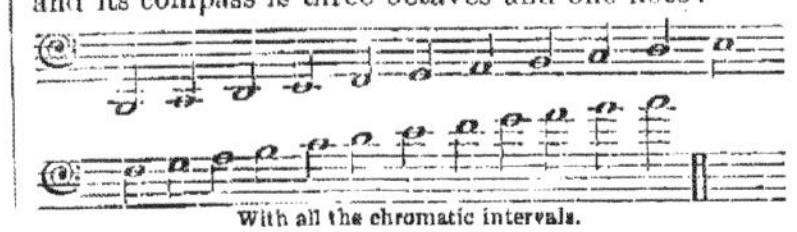

With all the chromatic intervals.

In the hands of a skilful artist, the major and minor shakes are possible on the subjoined part of its scale; as proved by M. Caussinus in the excellent work which he has just published:—

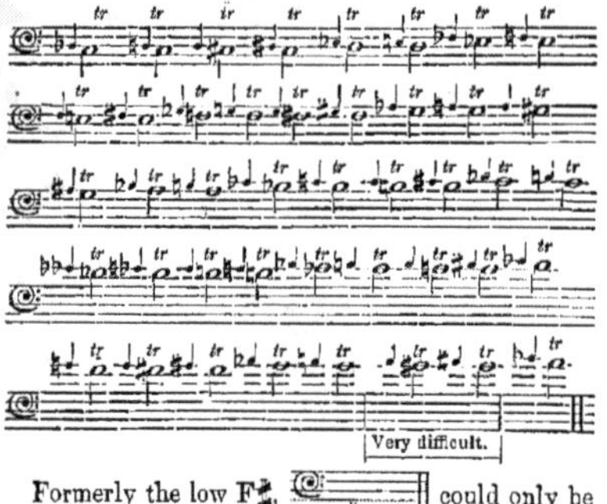

Formerly the low F♯, could only be produced in an incomplete way with the lips; this note essentially lacked correctness and steadiness; but M. Caussinus added to the instrument a key which rendered it as good as the others.

Passages of a certain rapidity, diatonic, and even chromatic, are practicable in the three upper octaves of the ophicleide; but are excessively difficult below, where they moreover produce no other than a detestable effect:—

Staccato passages are much less easy,—nay, almost impossible—in a quick movement. There are bass ophicleides in two keys, in *C* and in *B♭*; and there are some even made at present in *A♭*. These last will be of great utility, on account of the extreme depth of their lower notes, which form a unison with the three-stringed double-basses. The ophicleide in *B♭* has already rendered eminent service in this respect. They are each of them written for in transposition, like all transposing instruments:—

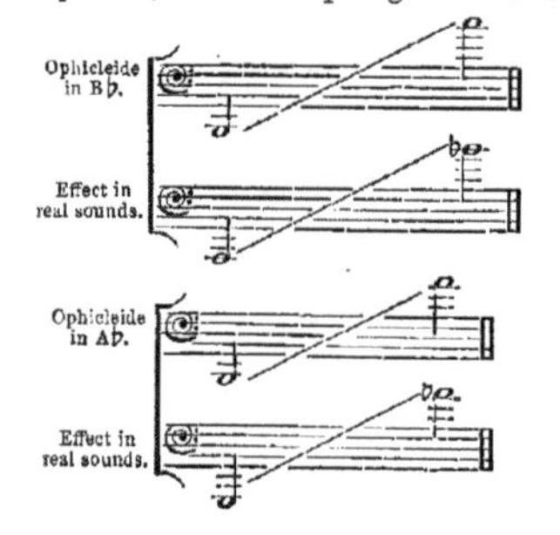

The first low G, it will be observed, is the unison of this on the double-bass. It is a pity that the ophicleide in *A♭* should be so little employed.

The quality of these low sounds is rough; but it does wonders—in certain cases—beneath masses of brass instruments. The very high notes have a wild character, of which perhaps sufficient advantage has not yet been taken. The medium notes—especially when the player is not very skilful,—too much recall the sounds of the cathedral serpent,* and of the cornet-à-bouquin. I think they should rarely be allowed to have prominence. There is nothing more coarse—I might almost say, more monstrous,—or less fit to harmonise with the rest of the orchestra, than the passages, more or less rapid, written in the form of *solos* for the ophicleide medium in some modern operas. It is as if a bull, escaped from its stall, had come to play off its vagaries in the middle of a drawing-room.

The Alto Ophicleide.

There are alto ophicleides in *F* and in *E♭*, and their compass is the same as that of the bass ophicleides; they are both written for on the G clef, like horns; and, in the same way as for horns, this clef represents in the octave below the written note. Thus, this C, corresponds with that of the F clef, which in reality sounds that of the G clef, Bearing in mind at present the transposition produced by the diapason of their specific keys, here is, in real sounds, the result of their written scale:—

[* An instrument much used in French churches.—*Translator.*]

They are employed in some kinds of military music to fill up the harmony, and even to execute certain phrases of melody; but their quality is generally disagreeable, and not noble, and they lack precise intonation; hence the almost complete neglect into which these instruments have now fallen.

The Double-Bass Ophicleide

The double-bass ophicleides, or monster ophicleides, are very little known. They may be useful in very large orchestras; but, until now, no one has been willing to play them in Paris. They require an amount of breath which would exhaust the lungs of the most robust man. They are in *F* and in *E♭*, a fifth below the bass ophicleides in *C* and in *B♭*; and an octave below the alto ophicleides in *F* and in *E♭*. They must not be made to go higher than the F.

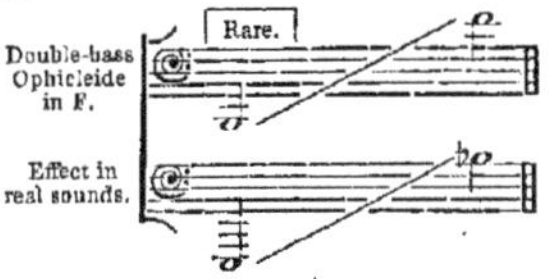

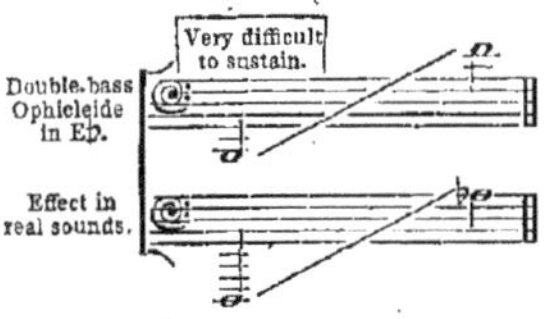

It is needless to state that shakes and rapid passages are incompatible with the nature of such instruments.

The Bombardon.

This is a low instrument, without keys, and with three cylinders. Its quality differs but little from that of the ophicleide.

Its compass is this:—

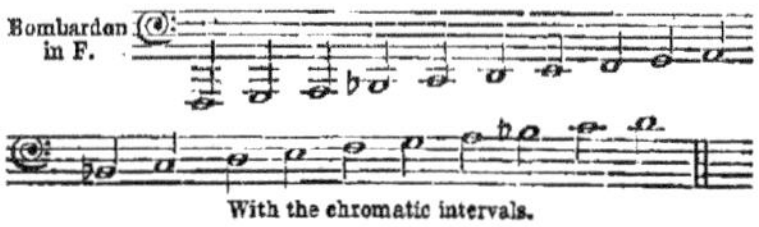

With the chromatic intervals.

It possesses five other notes, both above and below; but they are of uncertain emission, and better avoided.

This instrument—the sound of which is very powerful—can only execute passages of moderate movement. Florid phrases and shakes are precluded. It produces a good effect in large orchestras where wind instruments predominate. Its tube gives naturally the notes of the chord of F, hence it is called in *F*; nevertheless, the custom is, in Germany, to treat it, like the trombone, as *non-transposing*, and to write for it only real sounds.

The Bass-Tuba (the Double-Bass of Harmony).

It is a species of bombardon, the mechanism of which has been improved by M. Wibrecht, master of the King of Prussia's military bands. The bass-tuba,—much used at present in the North of Germany, particularly at Berlin—possesses an immense advantage over all other low wind instruments. Its quality of tone, incomparably more noble than that of ophicleides, bombardons, and serpents, has something of the vibration of the *timbre* of trombones. It has less agility than the ophicleides; but its sonority is more powerful than theirs, and its low compass is *the largest existing in the orchestra*. Its tube gives—like that of the bombardon—the notes of the chord of F; nevertheless, Adolphe Sax now makes bass-tubas in *E♭*. Notwithstanding this difference they are all treated, in Germany, as *non-transposing* instruments. The *bass-tuba* has five cylinders, and its compass is four octaves. For some years past these instruments have been used in France, where they are written for, like horns and trumpets, as transposing instruments.

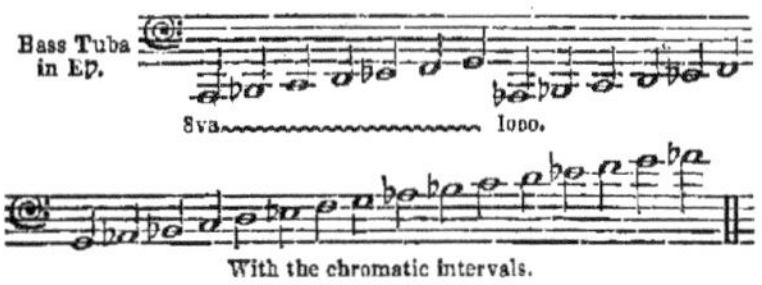

With the chromatic intervals.

In France the preceding scale would be written a third below.

The bass-tuba can produce some few notes higher, and even lower than the above, by the aid of the cylinder mechanism. Those which are extremely high are very dangerous; while those extremely low are scarcely to be heard; the C, the B♭, and the A, which I have just marked in its scale, are only to be distinguished by doubling them in the octave above with those of another bass-tuba, which both imparts to them and acquires from them additional sonority.

It must be well understood that this instrument is not better adapted than the bombardon to shakes and rapid passages. It can play certain measured melodies. An idea can hardly be formed of the effect produced in grand military harmonies by a mass of bass-tubas. It has at once something of the trombone and of the organ.

Instruments with a Mouth-piece, and of Wood.

The Serpent

Is a wooden instrument covered with leather, and having a mouth-piece; it has the same compass as the bass ophicleide, with rather more agility, precise intonation and sonority. There are three notes,—

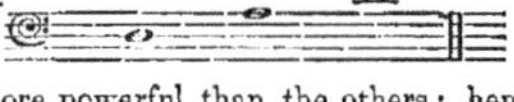

much more powerful than the others; hence those startling inequalities of tone which its players should apply themselves with all care to overcome as much as possible. The serpent is in *B*♭; consequently, it must be written for a whole tone above the real sound, like the ophicleide in *B*♭.

The essentially barbarous quality of tone which distinguishes this instrument would have suited better the rites of the sanguinary Druidical worship than those of the Catholic religion; wherein it always figures as a monument of the want of intelligence, and of the coarseness in sentiment and taste which, from time immemorial, have marked in our temples the applications of Musical Art to Divine Service. Exception must be made in favor of cases where the serpent is employed, in masses for the dead, to double the terrible plain-chant of the *Dies Iræ*. Its frigid and abominable blaring doubtless then befits the occasion; it seems invested with a kind of lugubrious poetry, when accompanying words expressive of all the horrors of death, and the vengeance of a jealous God. It would be no less well placed in profane compositions, if ideas of the same nature had to be expressed; but then only. It mingles ill, moreover, with the other *timbres* of orchestra and voices; and, as forming the bass to a mass of wind instruments, the bass-tuba, and even the ophicleide, are greatly preferable.

The Russian Bassoon

Is a low instrument of the serpent kind. Its *timbre* has nothing very characteristic, its sounds lack steadiness and consequently precision in tune; and, in my opinion, it might be withdrawn from the family of wind instruments without the smallest injury to Art. Its general compass is this:

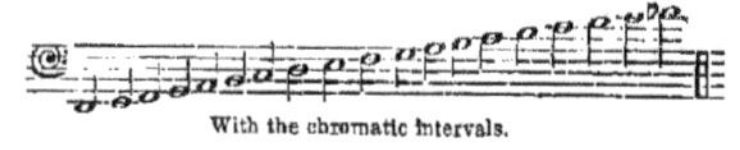

With the chromatic intervals.

Some instruments go down to C, and up to the high D, ; but these are exceptions, of which no practical account can be made. The best notes of the Russian bassoon are D and E♭. Only detestable effects are to be obtained from shakes on this instrument. Russian bassoons are found in military bands; but it is to be hoped that they will not figure there when the bass-tuba becomes more known.

Voices.

Voices are naturally divided into two great classes—male voices, or low voices; and female voices, or high voices. The latter comprise not only the voices of women, but also the voices of children of both sexes, and the voices of artificial sopranos. Both the one and the other are subdivided into two distinct species, which a generally received theory considers as being of the same compass, and differing only among themselves in degree of depth. According to established custom in all the schools of Italy and Germany, the lowest male voice (the bass) will reach from F below the stave (F clef) up to D and E♭ above; and the highest (the tenor), placed a fifth above the preceding, will consequently go from the C below the stave (C clef on fourth line) up to the A and B♭ above. The voices of women and children will, in the same order, range precisely an octave higher than the two male voices, dividing themselves under the names of contralto and soprano; the first corresponding with the bass voice, the second with the tenor voice. Thus, the contralto will go, like the bass, from the low F to the high E♭ (nearly two octaves); and the soprano, like the tenor, from the low C to the high B♭.

Doubtless this regular disposal of the four most characteristic kinds of the human voice is very seductive; but, unfortunately, it must be acknowledged as in some respects insufficient and hazardous, since it would deprive the composer of a great number of precious voices, if it were admitted without restriction in writing for choirs. Nature, in fact, does not proceed in the same manner in all climates; and if it be true that in Italy she produces many contralto voices, it cannot be denied that in France she is very sparing of them. Tenors that can easily go up to A and B♭ are common in France and Italy, but are rarer in Germany, where—as compensation—they have in their bass notes more sonority than anywhere else. It therefore appears to me absolutely imprudent to write choruses in four real parts of equal importance, according to the classical division of voices into *Sopranos*, *Contraltos*, *Tenors*, and *Basses*. It is at least certain that in *Paris*, in a chorus thus arranged, the contralto part—comparatively with the other parts, especially in a large mass of voices—would be so weak as to miss the greater portion of the effects assigned to it by the composer. Neither is it to be doubted that in Germany, and even in Italy and France, if the tenor were to be written within the established limits—that is to say, a fifth above the bass,—a good number of those voices would stop short at passages wherein the composer requires them to go up to the high A and B♭, or else would only give utterance to notes false, forced, and of bad quality. The same observation holds good in the case of bass voices, many of them lose much of their sonority after the low C or B, and it is useless to write for them either G's or F's. As Nature everywhere produces sopranos, tenors, and basses, I think it infinitely more prudent, more rational, and even more musical, *if the object be to make all the voices useful,* to write choruses either in six parts—first and second sopranos, first and second tenors, barytones, and basses (or first and second basses)—or in three parts, taking care to divide the voices each time that they approach the extremes of their respective compass, by giving to the first bass a note higher by a third, by a fifth, or by an octave, than the too-low note of the second bass, or to the second tenor and the second soprano intermediate sounds, when the first tenor and first soprano rise too high. It is less essential to separate the first sopranos from the second sopranos when the phrase extends very low than in the contrary case, the high voices lose, it is true, all their power, and their distinctive quality of tone, when they are made to sing notes proper only to a contralto or a second soprano voice, but at least they are not compelled to give forth bad sounds, like the second sopranos, when they are forced up too high, and it is the same with the two other voices. The second soprano, the second tenor, and the first bass, are generally placed a third or a fourth below and above the principal voice of which they bear the name, and possess a compass almost equal to theirs, but this is true more as regards the second soprano than as regards the second tenor and the first bass If the second soprano be given as its compass an octave and a sixth, beginning from the B below the stave up to the G above—

Second Soprano

all the notes will sound well and without difficulty It would not be the same with the second tenor, if given a scale of like extent its low D's, C's, and B's would have scarcely any sonority: and unless with set intention, and for a particular effect, it is better to avoid these low notes, which can be easily given to either the first or second basses, whom they perfectly suit The contrary holds good for the first basses, or barytones. If—supposing them to be a third above the second basses—their part extend from the low A to the high G, the low A will be heavy, and vague, and the high G excessively forced, to say the least This latter note is really only fit for the first and second tenors. Whence it follows that the most limited voices are the second tenors; which do not ascend as high as the first tenors, nor descend much lower; and the first basses, which, without going any higher than the second basses, cannot descend so low In a chorus written in six parts—as I propose—the true contralto voices (for there are always more or less in every choral body) must necessarily sing the second soprano part, and this is why I think it well, when the music goes beyond the high F, to subdivide them again, in order that the *contraltos* may not be forced to scream out notes too high for them.

Subjoined is the most sonorous compass of the seven different voices to be found in nearly all great choral bodies,—I abstain from indicating the extreme upper or lower notes possessed by certain individuals, which should only be written exceptionally —

Choruses of women in three parts have an enchanting effect in pieces of a tender and religious character, they are then disposed in the order of the three voices just stated,—first soprano, second soprano, and third soprano, or contralto

Sometimes a tenor part is given as bass to these three-part female voices Weber has done so with great success in his chorus of spirits (*Oberon*), but it can only be good in a case where the object is to produce a soft and calm effect, such a chorus having naturally but little energy. On the contrary, choruses composed of men's voices only have much power, the more because the voices are deeper and less divided The division of the basses into firsts and seconds (to avoid the high notes) is less necessary in rude and fierce accents, with which sounds forced and exceptional—like the high F and F♯—agree better from their peculiar character than the more natural sounds of the tenors upon the same notes But it is necessary to lead to these notes, and to bring them in dexterously, taking care not to make the voices pass abruptly from the medium or depth to the extreme upper register. Thus, Gluck, in his terrible chorus of Scythians, in the first act of *Iphigenia in Tauride*, gives the high F♯ to all the basses joined with the tenors, on these words '—' Ils nous amènent des victimes", but the F♯ is preceded by two D's, and the voice can easily be *carried on,* by binding the last D with the F♯ on the syllable " nous".—

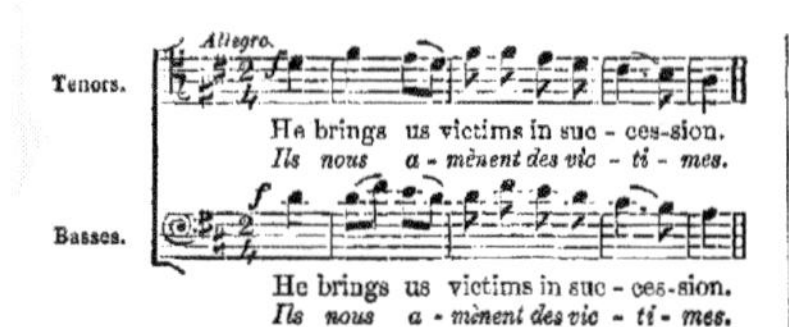

The sudden unison of the tenors and basses in this passage gives to the phrase, moreover, such a volume of sound, and so powerful an accent, that it is impossible to hear it without shuddering. Here we have another of the touches of genius which are to be met with in almost every page of the scores of this giant of dramatic music.

Independently of the expressive idea, which here seems to predominate, the common exigences of vocal scoring may frequently introduce unisons of this kind into choruses. If the direction of the melody, for instance, leads the first tenors towards the B♮s (a very dangerous note, and one to be shunned), the composer may bring in, for this phrase only, the *second sopranos and contraltos*, which can sing without difficulty in unison with the tenors, and blend with, while they confirm their intonations.

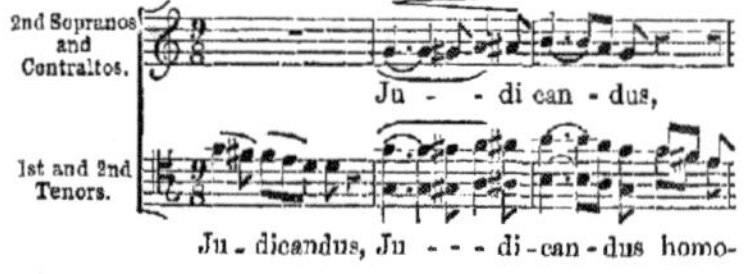

When, on the contrary, the tenors are compelled by the exigence of a melodic design to descend too low, the first basses are there to serve them as auxiliaries, and to strengthen them without perverting their vocal character by a marked difference in quality of tone. It would not be the same if the composer were to give the tenors—still less, the basses —as auxiliaries to the contraltos and the second sopranos: the female voice would then be almost eclipsed, and from the moment of the male voice's entrance, its character of vocal sonority would change abruptly, so as to destroy unity of execution in the melody. Juxtapositions of this kind—one voice coming to the aid of another—are therefore not good with all *timbres* indiscriminately, when the character of the voice which commenced and continued the phrase is to be preserved. For, I repeat, if the contraltos in the medium register become lost, when sustaining the unison of the tenors in the high register, the tenors in the medium would cover—to the point of hiding them altogether—the second sopranos in the low register, if united suddenly with them. In a case where the composer desires simply to add the compass of one voice to the compass of another voice, in a melodic descending progression, for instance, he must not make a mass of heavy *timbres* suddenly succeed to one of lighter quality, since the joining-point would be too apparent. It would be better first to let the higher half of the high voices cease, substituting for them the upper half of the low voices, and reserving until a little later the interweaving of the two other halves. Thus, supposing a long descending scale, beginning with the high G by the first and second sopranos together,—at the moment when the scale reaches the E a tenth below the first G, let the first soprano stop, and bring in the first tenors on the D (a whole tone below the last E of the first sopranos); the second sopranos continuing to descend, thus united with the first tenors, will cease upon the low B, after which the second tenors should come in upon the A in unison with the first tenors; the first tenors ceasing upon the F to make room for the first basses; the interweaving of the second tenors with the second basses will take place on the lower D or C; then the united basses will continue to descend as far as the G, and the result for the hearer will be a descending scale of three octaves' extent, during which the voices will have succeeded each other in such a way that the passing from one voice to the other shall have scarcely been perceived:—

After these observations, it will easily be conceived that the composer has to make his choice of the register of voices subservient to the character of the piece in which he employs them. He should use only notes of the medium in an Andante of soft and sustained sounds; those alone possess the suitable quality of tone, move with calmness and precision, and can be sustained without the least effort in a *pianissimo*. This is what Mozart has done in his celestial prayer:—"Ave verum corpus."

No. 52.

Ave verum.—MOZART.

Cu - - jus la - tus per - fo - - ra - tum un - - da - flu - xit et
Cu - - jus la - tus per - - fo - ra - tum un - - da - flu - xit et
Cu - - jus la - tus per - fo - - ra - tum un - da - flu - xit et
Cu - - jus la - tus per - - fo - ra - tum un - - da - flu - xit et
san - - gui - ne es - - to no - bis præ gus - ta - tum in
san - - gui - ne es - - to no - bis præ gus - ta - tum in
san - - gui - ne es - - to no - bis præ gus -
san - - gui - ne es - - to no - bis præ gus -
mor - - - - tis ex - a - - mi - ne, in mor - - - - - -
mor - - - - tis ex - a - - mi - ne, in mor - - -
- - ta - tum in mor - tis ex - a - - mi - ne, in mor - - -
- - ta - tum in mor - tis ex - a - - mi - ne, in mor - - -

Fine effects are always to be obtained from the extreme low notes of the second basses, such as the E♭, and even the D below the stave, which many voices can easily intone, when they have time to take them firmly, when the notes are preceded by sufficient time for breath, and written upon a sonorous syllable. Brilliant, pompous, or violent choruses should, on the contrary, be written rather higher: without, however, letting the prevalence of high notes be too constant, and without giving the singers many words to pronounce rapidly. The extreme fatigue resulting from this mode of writing would soon induce bad execution; besides, a continuance of high notes, on syllables articulated with difficulty, is not at all agreeable to the hearer.

We have not yet spoken of those very high notes of the voice called *head notes* or *falsetto.* They are of great beauty in tenor singers, whose compass they considerably augment; many artists being able without difficulty to reach, by head notes, up to E♭ and F above the stave. Frequent and valuable use might be made of these notes in choruses, if choralists were more proficient in the art of singing. Head notes are of good effect for basses and barytones only in an extremely light style of music, such as that of our French comic operas. High and feminine-toned sounds, so dissimilar from the *natural notes*—called *chest notes*—of the low voices, have, in fact, something revolting, everywhere but in buffo music. There has never been any attempt to introduce them into a chorus, or into any theme pertaining to the noble in style. The point where the chest voice ends, and the head voice begins, cannot be exactly determined. Clever tenor singers, moreover, give, *forte*, certain high notes such as A, B, and even C, in *head voice*, or in *chest voice*, at pleasure; nevertheless, for the majority, I believe, the B♭ must be fixed as the limit of a tenor singer's chest voice. And this again proves that the tenor voice is not strictly a fifth above the bass, as is stated to be the case by school theories; since, of twenty basses taken at random, ten of them, at least, could give, in chest voice, a high F♯, if properly led up to; while in the same number of tenors, one would not be found who could give, in chest voice, a tolerably good high C♯.

The ancient masters of the French school,—who never employed the head voice,—have written in their operas a part which they call "*haute-contre*"; and foreigners, deceived by the natural interpretation of the Italian word *Contralto,* often take it for the low voice of women. This name, however, denoted the voice of a man accustomed to sing almost exclusively, and in chest voice, the five high notes (including the B♮) of the first tenor's compass. The pitch was—as is generally believed—lower by a whole tone than the present pitch, but the proofs of this do not appear to me to be unimpeachable; and a doubt on the point is still allowable. At the present time, when a B♮ occurs in a chorus, the majority of tenor singers take it in head voice; but the very high tenors (the *haute-contres*) still take it without hesitation in chest voice.

Children's voices are of excellent effect in large choirs. Boys' soprano voices have even something penetrating and crystalline which is wanting in the *timbre* of women's sopranos. In a soft, smooth, calm composition, however, the latter, fuller and less piercing, always appear to me preferable. As for artificial sopranos—to judge from those I have heard in Rome—it does not seem that their almost entire abandonment is much to be regretted.

There are in the North of Germany, and in Russia, basses so deep that composers do not fear giving them, without preparation, D's and C's below the stave to sustain. This valuable kind of voice—called *basso profondo,*—contributes powerfully to the prodigious effect of the choir in the Imperial Chapel at St. Petersburgh,—the first choir in the world, according to those who have heard it. A *basso profondo* can hardly ever go beyond B or C above the stave.

For the effective employment of the very low notes of bass singers, they should never have a too rapid succession of notes, or be too much overcharged with words. Besides, choral vocalisations in the lowest part of the scale are of detestable effect. They are not it is true, much better in the medium; and let us hope that, notwithstanding the example set by the majority of the great masters, those ridiculous roulades on the words "Kyrie eleison," or on the word "Amen," which make vocal fugues in church music an indecent and abominable buffoonery, will be banished in future from every sacred composition worthy of the name. Slow and soft vocalisations of sopranos alone, accompanying a melody of the other voices placed beneath, have, on the contrary, a pious and angelic expression. It should not be forgotten to intersperse them with short rests, to afford breathing-time for the chorus-singers.

Those modes of emission which produce from men voice-sounds called *mixed*, and *veiled*, are extremely valuable; and give much character to both solo-singing and choral-singing.

The *mixed* voice combines somewhat the quality of chest notes and head notes; but—in the same way as for these latter—it is impossible to assign fixed limits for the mixed voice, either above or below. Such and such a voice may be able to take the *mixed* quality very high; while such another can only employ it upon lower notes. As for the *veiled* voice—of which the name indicates the character—it depends not only on the mode of utterance, but also on the degree of force, of execution, and of feeling, which animates the singers. A chorus of a somewhat agitated character, and properly called *sotto voce*, would be very easily executed in *veiled* voice, provided the chorus-singers possessed intelligence, expression, and practice in singing. This kind of vocal execution, contrasted with that of the powerful and brilliant sounds of the high *forte*, always produces a fine effect. As a magnificent example of this, Gluck's chorus in *Armida*:—"Follow Love, since you thus persist," should be cited. Here the two first stanzas, uttered in *veiled* voice, give terrible potency to the peroration, taken in full voice, and *fortissimo*, on the return of the phrase:—"Follow Love." It is impossible better to characterise suppressed menace, and then a sudden explosion of fury. It is thus that *Spirits of Rage and Hate* should sing:—

No. 53.

sf sf sf sf
sf sf sf sf
Love, who mis-leads you to take this fa-tal step, to take this fa - - - - - tal step.
-mour, qui te gui-de dans un abime affreux, dans un a-bime af-freux.
Vcello.
D.B.
La Haine.
In these wild desert paths 'tis in vain thou con-ceal - - - est how this hero has touch'd thy
Sur ces bords é-car-tés c'est en vain que tu-ca - - - ches le hé-ros dont ton cœur s'est
too - - - con-fi-ding heart; will Fame, from whom thou hast torn him, not regain her for-mer
trop . . . lais-sé tou-cher la gloire à qui tu l'ar-ra - - - ches doit bientot te l'ar-ra-

sway? Spite of thy care, and in spite of thy weep - - ing, thou shalt behold him es -
- - cher mal-gré tes soins au mé-pris de tes lar - - - mes, tu le ver-ras é-chap-
Chorus. p
- cape thine endear - ments. Follow Love, since you thus per-sist, un - for-tunate Ar - mi - da, follow
- per à tes char - mes. Suis l'a - mour puisque tu le veux, in - for-tu-née Ar - mi - de, suis l'a-
p
p
p

Love who mis-leads you to take this fa - tal step, to take this fa - tal step.
- mour qui te gui - de dans un a-bime af - freux, dans un a - bime af - freux.
La Haine.
Mark well my words this day; my warn - ing bear in mind; defeat shall wait on each en - dea - vour. I
Tu me rappel - le - ras peut ê - tre dès ce jour et ton at - ten - te se - ra vai - ne. Je

Unis.

quit thee, ne-ver to re-turn; no greater punishment can I inflict up-on thee, than leave thee to the gnaw - ing re-
vais te quit-ter sans re-tour je ne puis te pu - nir d'une plus ru - de pei - ne que de t'a-ban-don-ner pour ja-

sf sf sf

Col. 1mo.

CHORUS.

- grets born of Love. Follow Love, since you thus per-sist, un-for-tu-nate, Ar-mi - da, follow
- *mais à l'a-mour. Suis l'a-mour puisque tu le veux in-for-tu-née Ar-mi - de, suis la*

ff ff ff

Our remarks on the voice have been limited, we need hardly say, to its employment in choral bodies. The art of writing for single voices is really influenced by a thousand circumstances, very difficult to determine, but which it is necessary to take into account, and which vary with the organisation belonging to each singer. The showing how to write for Rubini, for Duprez, for Haitzinger—who are all tenor singers—is easy; but it would be difficult to indicate the mode of writing a tenor part equally favourable to, or perfectly suitable for, the three.

The solo tenor is, of all the voices, the most difficult to suit, on account of its three registers, comprising chest notes, mixed notes, and head notes, the extent and facility of which—as I have already said—are not the same in all singers. Such and such a performer uses his head voice a great deal, and can even give to his mixed voice much power of vibration; such and such another will sing with ease high and sustained phrases in all degrees of loudness, and in all degrees of rapidity; he will like the *e* and the *i*; while such another, on the contrary, uses the head voice with difficulty, and prefers singing constantly full vibrating chest notes; such another excels in impassioned pieces, but requires that the movement be sufficiently measured to permit the emission—naturally rather slow—of his voice; he will prefer open syllables, sonorous vowels—like "*a*"—and dreads having high notes to execute; a sostenuto of a few bars upon G will appear to him both difficult and dangerous. The first,—thanks to the flexibility of his mixed voice,—can take abruptly a high and loud note; the other, on the contrary, in order to give a high note in all its power, will require to have it gradually led up to, because in this case he employs his chest voice, reserving the mixed notes and head notes exclusively for half-effect and for tender accents. Another—whose tenor is of that kind formerly called in France *haute-contre*,—will have no fear of high notes, taking them in chest voice without preparation and without danger.

The first soprano voice is rather less difficult to treat than the first tenor; its head notes are scarcely different from the rest of the voice. Still, it is well to know the singer for whom one writes, on account of the inequalities in certain sopranos; some being vague and dim in the medium, or in the lower part, thus compelling the composer to select the registers carefully upon which he places the predominant notes of his melody. Mezzo-soprano (second soprano) and contralto voices, are generally more homogeneous, more equal, and consequently more easy to employ. Nevertheless care should be taken, for both of them, not to place many words on phrases that run high; the articulation of syllables then becoming very difficult, and sometimes impossible.

The most convenient voice is the bass, on account of its simplicity. Head notes being banished from its repertory, there need be no anxiety as to changes of *timbre;* and the choice of syllables becomes also —on this very account—less important. Every singer who assumes to be gifted with a true bass voice ought to be able to sing all reasonably written music, from the low G to the E♭ above the stave. Some voices descend much lower—like that of Levasseur, who can sing the low E♭, and even the D; others—like that of Alizard—can rise, without losing any of the purity of their quality, up to the F♯, and even to the G; but these are exceptions. On the other hand, voices which, without going up to the high E♭, cannot make themselves heard below the C (within the stave), are but incomplete voices —fragments of voices, of which it is difficult to make use, whatever may be their power or their beauty. Baritones are often in this condition; they are very limited voices, singing almost always within a single octave (from the middle E♭ to the E♮ above), which places the composer in the predicament of being unable to avoid an awkward monotony.

The excellence or mediocrity of vocal execution in choral bodies, or in solo-singers, depends not only on the art with which the registers of the voices are chosen, on that with which means are contrived for them to take breath, and on the words given them to sing, but also very much on the manner in which composers dispose their accompaniments. Some overwhelm the voices by an instrumental uproar which might be of very happy effect either before or after the vocal phrase, but not while the singers are endeavouring to make it heard; others, without burdening the orchestra beyond measure, take delight in displaying some particular instrument, which, performing passages, or an elaborate theme, during an air, distracts the hearer's attention from the main point, and annoys, embarrasses, and vexes the singer, instead of aiding and supporting him. We do not mean that simplicity of accompaniment should be carried to such an excess as to preclude orchestral design, the expression of which is eloquent, and the musical interest really maintained; particularly when it is interspersed with brief rests which give a little rhythmical latitude to the vocal movements, and do not necessitate a metronomical exactitude of measure. Thus—whatever may be said by several great artists—the plaintive figure of the violoncellos in the pathetic air of the last act of Rossini's *Guillaume Tell:* "Sois immobile," is of touching and admirable effect; it renders the idea of the piece complex, undoubtedly; but without fettering the air, the affecting and sublime expression of which it, on the contrary, enhances.

No. 54.

A single instrument playing in the orchestra some phrase constructed like a vocal melody, and forming with the voice a sort of duet, is also very often of excellent effect. The horn solo in the second act of Spontini's *La Vestale,* which murmurs in duet with Julia's sorrowfully impassioned air: "Toi que j'implore," gives added intensity to the accent of the vocal part; the mysterious quality of tone—veiled and somewhat painful—of the horn in *F* was never more ingeniously or more dramatically employed.

We have another example in Rachael's cavatina, accompanied by a solo on the corno inglese, in the second act of Halévy's *Juive.* The feeble and touching voice of the instrument mingles incomparably well here with the supplicating voice of the young girl.

No. 55.

Largo espressivo.
La Vestale.—SPONTINI.
Horns in E♭.
Solo Horn in F.
Cres
Flutes.
pp
Clarinets.
pp
Fagotti.
Violins.
a punta d'arco.
Viola.
JULIA.
Violoncello.
Double-bass.
pp

ppp
Trem - bling I pray in my deep dis - tress, To thee, ter - - rible
Toi . . . que j'im - plo - re a - vec . . . ef - froi. re - dou - ta - - ble dé -

As for single instruments that perform passages, arpeggios, or variations, during a strain of song, they are, I repeat, of such inconvenience to the singer, as well as to the hearers, that it requires extreme art and evident appropriateness to make them tolerable. I declare, at any rate, that with the single exception of the viola solo in Annette's ballad, in the third act of the *Freyschütz*, they have always appeared to me insufferable. Moreover, it is seldom good—notwithstanding the example set by Mozart, Gluck, the majority of masters of the ancient school, and some composers of the modern school—to double the vocal part by an instrument in the octave or unison, particularly in an *Andante*. It is almost always useless, the voice being sufficient for the enunciation of a melody; it is rarely agreeable, the inflexions of singing, its delicacies of expression and subtle gradations, being more or less overborne or dimmed by the juxtaposition of another melodic part; and, lastly, it is fatiguing for the singer, who, if he be clever, will deliver a fine air all the better for being left entirely to himself.

In choruses, or in grand tutti pieces, it is sometimes the fashion to form a sort of vocal orchestra; one portion of the voices then adopts an instrumental style, executing beneath the theme accompaniments rhythmed and figured in various ways. It almost always produces charming effects. Witness the chorus during the dance in the third act of *Guillaume Tell*:—"Toi que," &c.

No. 56.

Guillaume Tell—ROSSINI.

Here a good opportunity offers to point out to composers that, in choruses accompanied by instruments, the harmony of the voices should be correct, and treated as though they were alone. The various *timbres* of the orchestra are too dissimilar from those of the voices to fill in respect of them the office of a bass harmony, without which certain successions of chords become defective. Thus Gluck, who in his works often employed progressions of thirds and sixths in three parts, has made use of them even in his priestess choruses of *Iphigenia in Tauride*, which are soprano choruses written in two parts only. In these harmonic successions, as is well known, the second part occurs a fourth beneath the first part; the effect of the series of fourths being softened only by that of the bass written a third below the intermediate part, and a sixth below the upper part. Now, in the choruses of Gluck just alluded to, the women's voices execute the two high parts, and are therefore written in successions of fourths; while the low part, which completes the chords and renders them harmonious, is given to the instrumental basses, the sound of which differs essentially from that of the sopranos, and is moreover too distant from them, by reason of its extreme depth and point of departure. Hence it follows that, instead of sounding consonant chords, the voices, isolated on the stage and remote from the orchestra, give out a series of fourths rendered dissonant—or, at least, extremely harsh—by the apparent absence of the sixth.

If the harshness of these successions be of dramatic effect in the chorus of the first act of the opera in question—"O songe affreux," &c.—it is not so when the priestesses of Diana come (in the fourth act) to sing the hymn, so antique and so fine in colour nevertheless: "Chaste fille de Latone." We must bear in mind that, here, purity of harmony was absolutely indispensable. The series of fourths left uncovered in the voices is, then, an error of Gluck's—an error which would disappear were a third vocal part added, beneath the second, an octave above the basses of the orchestra.

No. 57.

Iphigenia in Tauride.—GLUCK.

No. 58.

Iphigenia in Tauride.—GLUCK.

In the heav'ns, and throughout nature all things con - form to thy law,
Dans les Cieux et sur la ter - re, tout est sou - mis à ta loi.
In the heav'ns, and throughout nature all things con - form to thy law,
Dans les Cieux et sur la ter - re, tout est sou - mis à ta loi.
dim.
All that E - re - bus con - - tain - eth, at thy name are struck with fear.
tout ce que l'E - rèbe en - - - ser - re à ton nom pâ - - lit d'ef - - froi.
All that E - re - bus con - - tain - eth, at thy name are struck with fear.
tout ce que l'E - rèbe en - - - ser - re à ton nom pâ - - lit d'ef - - froi.
Doux.
In all straits each one con - sults thee, Be it peace, or be it war.
En tout tems on te con - sul - te, dans la paix dans les com - - bats.
In all straits each one con - sults thee, Be it peace, or be it war.
En tout tems on te con - sul - te, dans la paix dans les com - - bats.

Male-voice unison choruses, introduced into dramatic music by the modern Italian school, give occasionally some fine results; but we must allow that the device has been greatly abused, and that if some masters still adhere to it, they do so solely because it favors their idleness, and lends itself conveniently to several choral bodies ill fitted for rendering well a piece in several parts.

Double choruses are, on the contrary, of a richness and pomp quite remarkable; they are certainly not hackneyed nowadays. They are, for expeditious musicians—both composers and performers—too long to write and to learn. To say the truth, the ancient authors, who made the most frequent use of them, generally composed merely two dialogue choruses, in four parts; choruses in eight real continuous parts are rather rare, even in their works. There are compositions for three choirs. When the idea they have to render is worthy of so magnificent an investiture, such bodies of voices, divided into twelve, or at least nine, real parts produce impressions the memory of which is ineffaceable, and cause grand choral music to rank as the highest among arts.

Instruments of Percussion.

These are of two kinds: the first comprises instruments of fixed sound, and musically appreciable; the second includes those of which the less musical product can be ranked only among noises destined to produce special effects, or to colour the rhythm.

Kettle-drums, bells, the glockenspiel, the keyed harmonica, and small ancient cymbals, have fixed sounds.

The long drum, the side-drum, the tambour, the tambour basque (or tambourine), the common cymbals, the tam-tam, the triangle, and the pavillon chinois, merely make noises variously characterised.

Kettle-Drums.

Of all the instruments of percussion, kettle-drums appear to me to be the most valuable; at least they are in most general use, and from them modern composers have derived the most picturesque and dramatic effects. Ancient masters used them only to strike the tonic and the dominant on a rhythm more or less common, in pieces of a brilliant character, or of warlike import; and therefore almost always combined them with trumpets.

In the majority of present orchestras there are but two kettle-drums, the larger of which is used for the lowest sound.

The custom is to give them the first and the fifth note of the key of the piece in which they are to figure. Some masters had the habit, not many years ago, of invariably writing [music] for the kettle-drums; contenting themselves with indicating at the commencement the real sounds that these notes were to represent; so that they wrote thus:—Kettle-drums in *D*; thence making G C signify [music];—Kettle-drums in *G*, and then G C meant [music]. These two examples will suffice to demonstrate the vices of such a system. The compass of kettle-drums is one octave, from [music] to [music]; that is to say, by means of the screws which compress the circumference—called the brace—of each kettle-drum, and which augment or diminish the tension of the parchment, the low kettle-drum can be tuned in the following keys :—

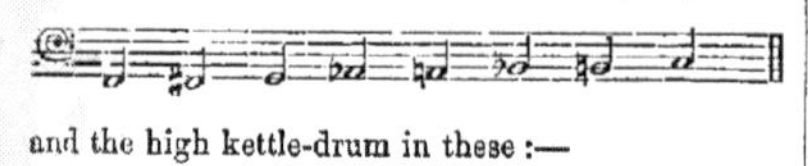

and the high kettle-drum in these :—

Now, supposing that kettle-drums are intended to sound only the tonic and the dominant, it is very evident that the dominant will not occupy in all keys the same relative position with the tonic; and that kettle-drums should therefore be tuned sometimes in fifth, sometimes in fourth. In the key of *C*, they will be in fourth, the dominant necessarily occurring below, since there is no high G (although there might be one); and it will be the same in *D*♭, in *D*♮, in *E*♭, and in *E*♮. But in *B*♭, the composer is at liberty to have his drums tuned in fifth or in fourth, and to place the tonic above or below, since he has two Fs at his disposal. Tuning in fourth, will be dull, the parchment of the two kettle-drums being then very little strained; the F, particularly, will be vapid and of bad quality. Tuning in fifth, becomes sonorous for the opposite reason. It is the same with kettle-drums in *F*♮, which may be tuned in two ways; in fifth, or in fourth, In the keys of *G*, *A*♭, and *A*♮, on the contrary, the tuning must be in fifth, because there is no low D, E♭, or E♮. There is no need, it is true, to mention in this case the tuning in fifth, since the drum-player will be obliged to adopt it; but is it not absurd to write movements of fourth when the performer has to play movements of fifth: and to present to the eye as the lowest note that which, to the ear, is the highest, and vice-versa?

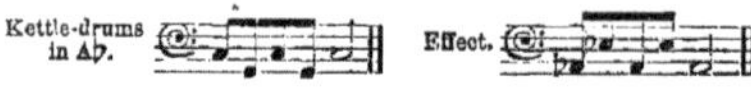

The principal cause of this strange custom of treating the kettle-drum as a transposing instrument is doubtless the idea, which all composers once took up, that kettle-drums ought only to give the tonic and the dominant; but when the fact appeared that it was frequently useful to give them other notes to play, it became necessary to write the real sounds. Accordingly, kettle-drums are now tuned in all sorts of ways,—in minor third or major, in second, in fourth true or augmented, in fifth, in sixth, in seventh, and in octave. Beethoven has drawn charming effects from the tuning in octave *F F*, in his eighth Symphony, and in his ninth (choral). Composers complained for many years of the vexatious necessity in which they found themselves—for want of a third sound in kettle-drums—of never employing the instrument in chords of which neither of these two notes formed a part; they never asked themselves whether a single drummer might not play upon three drums. At length, one fine day, the drum-player at the Paris opera having shown that the thing was easy, they ventured to try the audacious innovation; and since then, composers who write for the opera have at their disposal three kettle-drum notes. It required seventy years to reach this point! It will be still better, evidently, to have two pairs of kettle-drums and two drummers; and this method has been pursued in the orchestration of several modern symphonies. But progress is not so rapid in theatres; and there it will take some score of years to attain.

As many drummers may be employed in the orchestra as there are drums, so as to produce at pleasure, according to their number, rolls, rhythms, and simple chords, in two, three, or four parts. With two pairs, if one be tuned in *A*♮ *E*♭, for instance, and the other in *C F*, there may, with four drummers, be played the following chords in two, three, and four parts :—

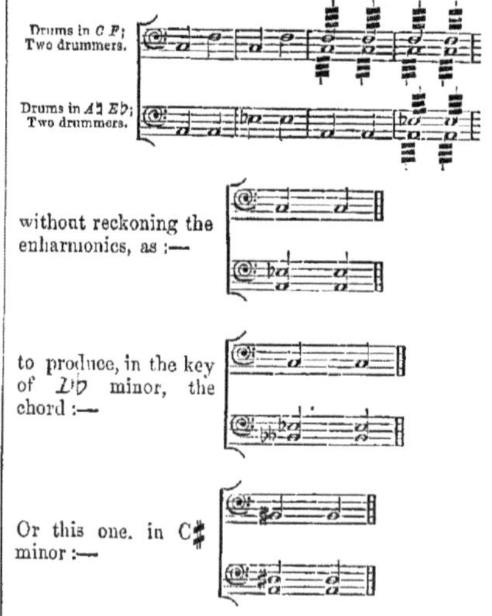

without reckoning the enharmonics, as :—

to produce, in the key of *D*♭ minor, the chord :—

Or this one, in C♯ minor :—

and the advantage of having at least one note to place in almost all the chords which are not too remote from the principal key. In order thus to obtain a certain number of chords in three, four, and five parts, more or less doubled, and moreover a striking effect of very close rolls, I have employed in my grand requiem mass eight pairs of drums tuned in different ways, and ten drum-players.

No. 59.—TUBA MIRUM.

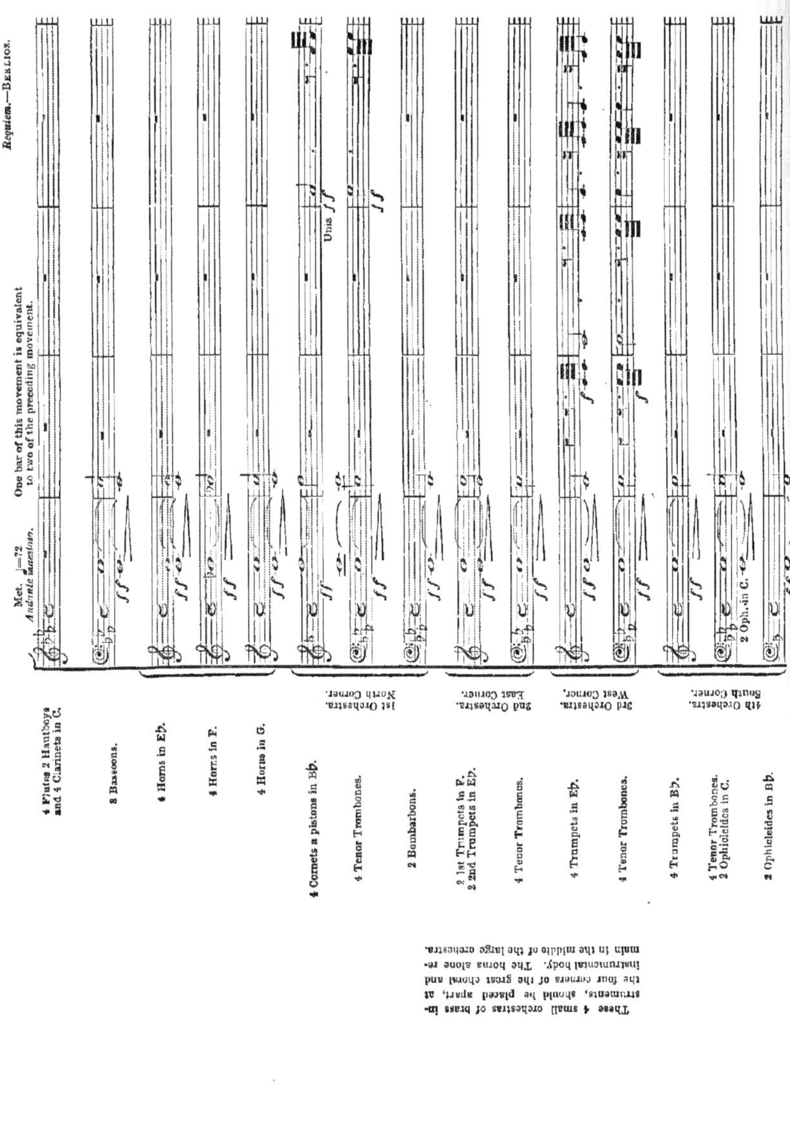

Requiem.—BERLIOZ.

Met. ♩=72 *Andante maestoso.*

One bar of this movement is equivalent to two of the preceding movement.

4 Flutes 2 Hautboys and 4 Clarinets in C.

8 Bassoons.

4 Horns in E♭.

4 Horns in F.

4 Horns in G.

1st Orchestra. North Corner.

4 Cornets a pistons in B♭.

4 Tenor Trombones.

2 Bombarbons.

2nd Orchestra. East Corner.

2 1st Trumpets in F.
2 2nd Trumpets in E♭.

4 Tenor Trombones.

3rd Orchestra. West Corner.

4 Trumpets in E♭.

4 Tenor Trombones.

4th Orchestra. South Corner.

4 Trumpets in B♭.

4 Tenor Trombones.
2 Ophicleides in C.

2 Ophicleides in B♭.

ff

Unis ff

2 Oph. in C.

These 4 small orchestras of brass instruments, should be placed apart, at the four corners of the great choral and instrumental body. The horns alone remain in the middle of the large orchestra.

Two drummers on one pair of drums in D♭, F♮.
Tuned in minor thirds.

Two drummers on one pair of drums in G, E♭.
Tuned in minor sixths.

One pair of drums in G♭, B♭
tuned in major thirds.

One pair of drums in B♮, E♮.
tuned in fourths.

One pair of drums in A♮, E♭.
tuned in diminished fifths.

One pair of drums in A♭, C♮.
tuned in major thirds.

One pair of drums in G♮, D♭.
tuned in diminished fifths

One pair of drums in F♮, B♭.
tuned in fourths.

Each of these six pairs should have one drummer; making in all, 10 drummers, and 8 pairs of drums.

All the drummers should have drumsticks with sponge ends.

This long drum should be set upright, and the rolls made with two kettle-drum-sticks.

Long drum in B♭.

A long drum with two padded drum-sticks.

Tamtam and Cymbals, (3 pairs.)
Struck like the Tamtam, with drum-stick, or wadded-stick.

Allegro.

1st Violins. *cres. molto. ff*

2nd Violins. Col. 1mo. *cres molto. ff*

Violas. *ff*

Soprano.

Tenor.

Bass.

Violoncellos and Double basses. *cres. molto. ff*

Let the movement become rather animated.
Together.
ff
Trumpets in E♭.

Trumpets in F.

The Flutes and Hautboys count always.
The Clarinets alone.
Together.
Together.
Divis.
Together.
Without Ophicleide.
Divis.
Ophl.
Ophl.

Flutes.
Hautboys.
Clar.
Met. 𝅗𝅥 = 86.
Slower.
cres. molto.
Divis.
Trumpet in F.
Trumpet in E♭.
Together.

Sticks of sponge.

ff

Sticks of sponge.

Sticks of sponge.

f

ff

Sticks of sponge.

Sticks of sponge.

ff

Sticks of sponge.

ff

Sticks of sponge.

ff

Sticks of sponge.

ff

Strike with the two drumsticks alternatively on each side.

dim.

The Tam-tam and the Cymbals count.

ff

f

ff

f

Slower.

Et . . i - te - rum ven - tu-rus est cum

ff

ff

The Flutes and Hautboys count.
Clarinets alone.

Let the movement become rather animated.

Unis.

Tromb.

Ophicl.

Oph.

Tantam and Cymbals.

f decrescendo p f p f p

glo - ri - a ju - di - ca - re vi - vos, vi - - vos et mor - - - tu - os,

Violoncellos and Double-basses.

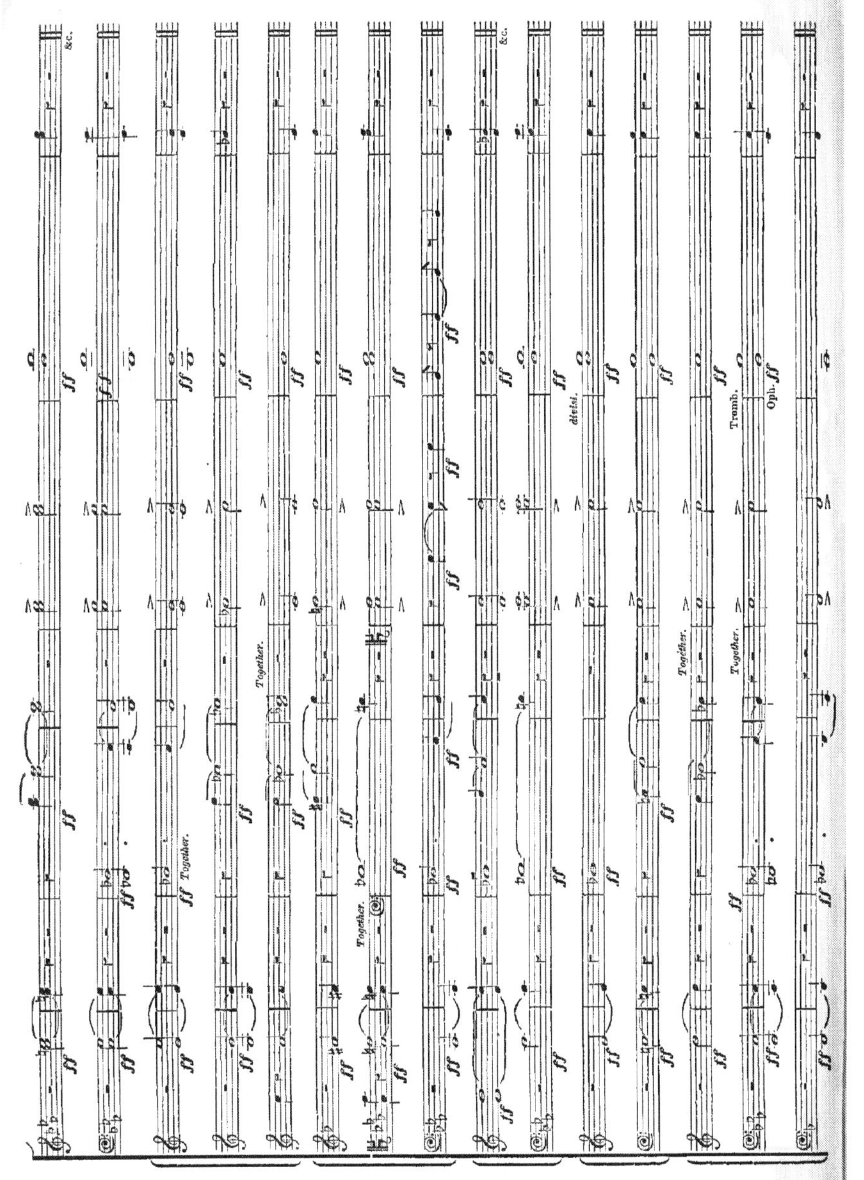
&c.
Together.
Together.
Together.
&c.
divisi.
Together.
Together.
Tromb.
Oph.

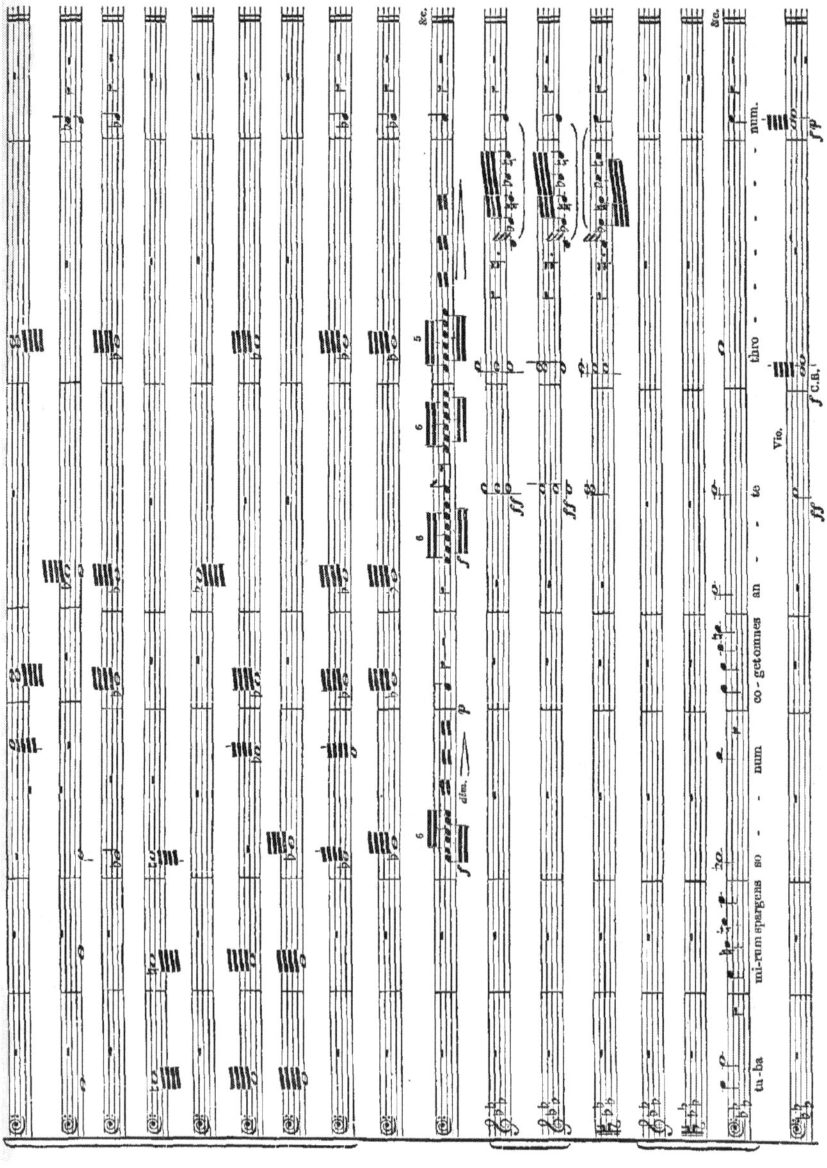

&c.

6 6 5

f *dim.* *p* *f*

ff *ff*

&c.

tu-ba mi-rum spargens so - - num co-get omnes an - - te thro - - - - - num.

Vio.

ff *f* C.B. *fp*

We said just now that kettle-drums have but one octave compass; the difficulty of getting a parchment sufficiently large to cover a vessel bigger than the great bass kettle-drum is perhaps the reason which prevents our obtaining sounds lower than F. But this does not hold good with regard to the high kettle-drums: assuredly, by diminishing the size of the metallic vessel, it would be easy to obtain the high G, A, and B♭. These small kettle-drums might be, on numerous occasions, of the happiest effect. Formerly, drum-players were hardly ever obliged to change the tuning of their instrument in the course of a piece; but now composers do not hesitate to subject the tuning, during a very short space of time, to a tolerably large number of modifications. They might be spared the employment of this means—which is troublesome and difficult for the performers—if there were, in all orchestras, two pairs of kettle-drums, and two drummers; at any rate, when recourse is had to it, care should be taken in the first place to give the drum-player a number of rests proportioned to the importance of the change demanded from him, so that he may have time to effect it conveniently; in this case, also, it is necessary to indicate a tuning nearest to that which is quitted.

For example, if the kettle-drums being in *A E*, it be wished to go into the key of *B♭*, it would be an egregious piece of awkwardness to indicate the new interval *F B♭* (fourth), which compels letting down the low kettle-drum a third, and the high kettle-drum an augmented fourth, when *B♭ F* (fifth), merely necessitates the raising both a half tone. It may easily be conceived, besides, how difficult it is for the drum-player to give a precisely correct new tuning to his instrument, obliged as he is to turn the keys or screws compressing the brace during the performance of a piece full of modulations; which may make him sound the key of *B*♮ major at the very moment when he is seeking the key of *C* or the key of *F*. This proves that, independently of the particular talent which the drummer should possess in the manipulation of his drumsticks, he ought to be an excellent musician, and endowed with an ear of extreme delicacy. This is why good drum-players are so rare.

There are three kinds of drumsticks, the use of which so changes the nature of the drum's sound that it is worse than negligence on the part of composers if they fail to indicate in their scores the kind which they desire the performer to use.

Drumsticks with *wooden ends* produce a harsh, dry, hard sound; scarcely good for anything but to strike a violent blow, or to accompany a great noise of the orchestra.

Drumsticks with *wooden ends covered with leather* are less hard; they produce a sound less startling than the preceding, but very dry nevertheless. In numerous orchestras these drumsticks alone are used; which is a great pity.

Drumsticks with *ends made of sponge* are the best, and are those of which the use—musical, rather than noisy—should be more frequent. They give to the kettle-drum a grave, velvety quality of tone, which, making the sounds very neat, renders therefore the tuning very distinct, and suits a large number of gradations soft or loud in execution, wherein the other drumsticks would produce a detestable—or, at least, an insufficient effect.

Whenever the object is to play mysterious sounds, dimly menacing,—even in a *forte*—recourse should be had to the drumsticks with sponge ends. Moreover, as the elasticity of the sponge aids the rebound of the drumstick, the player need only touch the parchment of the kettle-drums to obtain, *in pianissimo*, delicate rolls, very soft and very close. Beethoven, in his Symphonies in *B♭* and in *C* minor, has deduced from the *pianissimo* of the kettle-drums a marvellous effect; and these admirable passages lose much by being played with drumsticks without sponge ends,—although the author in his scores has specified nothing on this point.

Hautboys.
Imo.
Imo. cres.
Trumpets in E♭.
cres.
Imo.
Kettle-drums in E♭.
cres.
Arco.
cres.
Arco.
Arco.
cres.
Arco.
p cres.
ff
Solo.
pp
Pizz.
Arco.
Col. Violoncello.
Together.

No. 61.

Symphony in C minor.—BEETHOVEN.

Sempre pp
Sempre pp
Sempre pp
pp Arco.
Sempre pp
Sempre pp

pp
cres.
p
cres.
p
cres.
pp
cres.
cres.
8ves.
cres.
cres.
cres.
cres.

In the works of the ancient masters especially, there is frequently found this indication:—Kettle-drums *muffled*, or *covered*. It signifies that the parchment of the instrument is to be covered with a piece of cloth; the effect of which is to deaden the sound, and to render it extremely lugubrious. The drumsticks with sponge ends are preferable to the others in this case. It is sometimes well to indicate the notes that the drummer should play *with two drumsticks at once*, or with a *single drumstick*:—

The nature of the rhythm, and the place of the loud accents, should decide the choice.

The sound of kettle-drums is not very low; it is heard as it is written on the F clef; in unison therefore with the corresponding notes on the violoncellos, and not an octave below, as some musicians have supposed.

Bells.

These have been introduced into instrumentation for the production of effects more dramatic than musical. The *timbre* of low bells is appropriate only to solemn or pathetic scenes; that of high bells, on the contrary, gives rise to more serene impression; they have something rustic and simple about them, which renders them particularly suitable to religious scenes of rural life. This is why Rossini has employed a little bell in high *G*, to accompany the graceful chorus in the second act of *Guillaume Tell*, of which the burden is "voici la nuit"; while Meyerbeer has had recourse to a bell in low *F*, to give the signal for the massacre of the Huguenots, in the fourth act of the opera of that name. He has taken care, moreover, to make of this F the diminished fifth of the B♮ struck below by the bassoons; which, aided by the low notes of two clarinets (in *A* and in *B♭*), give that sinister quality of tone which awakens the terror and alarm pervading this immortal scene.

No. 62.

Maestoso molto.
Les Huguenots.—MEYERBEER.
Violins.
Violas.
Flutes.
1 Hautboy.
1 Corno Inglese.
1 Clar. in B♭
1 Clar. in A.
Bassoons.
Horns in F.
Trombones.
Ophicleide.
Bell in F.
VALENTINE.
Yes, they freeze my very
Ils me gla-cent de ter-
RAOUL.
Hearest thou those sounds of mourning?
En-tends tu ces sons fu-nè-bres
Violoncello.
Double-bass.

Changes on B♭.
blood.
- - reur.
Near to
Près de
From out the mid - night dark - ness There comes a cry of rage. Oh! where was I then,
Du sein des noi - res té - nè - bres s'é - lève un cri de fu-reur où donc é - tais - je,

8ves
Col Flauto 2do.
Col Flauti, 8ve lower.
2nd Bell in C.
me, dear Ra-oul,
moi cher Ra-oul,
Ah, still the fa - - - tal thought how they massacred my brothers. 'Tis the hor-rid sig -
Ah, sou - ve - nir fa - tal du mas - sa-cre de mes frères c'est l'hor-ri - ble si -
divisi.

Sets of Bells.

Felicitous effects are obtained, especially in military music, from a set of very small bells (similar in quality to those of chimney-clocks), fixed one above another on a frame of iron, numbering eight or ten, and ranged diatonically in the order of their size: the highest note naturally being at the summit of the pyramid, and the deeper ones below. These chimes, which are struck by a little hammer, can execute melodies of moderate quickness, and small compass. They are made in different scales. The highest are the best.

The Glockenspiel.

Mozart has written, in his opera of the *Magic Flute*, an important part for a keyed instrument that he calls Glockenspiel, composed doubtless of a great number of very small bells, arranged in such a manner as to be put in vibration by a mechanism of keys. He gave it the following compass; and wrote for it upon two lines and two clefs, like the pianoforte :—

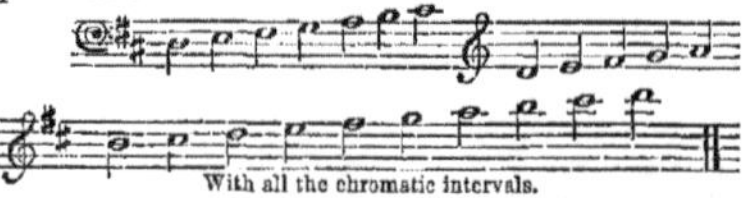

When they got up, at the Paris opera, the imperfect Pasticcio known under the name of the *Mysteries of Isis*, in which was introduced—more or less disfigured—a portion of the music in the *Magic Flute*, they procured, for the glockenspiel piece, a little instrument, the hammers of which, instead of striking on bells, struck upon bars of steel. The sound is produced an octave above the written notes; it is sweet, mysterious, and of extreme delicacy. It adapts itself to the most rapid movements; and is incomparably better than that of little bells.

No. 63.

The Magic Flute.—MOZART.

la ra la la la la la la All anger dis - perseth at me - lo - dy's might, la ra
la ra la la la la la la la, rabbia va vi - a o per - de il po - ter, la ra
la la la la, ra la la la la ra la, All an-ger dis - perseth at me - lo - dy's
la la la la, ra la la la la ra la, la rab-bia va vi - a o per - de il po -

The Keyed Harmonica

Is an instrument of the same kind as the preceding; the hammers striking upon plates of glass. Its quality of tone is of an incomparably voluptuous delicacy, of which the most poetical application might frequently be made. Like that of the key-board of steel bars I have just mentioned, its sonority is extremely weak, and the fact should be kept in mind, when associating it with other instruments of the orchestra. The softest *mezzo forte* of the violins alone would suffice to cover it entirely. It would blend better with light accompaniments of *pizzicato*, or harmonics; and with some very soft middle notes of the flutes.

The sound of the keyed harmonica comes out as it is written. It can hardly be given more than two octaves; all the notes beyond the high E, [musical example] being scarcely perceptible, and those beyond the low D, [musical example] having a very poor tone, still more weak than the rest of the scale. This defect in the low notes might perhaps be remedied by giving them glass plates of greater thickness than the others. Pianoforte-makers are the usual manufacturers of this delicious and too little known instrument. It is written for, like the preceding, on two lines and two G clefs.

It is needless to add that the mechanism of execution on these two little key-boards is exactly the same as that of the pianoforte, and that all the passages, arpeggios, and chords may be written for them, within their respective compass, which would be written for a very small pianoforte.

Ancient Cymbals.

These are very small, and their sound becomes higher in proportion as they are thicker and less in size. I have seen some in the Pompeïan Museum at Naples which were no larger than a dollar. The sound of those is so high, and so weak, that it could hardly be distinguished without the complete silence of the other instruments. These cymbals served, in ancient times, to mark the rhythm of certain dances,—like our modern *castanets*, doubtless.

In the fairy-like scherzo of my Romeo and Juliet Symphony I have employed two pairs, the same size as the largest of the Pompeïan cymbals; that is to say, rather less than the size of the hand, and tuned the one a fifth from the other. The lowest gives this B♭, [musical example] and the highest this F, [musical example] To make them vibrate well, the player should—instead of striking the cymbals full one against the other—strike them merely by one of their edges. All bell-founders can manufacture these small cymbals; which are first cast in brass or copper, and then turned, to bring them into the desired key. They should be of at least three lines and a half in thickness. There is also a delicate instrument of the nature of the keyed harmonica; but its sound is louder, and can easily be heard through a large orchestra playing either *piano* or *mezzo forte*.

The Long Drum.

Among instruments of percussion having an indefinite sound, the long drum is assuredly that which has done the greatest mischief, and brought the largest amount of nonsense and barbarism into modern music. None of the great masters of the last age thought of introducing it into the orchestra. Spontini was the first to make it heard, in his triumphal march in the *Vestale;* and a little later in some pieces of his *Fernand Cortez:* where it was well placed. But to write for it as it has been written for these fifteen years, in all full pieces, in all finales, in the slighest chorus, in dance-tunes, even in cavatinas, is the height of folly, and (to call things by their right names) of brutal stupidity; the more because composers, in general, have not even the excuse of an original rhythm, which they might be supposed to wish to display and make predominant over the accessory rhythms. Instead of this they strike senselessly the accented parts of each bar, they overwhelm the orchestra, they overpower the voices; there is no longer either melody, harmony, design, or expression; hardly does the prevailing key remain distinguishable! And then they innocently think they have produced an *energetic* instrumentation, and have written something very fine!

It is needless to add that the long drum used in this style is scarcely ever unaccompanied by cymbals; as if these two instruments were in their nature inseparable. In some orchestras they are even played by one and the same musician, who, a cymbal being attached to the long drum, can strike it with the other in the left hand, while in the right he flourishes his drumstick. This economical proceeding is intolerable; the cymbals, losing thus their sonority, produce a noise which might be compared to the fall of a sack full of ironmongery and broken glass. It has a trivial character, deprived of all pomp or brilliancy, and is fit for nothing better than to make dance-music for monkeys, or to accompany the feats of jugglers, mountebanks, and swallowers of swords and serpents, in the public streets and alleys.

The long drum has nevertheless an admirable effect when judiciously employed. It should, for example, be introduced in a full piece, in the midst of a large orchestra, merely to augment little by little the force of a lofty rhythm already established, and gradually reinforced by the successive entrance of groups of the most sonorous instruments. Its introduction than does wonders; the *swing* of the orchestra becomes one of unmeasured potency; the noise, thus disciplined, is transforced into music. The *pianissimo* notes of the long drum, united with the cymbals, in an andante, and struck at long intervals, have something very grand and solemn about them. The *pianissimo* of the long drum *alone*, is, on the contrary, gloomy and menacing (if the instrument be well made, and of large size); it resembles a distant sound of cannon.

I have employed, in my Requiem, the long drum *forte* without cymbals, and with two drumsticks. The performer, striking a blow on each side of the instrument, can thus sound a tolerably rapid succession of notes, which, mingled—as in the work I have just mentioned—with rolls on the kettle-drums in several parts, and with an orchestration where accents of terror predominate, give the idea of the strange and awful noises that accompany great cataclysms of nature. (See No. 59, page 200.)

On another occasion, in order to obtain in a symphony a dull roll much deeper than the lowest sound of the kettle-drums could be, I caused it to be given by two drummers playing together on a single long drum placed upright like a small drum.

Cymbals.

Cymbals are very often united with the long drum; but, as I have just said, they may be treated apart with the greatest success on numerous occasions. Their quivering and shrill sounds,—the noise of which predominates over all the other noises of the orchestra,—ally themselves incomparably well, in certain cases, either with sentiments of extreme ferocity (then united to sharp whistlings of piccolo flutes, and to the strokes of the kettle-drum or small drum), or with the feverish excitement of a bacchanalian orgy, where revelry verges upon frenzy. Never has there been a finer effect of cymbals produced, than in the chorus of Scythians: "Les dieux," in Gluck's *Iphigenia in Tauride.*

No. 64.

Col. Vno. 1mo.
Col. Vno. 1mo.
CHORUS.
1st Tenors (Hautes Contre.)
The gods a - - bate their
Les dieux ap - - pai - sent
2nd Tenors.
Basses.
an - ger - now; They bring us victims, vic - tims wor - - thy; The
leur cour - roux; ils nous a - mènent des vic - ti - - - mes les

Col. Vno. Imo.
Gods a - bate their an - - ger now; They bring us victims, victims
Dieux ap - - pai - - sent leur cour - roux ils nous a - - mènent des vic -
wor - - thy; To these just a - ven - gers of e - - - vil Let their
- ti - - mes à ces ju - tes ven - geurs des cri - - - mes que leur

A vigorous and well-marked rhythm gains greatly in an immense chorus, or in the dance-tune of an orgy, if executed, not by a single pair of cymbals, but by four, six, ten pairs, and even more, according to the space, and to the mass of other instruments and voices. The composer should always be careful to determine the length that he wishes his cymbal notes to last, followed by a rest; in case he wish to have the sound prolonged, he must write long and sustained notes, as:— with this indication:—"let them vibrate;" but, in the contrary case, he must place a quaver or a semiquaver, as:— with these words:—"damp the sound;" which the player does by bringing the cymbals against his chest as soon as he has struck them. Sometimes, a drumstick with a sponge end, or that of a long-drum, is used to strike a cymbal suspended by its leather strap. This produces a metallic quiver of moderate length; sinister, though without the formidable accent of a stroke of the gong.

The Gong.

The gong, or tam-tam, is employed only in funereal compositions and in dramatic scenes where horror is carried to its height. The vibrations of the gong, mingled *forte* with the thrilling chords of the brass instruments (trumpets and trombones), make the hearer shudder; its pianissimo strokes, heard nearly by themselves, are no less fearful from their lugubrious sound. M. Meyerbeer has proved this in his magnificent scene of *Robert le Diable*, the Resurrection of the Nuns:—

No. 65.

Robert le Diable.—MEYERBEER.

The Tambour Basque (or Tambourine).

This favourite instrument of the Italian peasantry, who use it in all their festivities, is of excellent effect when employed in masses, striking like cymbals, and with them, a rhythm in a dance scene or orgy. It is seldom introduced *alone* in the orchestra; unless in a case where the subject of the piece renders it illustrative of the manners of the people who habitually use the instrument—such as wandering Bohemians, or gypsies; the Basque nation; the Roman peasants; and those of the Abbruzzi and Calabria. It produces three kinds of very different noises: when it is simply struck with the hand, its sound has not much effect (unless employed in numbers); and the tambourine thus struck is not distinguishable unless left nearly alone by the other instruments: if it be played by rubbing its parchment with the ends of the fingers, there results a roll in which the noise of the small bells hung round its edge is chiefly heard. The roll is thus written, but should be very short, because the finger which rubs the parchment of the instrument soon, as it advances, reaches the edge, where an end is put to its action.

A roll like this, for instance, would be impossible—

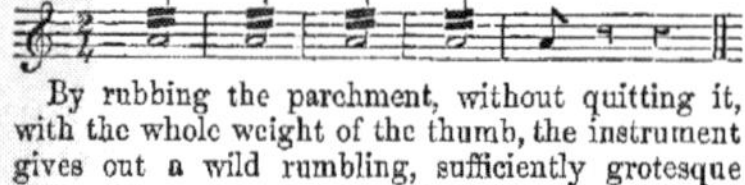

By rubbing the parchment, without quitting it, with the whole weight of the thumb, the instrument gives out a wild rumbling, sufficiently grotesque and ugly, but of which it is not absolutely impossible to make use in some masquerade scene.

The Drum.

Drums, properly so termed—called also "caisses claires"—are rarely well placed in other than large orchestras of wind instruments. Their effect is the better and nobler in proportion as they are more numerous; a single drum—particularly when it figures in the midst of an ordinary orchestra—has always appeared to me mean and vulgar. Let us own, nevertheless, that M. Meyerbeer has known how to derive a peculiar and terrible sonority from the association of a drum with the kettle-drums for the famous *crescendo* roll in the Benediction of the Daggers (*Les Huguenots*). But eight, ten, twelve, or more drums executing, in a military march, rhythmical accompaniments, or *crescendo* rolls, prove magnificent and powerful auxiliaries to the wind instruments. Simple rhythms, without either melody, harmony, key, or anything that really constitutes music, serving only to mark the step of soldiers, become attractive when performed by a body of forty or fifty drums alone. And perhaps we may here take occasion to remark the singular as well as actual charm for the ear, which arises from a multiplicity of unisons, or from the simultaneous reproduction, by a very large number of instruments of the same kind, of the noise they individually produce. This may have been observed in attending infantry soldiers' exercise. At the word of command to "shoulder arms" or to "ground arms," the slight clink of the firelocks, and the dull sound of the butt-end of the muskets as they drop on the ground, signify nothing at all when one, two, three, ten, or even a score of men produce them; but let the action be performed by a thousand men, and immediately the thousand unisons of an insignificant noise will give a brilliant aggregate which involuntarily attracts and captivates the attention—which pleases, and in which I find even some vague and occult harmonies.

Drums are used *muffled*, like kettle-drums; but instead of covering the parchment with a piece of cloth, the players often content themselves with loosening the braces of the drum, or with passing a leather strap between them and the lower parchment, in such a way as to check the vibrations. The drums then acquire a dim, dull sound, somewhat analogous to that produced by muffling the upper parchment; and are thus rendered fit for compositions of a funereal or terrible character.

The Caisse Roulante, or Side-Drum.

The *side-drum* is a drum rather longer than the preceding one, the body being of wood instead of brass. Its sound is dull and somewhat like that of the drum *without tone*, or *muffled*. It produces a sufficiently good effect in military music; and its subdued rolls serve as a kind of background to those of the drums. It is a *side-drum* that Gluck has employed for striking the four continued quavers whose rhythm is so barbarous in the chorus of Scythians (*Iphigenia in Tauride*). (See No. 64, page 226.)

The Triangle.

At the present time as deplorable a use is made of this instrument as of the long drum, cymbals, kettle-drums, trombones, and, in short, of all that thunders, sounds, and resounds. It is, however, still more difficult to find fit occasion for introducing it into the orchestra than the others. Its metallic noise suits only pieces of an extremely brilliant character when *forte*, or of a certain wild whimsicality when *piano*. Weber has felicitously employed it in his gipsy chorus of *Preciosa*; and Gluck still better in the major of his terrible dance of Scythians, in the first act of *Iphigenia in Tauride*:—

Unis.
Col. Basso.
Solo.

The Pavillon Chinois,

With its numerous little bells, serves to give brilliancy to lively pieces, and pompous marches in military bands. It can only shake its sonorous locks, at somewhat lengthened intervals, that is to say, about twice in a bar, in a movement of moderate time.

We will say nothing here of certain instruments more or less imperfect, and little known; such as the Eolidicon, the Anémocorde, the Accordeon, the Poikilorgue, the ancient Sistrum, &c. referring those of our readers curious to know more of them, to M. Kastner's excellent *general treatise of instrumentation*. Our intention, in the present work, is merely to study the instruments used in modern music, endeavouring to discover according to what laws harmonious sympathies and striking contrasts may be established between them, and taking into particular account their powers of expression, and the appropriate character of each.

New Instruments.

The author of this work is doubtless not obliged to indicate the multitude of attempts of all kinds daily made by instrument-makers, and their pretended inventions, more or less disastrous, or to make known the futile specimens which they seek to introduce amidst the race of instruments. But he must point out and recommend to the attention of composers admirable discoveries made by ingenious artists, particularly when the excellent result of those discoveries has been generally recognised, and when their appreciation is already a thing achieved, in musical performance, throughout a portion of Europe. Such manufacturers are few in number, and Messrs Adolphe Sax and Alexandre rank at the head of them.

M. Sax—whose labours will first occupy our attention—has brought to perfection (as I have already remarked here and there in the course of this work) several ancient instruments. He has, besides, supplied many voids existing among the family of brass instruments. His principal merit, however, is the creation of a new family, complete since a few years only—that of the instruments with a single reed, with a clarinet mouth-piece, and in brass. They are called Saxophones. These new voices given to the orchestra possess most rare and precious qualities. Soft and penetrating in the higher part, full and rich in the lower part, their medium has something profoundly expressive. It is, in short, a quality of tone *sui generis*, presenting vague analogies with the sounds of the violoncello, of the clarinet and corno inglese, and invested with a brazen tinge which imparts a quite peculiar accent. The body of the instrument is a parabolic cone of brass, provided with a set of keys. Agile, fitted for the execution of passages of a certain rapidity—almost as much as for cantilena passages—saxophones may figure with great advantage in all kinds of music; but especially in slow and soft pieces.

The quality of tone of the high notes of low saxophones partakes something of the painful and sorrowful, while that of their bass notes is, on the contrary, of a calm and, so to speak, pontifical grandeur.

All of them,—the baritone and the bass principally—possess the faculty of swelling and diminishing their sound; whence results,—in the lower extremity of their scale,—effects hitherto unheard, and quite peculiar to themselves, at the same time bearing some resemblance to those of the "expressive organ." The quality of tone of the high saxophone is much more penetrating than that of clarinets in $B\flat$ and in C, without having the piercing and often shrill brilliancy of the small clarinet in $E\flat$. As much may be said of the soprano. Clever composers will hereafter derive wondrous effects from saxophones associated with the clarinet family, or introduced in other combinations which it would be rash to attempt foreseeing. This instrument is played with great facility, its fingering proceeding from the fingering of the flute and hautboy. Clarinet-players, already familiar with the mouthing, render themselves masters of its mechanism in a very short time.

Saxophones are six in number:—the high, the soprano, the alto, the tenor, the baritone and the bass saxophone.

M. Sax is about to produce a seventh,—the double-bass saxophone.

The compass of each of them is nearly the same; and here is their scale, written for all on the G clef, like that of clarinets, after the system proposed by M. Sax, and already adopted by composers:—

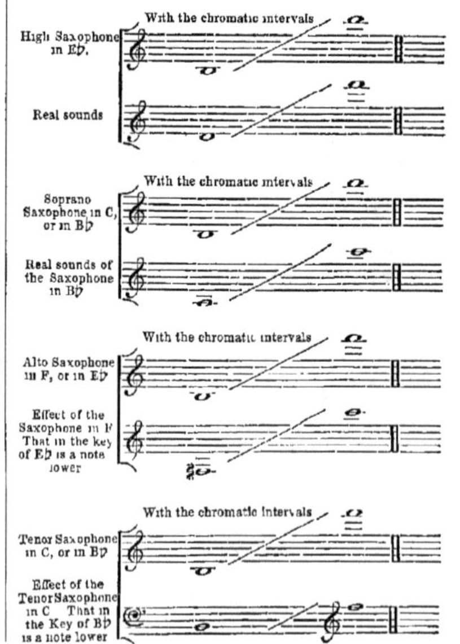

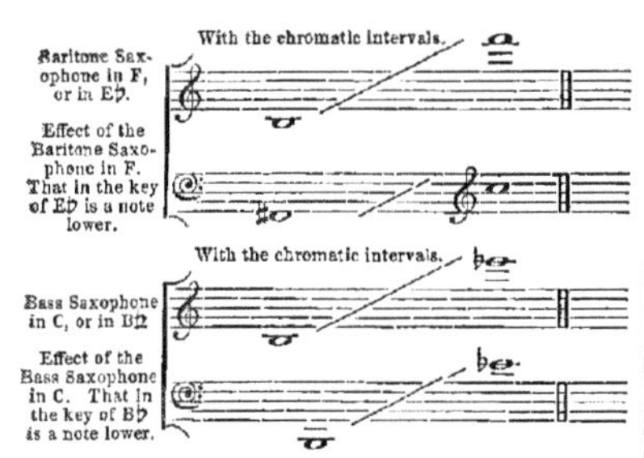

Major and minor shakes are practicable on almost all the extent of the chromatic scale of the saxophone. Here are those which it is well to avoid :—

M. Sax has also produced the family of sax-horns, of saxotrombas, and of sax-tubas,—brass instruments with a wide mouth-piece ; and with a mechanism of three, four, or five cylinders.

Sax-Horns.

Their sound is round, pure, full, equal, resounding, and of perfect homogeneousness throughout the extent of the scale. The changing keys of the sax-horn proceed, like those of the cornet à pistons, by descending ; commencing from the typical instrument, the *small very-high sax-horn in C,* which is an octave above the cornet in *C.* The custom has obtained in France of writing all these instruments—as well as saxotrombas and sax-tubas, the lowest and the highest—on the G clef, as horns are written ; with this difference only, that if, for the horn in low *C,* we have to represent the real sound an octave below the note written on the G clef, we must—for certain very low instruments of Sax—represent it two octaves below.

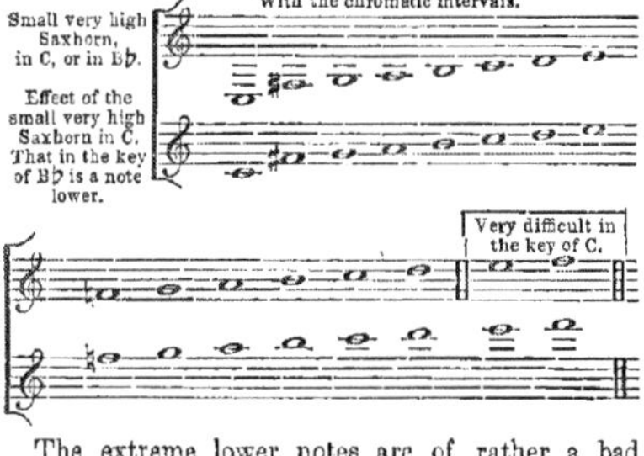

The extreme lower notes are of rather a bad quality of tone, and this instrument should rarely be employed beneath the low A. But there is nothing more brilliant, more neat, more devoid of shrillness—notwithstanding their vivid appeal—than all the notes of the higher octave. The quality of tone is besides so clear and so penetrating, that it allows a single very high sax-horn to be distinguished among a considerable mass of other wind instruments. The very high sax-horn in *B♭* is more used than the one in *C;* and, although it is a note lower than the other, there is still much difficulty—or at least much care is required—for the performer to bring out the two last sounds :—

One should, therefore, be very sparing of these precious notes, and introduce them with skill.

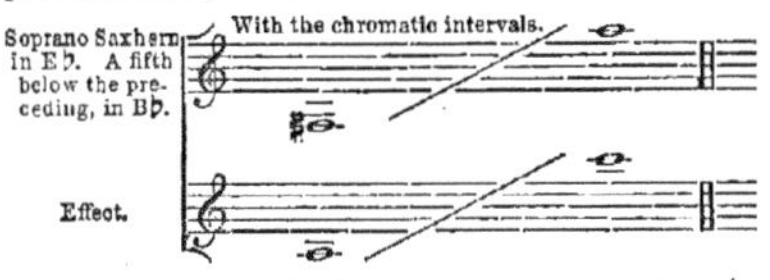

Commencing with the soprano sax-horn in *E♭,* we will no longer indicate the first low note of the tube's resonance. It is too bad to be employed.

We will merely warn composers that, if they indicate an instrument *with four cylinders,* the chromatic compass of the low part of this instrument no longer stops at the F♯, but goes down to the first C,

These two sax-horns,—the baritone and bass,—have the same compass in the high part of the instrument. The tube is rather smaller for the baritone. The bass, which has almost always four cylinders, has a tube somewhat wider, which allows of its descending lower and more easily.

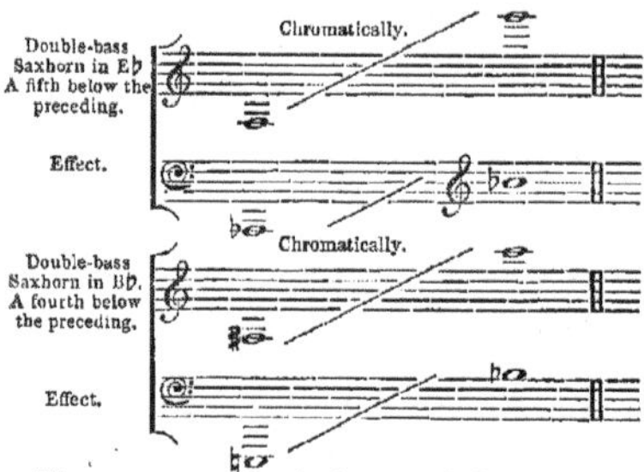

There are, moreover, the low double-bass sax-horn in *E♭*, and the drone sax-horn in *B♭*, which are an octave below the two preceding; but of which only the medium notes should be employed in a moderate movement.

Saxotrombas.

These are brass instruments with mouth-piece, and with three, four, or five cylinders, like the preceding. Their tube, being more contracted, gives to the sound which it produces a character more shrill,—partaking at once of the *timbre* of the trumpet and of the bugle.

The number of the members of the family of saxotrombas equals that of sax-horns. They are disposed in the same order, from high to low; and possess the same compass.

Sax-Tubas.

These are instruments with mouth-piece and a mechanism of three cylinders; they are of enormous sonority, carrying far, and producing extraordinary effect in military bands intended to be heard in the open air.

They should be treated exactly like sax-horns; merely taking into account the absence of the low double-bass in *E♭*, and of the drone in *B♭*.

Their shape—elegantly rounded—recalls that of antique trumpets on a grand scale.

The Concertina.

This is a small instrument, with tongues of brass put into vibration by a current of air. The accordeon, which for some years was a musical toy, formed the groundwork of the concertina, and, subsequently, that of the melodium. The sound of the concertina is at once penetrating and soft; notwithstanding its weakness, it carries tolerably far; it allies itself well with the *timbre* of the harp and pianoforte, and unites still more with the sound of the melodium, which is now the head of its family. But there would be little advantage in causing such an association; since the melodium has a quality of tone analogous to that of the concertina, produces the same effects, and moreover is capable of many others beyond the power of the concertina.

The concertina is a kind of small elastic box; which is held horizontally between both hands. It is played by means of knobs, pressed with the points of the fingers, and which, raising a valve, cause to pass over the plates or reeds of brass a column of air supplied by a bellows placed between the two sides of the box. These sides are formed by two tablets; which hold, on the outside, the key-board of knobs and, on the inside, the vibrating plates. The bellows, having no valve, can only fill and empty itself by means of the set of reed-valves, which inspire and expire, each in turn, the air necessary for the vibration of the reeds.

The concertina has its small family complete; independently of its relationship to the melodium. There is the bass concertina, the alto, and the soprano. The bass concertina has the compass of the violoncello; the alto, that of the viola; and the soprano, that of the violin. The soprano concertina is almost the only one used.

We will presently give the compass of the concertina, which, owing to its popularity in England, is called the English concertina.

It will be perceived, in these two chromatic scales (one of which represents the notes of the left tablet, and the other those of the right tablet) that the maker of the English concertina has established, in the three first octaves, enharmonic intervals between the A♭ and the G♯, and between the E♭ and the D♯, giving a little more elevation to the A♭ than to the G♯, and to the E♭ than to the D♯; thus conforming to the *doctrine* of the acousticians,—a doctrine entirely contrary to the *practice* of musicians.

This is a strange anomaly.

It is very evident that the concertina, being an instrument with fixed sounds, like the pianoforte, the organ, and the melodium, should, like these instruments, be tuned according to the law of temperament.

In its present state, its enharmonic notes in fact prevent it from being played with a pianoforte, organ, or melodium, without producing discords when the musical phrase or the harmony introduces unisons between the enharmonic A♭s or the G♯s, the E♭s or the D♯s, of the concertina, and the same notes as temperamented on the other instrument; since the A♭ and the G♯, as well as the E♭ and the D♯, are identical on the instruments tuned in temperament, while they are not so on the concertina; and that neither the one nor the other of the enharmonic sounds (A♭ and G♯ of the concertina) will be in strict unison with the A♭ or the G♯ of the temperamented instrument, which preserves the middle between the two sounds of the concertina. Moreover, the effect of this disposition of a portion of the scale will be still more frightful if the concertina play a duet with an instrument having movable sounds, such as the violin. Musical practice, musical sense, the ear, in short, of all people with whom modern music is cultivated, allows that, in certain cases, notes called "*leading*," obedient to the attraction exercised over them by their *upper tonic*, and *minor sevenths and ninths*, obedient to the attraction of the note upon which they make their resolution, may become—the first slightly sharper than it would be in temperamented scale, and the second slightly flatter.

The G♯ (*too flat*) of the concertina could not, then, be in tune with the G♯ (*too sharp*) of the violin; nor the A♭ (*too sharp*) of the one, with the A♭ (*too flat*) of the other—each of the performers, obeying two diametrically opposite laws (the law of the calculation of vibrations, and the musical law)—if the violinist, yielding to the necessity of effecting strict unison, did not play in such a manner as to assimilate with the sound (whatever it might be) of the instrument having fixed intonations—playing therefore falsely. This takes place—in less proportions, and without hurting the ear—unconsciously with violins when used with the pianoforte and other temperamented instruments. But a fantastic proceeding, which should reconcile the system of the English concertina with the musical system of ascending leading notes, and descending sevenths, would consist in adopting the exact reverse of the acoustician's opinion on the enharmonics, by employing the A♭ in place of the G♯, and vice-versa. The violin executing then this passage musically,—

would find itself nearly in unison with the concertina executing the same passage written in this absurd way,—

This ancient endeavour of the acousticians to introduce at all risks the result of their calculations into the practice of an art *based especially on the study of the impressions produced by sounds upon the human ear* is no longer maintainable.

So true is it, that Music rejects it with energy; and can only exist by rejecting it.

So true is it, even, that the various modifications of the interval *between two sounds which are mutually attracted* (in musical practice), are extremely delicate gradations, which artists and singers should employ with great precaution, from which orchestral performers should in general abstain, and which composers, with the due foresight of their office, should treat in an especial manner.

So true is it, in short, that the immense majority of musicians instinctively avoid them, in harmonious combinations. Whence it results that the sounds so-called irreconcilable by the acousticians, are perfectly reconciled by musical practice; and that those relations declared false by calculation, are accepted as true by the ear, which takes no account of inappreciable differences, nor of the reasonings of mathematicians. There is scarcely a modern score, in which, either to facilitate execution, or for some other reason,—nay, frequently without any reason,—the composer has not written harmonic or melodic passages, *in the sharpened key* for one portion of the orchestra or choir, and in the *flattened key* for the other:—

Or under the appearance of two different keys, of which only two notes are in enharmonic relation; as in this passage from Weber's *Freyschutz*:

Here, the violoncellos and the double-basses seem to play in *G* minor, while the trombones appear to play in *B♭* minor.

In this example, if the violoncellos and the double-basses made their F♯ too sharp, and if the trombones made their G♭ too flat, doubtless a discord would be heard; but supposing that the execution is good, this need not be the case; then, the two sounds,—each of which has a tendency contrary to that of the other, —will be perfectly in tune together.

On all such occasions, the orchestra becomes a large temperamented instrument. It becomes so in a number of other cases; and, sometimes, when the musicians who constitute it are not aware of the fact.

In the celebrated chorus of demons, in his *Orfeo*, Gluck has established an enharmonic relation between two parts, in an *indeterminate* key. I allude to the passage on which J. J. Rousseau and others have written so many follies, grounded upon the difference which they believed they discovered between the G♭ and the F♯.

If it were true that the execution permitted any difference to be perceived here between the F♯ of the chorus and the G♭ of the basses (pizzicato), this difference—I repeat—could produce only an intolerable and anti-musical discord; the ear would be revolted, and that is all. Far from this, the hearer is profoundly stirred by an emotion of awe,—most grand, and musical. He knows not, it is true, the precise key that he hears. Is it *B♭?* Is it *G* minor? He cannot tell,—he cares little; but nothing hurts his ear in the association of the various instrumental and vocal parts. The F♯ of the chorus, and of the second orchestra, produces the prodigious effect we feel, on account of the unexpected way in which it is introduced, and the accent of wildness imparted by this indefiniteness of key,—and not on account of its assumed and monstrous discord with the G♭. One must be, moreover, childishly ignorant of the phenomena of sound, not to be aware that this discord could not in any case cause the effect produced, since the G♭ pizzicato of several basses *playing piano* is necessarily covered,—or, more properly, extinguished,—by the sudden entrance of fifty or sixty men's voices in unison, and by all the rest of the mass of stringed instruments attacking (with the bow) the F♯ *fortissimo*.

These ridiculous arguings, these ramblings of men of letters, these absurd conclusions of the learned, possessed—all of them—with the mania of speaking and writing upon an art of which they are ignorant, can have no other result than that of making musicians laugh. But it is a pity: knowledge, eloquence, genius, should always remain surrounded by the admiration and respect due to them.

After this long digression, I return to the English concertina; of which, this is the barbarous scale:—

The concertina, notwithstanding the disposition of the preceding example, is written for on a single line, and on the G clef. The shake is practicable on all the notes of the scale; less easily, however, in the lower extremity. The double shake (in thirds) is easy.

Diatonic and chromatic passages, or arpeggios, of tolerable rapidity, may be executed on this instrument.

It is possible to add to the principal part, if not several other complicated parts, as on the pianoforte and organ, at least a second part, proceeding nearly parallel with the melody, and also chords of four to six notes; or richer still:—

The German concertina—much used also in England—is not constructed on the system of the preceding. Its scale, which extends lower (it goes down to C and B♭), contains no enharmonic interval. It is consequently constructed according to the law of temperament.

The compass of concertinas varies with the number of keys, knobs, or stops, given to them; and this number changes according to the caprice of the makers. Finally, this instrument—like the guitar —requires that the composer who would turn it to advantageous account should have a knowledge of its mechanism, and be able to play it himself, more or less well.

The Melodium Organ (Alexandre's).

This instrument has a key-board, like the organ built with pipes. Its sound results—like that of the concertina,—from the vibration of free metallic reeds, over which passes a current of air. This current of air is produced by a bellows, put in motion by the feet of the performer; and according to the mode in which the feet act upon this blowing mechanism, in certain conditions wherein the instrument may be placed, the sounds acquire more or less intensity.

The melodium organ possesses crescendo and diminuendo; it is *expressive.* Hence the name "Register of Expression," given to the particular mechanism it possesses. The fingering of the key-board is the same as that of the organ key-board. It is written for on two lines, and even on three; like the organ. Its compass is five octaves :—

The compass, however, is not limited to the above for melodiums with more than one stop. The number of stops is very variable. The most simple melodium—the one with a single stop, of which we have just shown the compass,—contains two different qualities of tone; the *timbre* of the *corno inglese* for the left half of the key-board, and that of the flute for the right half.

The others,—according to the will of the maker, —may have, by different combinations, bassoon, clarion, flute, clarinet, fife, and hautboy stops (so called on account of the analogy which exists between their quality of tone and that of the instruments after which they are named); and, moreover, the *Grand* stop, the *Forte*, and the *Expressive.* These stops give to the melodium a compass of seven octaves, although its key-board has only five.

They are placed at the command of the performer by means of a mechanism like that of the organ, arranged on each side of the body of the instrument, and put in action by drawing forward a wooden handle with either hand.

Some other stops are obtained by a similar mechanism, placed beneath the body of the instrument, and moved by pressure from left to right, and from right to left, with the knee of the performer. This mechanism constitutes what is called "the register."

The melodium does not possess the mixture stops of the organ, the effect of which excites in many people a traditional admiration; but which, in reality, have a horrible tendency to noise; it has only double and single octave stops, by means of which each key is made to give the octave and the double octave of its note, or the double octave without the single, or even the upper octave and the lower octave at the same time.

Many ignorant players and lovers of noise make deplorable use of these octave stops. Thence results also a barbarism, less, it is true, than that of the mixture stops of the organ, which give to each note the simultaneous sound of the two other notes of the major common chord, that is to say, of its major third, and of its fifth; but still an actual barbarism, because,—besides the harmonic thickening produced, —it necessarily introduces into the harmony the most frightful disorder, by the inevitable inversion and spreading of the chords. Ninths thus produce seconds and sevenths; seconds, sevenths and ninths; fifths, fourths; fourths, fifths, &c. In order to remain in true musical condition with such stops, it would be needful to use them only in pieces written in *counterpoint invertable in octave,*—which is not done.

It is to the ignorance of the middle ages, groping blindly for laws of harmony, that we must doubtless attribute the introduction of these monstrosities into organs. Mere custom has preserved and transmitted them to us, and we must hope they will by degrees disappear.

The sounds of the melodium being of rather slow emission, like the sounds of the organ with pipes, render it better adapted to the *legato* style than to any other; and peculiarly suitable to sacred music, to soft and tender melodies, of slow movement.

Pieces of a skipping, petulant, or violent character, executed on the melodium, will always attest—in my opinion—the bad taste of the performer, the ignorance of the composer, or the bad taste and ignorance of both.

To impart to the sounds of the melodium a religious and dreamy character,—to render them susceptible of all the inflexions of the human voice, and of the majority of instruments,—such is the object M. Alexandre has both proposed and accomplished.

The melodium is at once a Church instrument, and a Theatre instrument; a drawing-room, and a concert-room instrument. It occupies but little space; and it is portable. It is therefore a servant of indisputable utility to composers and amateurs. Since Messrs. Meyerbeer, Halévy, Verdi, have employed the organ in their dramatic works, how many provincial theatres in France, and even Germany, not possessing organs, have found difficulty in executing these works; and to how many mutilations and rearrangements (more or less clumsy) of scores, this absence of organs has given rise! The directors of these theatres would now be inexcusable were they to tolerate such misdeeds; since for a very moderate sum they may have—in lieu of an organ with pipes—a melodium organ very nearly sufficing to replace it.

The same thing applies to small churches, where music hitherto has not been possible. A melodium, played by a musician of good sense, might and could introduce there harmonic civilization; and cause, in time, a banishment of those grotesque howlings which still, in such places, mingle with religious service.

Pianos and Melodiums (by Alexandre) with prolonged sound.

The *prolongation of sound* is the most important recent musical invention that has been brought into key-board instruments. This invention, applied now-a-days to pianos and melodium organs, gives the player the power of sustaining for an indefinite time, by a simple movement of his knee, a note, a chord, or an arpeggio, in all the compass of the key-board, after his fingers have ceased to press the keys. And during this steady sustaining of a greater or less number of notes, the player, having his hands at liberty, can not only strike and make other notes speak which form no part of the sustained chord, but also the prolonged notes themselves. It will at once be perceived to what a multitude of various and charming combinations this invention affords scope on the melodium organ and piano. They are absolute orchestral effects, of the nature of those which are produced when the stringed instruments execute four or five parts diversely designed amidst a sustained harmony of the wind instruments (flutes, hautboys, and clarinets); or, better still, like those which result from a piece in several parts, played by wind instruments, during a harmonious holding-on of *divided violins;* or when the harmony and the melody are moving above or below a pedal point.

Moreover, the effect of prolongation may take place with different degrees of intensity on the melodium; according as the *Forte*-register which is appended to it be opened or shut.

Two *knee-pieces* are placed beneath the key-board in such a way as to be readily put in action by a touch of the player's knees. The one,—the right,—produces the prolongation of the sounds on the right half of the key-board; the other prolongs them on the other half. In order to prolong the sound, the key should be put down at the same time that the knee-piece is pressed; thus:—

If it be wished to stop the sustaining of the sounds, a second pressure of the knee stops it immediately; thus —

But if this fresh pressure on the knee-piece stop the effect of prolongation produced by the preceding pressure, it is also immediately replaced by a fresh effect, if one or more fresh keys be struck at the same time; thus:—

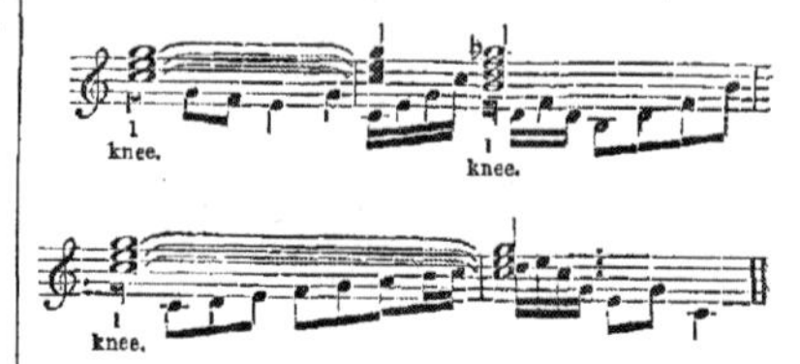

If it be wished, after a brief chord, to produce the prolongation of a single note of this chord, the movement of the knee must be made only after quitting the keys corresponding with the sounds that are not desired to be held on, but while the finger still presses the key of the note wished to be sustained; after which, the hand becomes entirely free. A similar series of movements is made for changing the notes held on; besides another supplementary movement, for stopping, while the finger still puts down the key of that note desired to be sustained, the prolongation of those notes of the chord not required to be held on.

This applies indifferently to both knee-pieces,—whether for the piano or for the melodium.

It is necessary, in writing for the piano or organ melodium with prolonged sounds, to employ at least three lines, and often four; reserving, in this latter case, the upper line for the high or intermediate sustained-notes, and the lower line for the low sustained-notes. The two middle lines then remain for the parts executed by the two hands:—

The Octo-bass.

M. Vuillaume, a musical-instrument maker of Paris, whose excellent violins are so much esteemed, has just enriched the family of stringed instruments by a fine and powerful member,—the octo-bass.

This instrument is not—as many imagine—the low octave of the double-bass; it is but the low octave of the violoncello. It consequently descends lower—by a third—than the four-stringed double-bass.

It has only three strings, tuned in fifth and fourth:

8va. bassa.

The left-hand fingers of the player not being sufficiently long, nor sufficiently strong, to act fitly on the strings (for the octo-bass is of colossal dimension), M. Vuillaume has contrived a set of movable keys, which, pressing the strings with energy, bring them on to frets placed on the neck of the instrument, for producing the tones and semitones. These keys are moved by levers, which the left hand seizes and draws up and down behind the neck of the instrument; and by seven other pedal-keys, upon which the foot of the player acts.

It suffices to say that the octo-bass cannot execute any rapid succession; and that it must have assigned to it a special part, differing in many respects from the double-bass part. Its compass is an octave and a fifth only:—

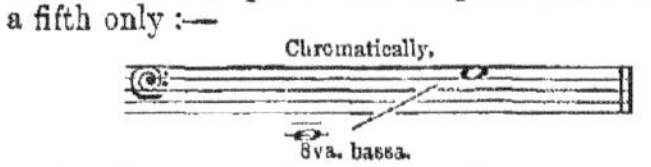

This instrument has sounds of remarkable power and beauty,—full and strong, without roughness. It would be of admirable effect in a large orchestra; and all Festival orchestras, where the number of the instrumentalists amounts to more than 150, should have at least three.

We shall not here contest the opinion that tends to consider the recent inventions of instrument-makers as fatal to musical art. These inventions exert, in their sphere, the influence common to all advances of civilisation; the abuse that may be made of them—that even which indisputably is made—proves nothing against their value.

The Orchestra.

The orchestra may be considered as a large instrument capable of uttering at once or successively a multitude of sounds of different kinds; and of which the power is mediocre or colossal according as it employs the whole or a part only of the executive means belonging to modern music, and according as those means are well or ill chosen and placed in acoustic conditions more or less favorable.

The performers of all kinds whose assemblage constitutes it thus seem to be its strings, its tubes, its pipes, its planes of wood or metal; machines, intelligent it is true, but subject to the action of an immense key-board, played upon by the conductor, under the direction of the composer.

I believe I have already said that it seemed to me impossible to indicate how fine orchestral effects are to be found; and that this faculty—developed doubtless by practice and rational observation—is like the faculties of melody, of expression, and even of harmony; and belongs to the number of those precious gifts which the musician-poet, the inspired inventor, must receive from nature herself.

But certainly it is easy to demonstrate, in a manner almost exact, the art of *making orchestras* fit to give a faithful rendering of compositions of all shapes and dimensions.

Theatrical orchestras and concert orchestras should be distinguished the one from the other. The former, in certain respects, are generally inferior to the latter.

The place occupied by the musicians, their disposal on a horizontal plane or on an inclined plane, in an enclosed space with three sides, or in the very centre of a room, with reverberators formed by hard bodies fit for sending back the sound, or soft bodies which absorb and interrupt the vibrations, and more or less near to the performers, are points of great importance. *Reverberators* are indispensable; they are to be found variously situated in all enclosed spaces. The nearer they are to the point whence the sounds proceed, the more potent is their influence.

This is why there is *no such thing* as music in the open air. The most enormous orchestra placed in the middle of an extensive garden open on all sides—like that of the Tuileries—would produce no effect. The reverberation from the palace walls even, were it placed against them, is insufficient; the sound instantaneously losing itself on all the other sides. An orchestra of a thousand wind instruments, with a chorus of two thousand voices, placed in a plain, would not have a twentieth part of the musical action that an ordinary orchestra of eighty players with a chorus of a hundred voices would have if well disposed in the concert-room at the Conservatoire. The brilliant effect produced by military bands in the streets of great towns comes in support of this statement, which it seems to contradict. But the music is not then in the *open air;* the walls of high houses skirting the streets right and left, avenues of trees, the fronts of grand palaces, neighbouring monuments, all serve as reverberators; the sound revolves and circulates freely in the circumscribed space thus surrounding it, before escaping by the points left open; but let the military band, pursuing its march, and continuing to play, leave the large street for a plain devoid of trees and habitations, and the diffusion of its sounds is immediate, the orchestra vanishes, there is no more music.

The best way of disposing the performers, in a room with dimensions proportioned to their number, is to raise them one above another by a series of steps, arranged in such a way that each row may send out its sounds to the hearer without any intermediate obstacle.

All well-organised concert orchestras should be thus arranged in steps. If the orchestra be erected in a theatre, the stage should be completely closed in at the back, at the sides both right and left, and above, by an enclosure of wooden planks.

If, on the contrary, it be erected in a room dedicated to the purpose, or in a church where it occupies one of the extremities, and if, as it frequently happens in such cases, the back of this space be formed of massive building which reflects with too much force and hardness the sound of the instruments placed against it, the force of the reverberation—and consequently the too great resounding—may easily be mitigated, by hanging up a certain number of draperies, and by bringing together at this point such bodies as will break the motion of the waves of sound.

Owing to the construction of our theatres, and to the exigences of dramatic representation, this amphitheatrical disposal is not possible for orchestras intended for the performance of operas. The instrumentalists brought together in lyric theatres, in the lowest central point of the building, before the footlights, and on a horizontal plane, are deprived of the majority of the advantages resulting from the arrangement I have just indicated for a concert orchestra; hence, what lost effects, what unperceived delicate gradations in opera bands, in spite of the most admirable execution! The difference is such that composers are almost compelled to bear it in mind, and not to instrument their dramatic scores quite in the same way as symphonies, masses, or oratorios, intended for concert-rooms and churches.

Opera orchestras were always formerly composed of a number of stringed instruments proportioned to the mass of other instruments; but this has not been the case for many years. A comic opera orchestra in which there were only two flutes, two hautboys, two clarinets, two horns, two bassoons, rarely two trumpets, and hardly ever any kettle-drums, was balanced then with nine first violins, eight second violins, six violas, seven violoncellos, and six double-basses; but as four horns, three trombones, two trumpets, a long drum, and cymbals figure there nowadays, without the number of stringed instruments having been increased, the balance is destroyed, the violins are scarcely to be heard, and the result of the whole is detestable. The orchestra of the Grand-Opéra, where there are, besides the wind instruments already named, two cornets-à-pistons and an ophicleide, the instruments of percussion, and sometimes six or eight harps—is not balanced either with twelve first violins, eleven second violins, eight violas, ten violoncellos, and eight double-basses; it should have at least fifteen first violins, fourteen second violins, ten violas, and twelve violoncellos, the extra instruments being left unused in those pieces where the accompaniments are very soft.

The proportions of a comic opera orchestra would suffice for a concert orchestra intended for the performance of Haydn's and Mozart's symphonies.

A larger number of stringed instruments would even be, sometimes, too much for the delicate effects which these masters have usually assigned to the flutes, hautboys, and bassoons.

For Beethoven's symphonies, Weber's overtures, and modern compositions conceived in the grand and impassioned style, there needs, on the contrary, the mass of violins, violas, and basses which I have just indicated for the grand opera.

But the finest concert orchestra, for a room scarcely larger than that of the Conservatoire,—the most complete, the richest in gradations, in varieties of tone, the most majestic, the most powerful, and at the same time the most soft and smooth, would be an orchestra thus composed:—

21 First Violins.
20 Second do.
18 Violas.
8 First Violoncellos.
7 Second do.
10 Double-Basses.
4 Harps.
2 Piccolo Flutes.
2 Large Flutes.
2 Hautboys.
1 Corno Inglese.
2 Clarinets.
1 Corno di Bassetto, or one Bass-Clarinet.
4 Bassoons
4 Horns with Cylinders.
2 Trumpets with Cylinders.
2 Cornets à Pistons (or with
3 Trombones {1 Alto, 2 Tenors,} or 3 Tenors.
1 Great Bass Trombone.
1 Ophicleide in $B\flat$ (or a Bass-Tuba).
2 Pairs of Kettle-Drums, and 4 Drummers.
1 Long Drum.

If a choral composition were to be executed, such an orchestra would require :—

46 Sopranos { Firsts and Seconds.	40 Tenors { Firsts and Seconds.	40 Basses { Firsts and Seconds.

By doubling or tripling this mass of performers, in the same proportions, and in the same order, a magnificent Festival orchestra might doubtless be obtained. But it is erroneous to believe that all orchestras should be constituted according to a system based on the predominance of stringed instruments; very admirable results may be obtained from a contrary plan. The stringed instruments—too weak to prevail over masses of clarinets and brass instruments,—then serve as a harmonious link with the thrilling sounds of the wind instruments; softening their brilliancy in some cases, and animating their effect in others, by means of the tremolo, which, by blending with them, renders musical even the roll of the drums.

Common sense tells the composer—unless he be compelled to a different course by any particular form of orchestra—that he should combine his mass of performers according to the style and character of the work he brings forth, and according to the nature of the principal effects which the subject demands. Thus, in a *Requiem*, and in order to deliver musically the grand images of this *hymn of the dead*, I have employed four small orchestras of brass instruments (trumpets, trombones, cornets, and ophicleides), placed apart from each other, at the four corners of the main orchestra, formed of an imposing body of stringed instruments, of all the other wind instruments doubled and tripled, and of ten drummers playing on eight pairs of kettle-drums tuned in different keys. It is quite certain that the particular effects obtained by this novel form of orchestra were absolutely unattainable by any other.

Here we have an opportunity to remark upon the importance of the various *points of procedure of the sounds*. Certain parts of an orchestra are intended by the composer to interrogate and answer each other; now, this intention can only be made manifest and of fine effect by causing the groups between which the dialogue occurs to be placed at a sufficient distance from one another. The composer should, therefore, in his score, indicate for them the disposition which he judges proper.

The drums, long drums, cymbals, and kettle-drums, if employed to strike certain rhythms all at once—after the common mode of proceeding—may remain together; but if they have to execute an interlocutory rhythm, of which one fragment is struck by the long drums and cymbals, and the other by the kettle-drums and drums, there is no doubt the effect will be made incomparably better, finer, and more interesting, by placing the two masses of instruments of percussion at the extremities of the orchestra, and consequently at a sufficient distance from one another. The constant uniformity of the executive masses is one of the great obstacles to the production of sterling and really new works; it besets composers more from old custom, routine, laziness, and want of reflection, than from motives of economy,—motives unfortunately but too important, in France especially, where Music is so far from forming a part of the moral being of the nation, where the government does everything for theatres, and nothing at all for music properly so called, where capitalists are ready to give 50,000f. and more for some great master's picture, *because that represents an intrinsic value*, yet would not lay out 50f. to render feasible, once a year, some solemnity worthy of a nation like ours, and fitted to display the very numerous musical resources which it really possesses without the capability of making them of use.

It would nevertheless be curious to try for once, in a composition written *ad hoc*, the simultaneous employment of all the musical forces which might be gathered together in Paris. Supposing that a master had these at his disposal, in a vast space adapted for the purpose by an architect who should be well versed in acoustics and a good musician, he ought, before writing, to determine with precision the plan and arrangement of his immense orchestra, and then to keep them always present to his mind while writing. It is obvious that it would be of the highest importance, in the employment of so enormous a musical mass, to take account of the distance or the nearness of the different groups which compose it. This condition is one of the most essential to deriving the utmost advantage from it, and in calculating with certainty the scope of its effects. Until now, at the Festivals, merely the ordinary orchestra and chorus have been heard, quadrupled or quintupled in their several parts, according to the greater or less number of the performers; but in the case proposed it would be quite another affair; and the composer who should attempt exhibiting all the prodigious and innumerable resources of such an *instrument*, would assuredly have to achieve an entirely new task.

Here, then, is how—with time, care, and the necessary *outlay*—it could be effected in Paris. The disposal of the groups would remain at the will, and subject to the particular intentions, of the composer; the instruments of percussion, which exercise an irresistible influence on the rhythm, and which always lag when they are far from the conductor, should be placed sufficiently near him to be able instantaneously and strictly to obey the slightest variations of movement and measure :—

120 Violins, divided into two, or three, and four parts.

40 Violas, divided or not into firsts and seconds; and of which ten at least should be ready to play, when needed, the Viole d'amour.

45 Violoncellos, divided or not into firsts and seconds.

18 Double-Basses with 3 strings, tuned in fifths (G, D, A).

15 other Double-Basses with 4 strings, tuned in fourths (E, A, D, G).

4 Octo-Basses.
6 Large Flutes.
4 Third-Flutes (in $E\flat$), improperly called in F.
2 Octave Piccolo Flutes.
2 Piccolo Flutes (in $D\flat$), improperly called in $E\flat$.
6 Hautboys.
6 Corni Inglesi.
5 Saxophones.
4 Bassons-quinte.
12 Bassoons.
4 Small Clarinets (in $E\flat$).
8 Clarinets (in C, or in $B\flat$, or in A).
3 Bass-Clarinets (in $B\flat$).
16 Horns (of which six should be with pistons).
8 Trumpets.
6 Cornets à Pistons.
4 Alto-Trombones.
6 Tenor-Trombones.
2 Great Bass-Trombones.
1 Ophicleide in C.
2 Ophicleides in $B\flat$.
2 Bass-Tubas.
30 Harps.
30 Pianofortes.
1 very low Organ, provided with stops of at least 16 feet.
8 Pairs of Kettle-Drums (10 Drummers).
6 Drums.
3 Long Drums.
4 Pairs of Cymbals.
6 Triangles.
6 Sets of Bells.
12 Pairs of Ancient Cymbals (in different keys).
2 very low Great Bells.
2 Gongs.
4 Pavillons Chinois.

467 Instrumentalists.

40 Children Sopranos (firsts and seconds).
100 Women Sopranos (firsts and seconds).
100 Tenors (firsts and seconds).
120 Basses (firsts and seconds).

360 Chorus-singers.

It will be perceived that in this aggregate of 827 performers the chorus-singers do not predominate; and even thus, there would be much difficulty in collecting in Paris three hundred and sixty voices of any excellence,—so little is the study of singing at present cultivated or advanced.

It would evidently be necessary to adopt a style of extraordinary breadth, each time the entire mass is put in action; reserving the delicate effects, the light and rapid movements, for small bands which the author could easily arrange, and make them discourse together in the midst of this musical multitude.

Beside the radiant colours which this myriad of different tone-qualities would give out at every moment, unheard-of *harmonic effects* would be deduced from them.

From the division of the 120 violins into eight or ten parts, aided by the 50 violas, in their high notes, the angelic aërial accent, and the *pianissimo* tint.

From the division of the violoncellos and double-basses below in slow movements, the melancholy religious accent, and the *mezzo forte* tint.

From the union, *in a small band*, of the very low notes of the clarinet family, the gloomy accent, and the *forte* and *mezzo forte* tints.

From the union, *in a small band*, of the low notes of the hautboys, corni inglesi, and bassons-quinte, mingled with the low notes of the large flutes, the religiously mournful accent, and the *piano* tint.

From the union, *in a small band*, of the low notes of the ophicleides, bass-tuba, and horns, mingled with the *pedals* of the tenor-trombones, with the lowest notes of the bass-trombones, and of the 16 feet stop (open flute) of the organ, profoundly grave, religious, and calm accents, and the *piano* tint.

From the union, *in a small band*, of the highest notes of the small clarinets, flutes, and piccolo flutes, the shrill accent, and the *forte* tint.

From the union, *in a small band*, of the horns, trumpets, cornets, trombones, and ophicleides, a pompous and brilliant accent, and the *forte* tint.

From the union, *in a large band*, of the 30 harps with the entire mass of bowed instruments playing *pizzicato*, and thus forming together another gigantic harp with *nine hundred and thirty-four* strings, graceful, brilliant, and voluptuous accents, in all tints and gradations.

From the union of the 30 pianofortes with the six sets of bells, the twelve pairs of ancient cymbals, the six triangles (which might be tuned, like the ancient cymbals, in different keys), and the four pavillons chinois, constituting a metallic *orchestra* of percussion, joyous and brilliant accents, and the *mezzo forte* tint.

From the union of the eight pairs of kettle-drums with the six drums, and the three long drums, forming a small *orchestra* of percussion, and almost exclusively *rhythmical*, the menacing accent, in all tints.

From the mixture of the two gongs, the two bells, and the three large cymbals, with certain chords of trombones, the lugubrious and sinister accent, in the *mezzo forte* tint.

How can I enumerate all the harmonic aspects under which each of these different groups, associated with other groups either sympathetic or antipathetic with them, would appear!

There might be grand duets between the band of wind instruments and the stringed band; between one of these two bands and the chorus; or between the chorus and the harps and pianofortes only.

A grand trio between the chorus in unison and in octave, the wind instruments in unison and in octave, and the violins, violas, and violoncellos also in unison and in octave.

This trio might be accompanied by a rhythmical form designed by all the instruments of percussion, the double-basses, the harps, and the pianofortes.

A simple chorus, double or triple, without accompaniment

An air for violins, violas, and violoncellos *together*, or for wooden wind instruments *together*, or for brass instruments *together*, accompanied by a *vocal band*

An air for sopranos, or tenors, or basses, or all the voices in octave, accompanied by an *instrumental band*

A small choir singing, accompanied by the large choir, and by some instruments

A small band playing, accompanied by the large orchestra, and by some voices

A grand deep melody, executed by all the bowed basses, and accompanied above by the violins divided, and the harps and pianofortes

A grand deep melody, executed by all the wind basses and the organ, and accompanied above by the flutes, hautboys, clarinets, and the violins divided.

Etcetera, etcetera, etcetera.

The system of rehearsals requisite for this colossal orchestra cannot be doubtful, it is that which must be adopted whenever there is an intention to get up a work of grand dimensions, the plan of which is complex, and certain parts or the whole of which offer difficulties in performance, it is the system of partial rehearsals This is how the conductor will have to proceed in his analytical operation

I take for granted that he knows *thoroughly, and in its minutest details*, the score which he is about to have performed. He will first appoint two sub-conductors, who should—marking the beats of the bar in the general rehearsals—keep their eyes continually upon him, in order to communicate the movement to the masses too far removed from the centre He will then select rehearsers for each of the vocal and instrumental groups

He will first make them rehearse themselves, that they may be well instructed in the way in which they will have to direct the portion of study allotted to them

The first rehearser will rehearse separately the first sopranos, then the seconds and then the firsts and seconds together

The second rehearser will practise in the same way the first and second tenors

The third rehearser will do the same by the basses After which, three choirs, each composed of a third of the total mass, will be formed, and then lastly, the whole chorus will be practised together

As an accompaniment to these choral studies, either an organ, or a pianoforte may be used, assisted by a few wind instruments, violins and basses.

The sub-conductors and the orchestral rehearsers will practise separately in the same way —

1stly The first and second violins separately, then all the violins together

2ndly The violas, violoncellos, and double-basses separately, then all together

3rdly The entire mass of bowed instruments.

4thly The harps alone.

5thly The pianofortes alone

6thly The harps and pianofortes together

7thly The wooden wind instruments alone

8thly. The brass wind instruments alone.

9thly. All the wind instruments together

10thly The instruments of percussion alone, particularly teaching the kettle-drummers to tune their kettle-drums well

11thly The instruments of percussion joined with the wind instruments.

12thly Lastly, the whole vocal and instrumental mass united, under the direction of the conductor himself

This method of proceeding will have the result of securing, first, an excellence of execution that never could be obtained under the old system of collective study; and next, of requiring from each performer but four rehearsals at most It should not be forgotten to have a profusion of tuning-forks of the exact pitch among the members of the orchestra; it is the sole means by which the accurate tuning of this crowd of instruments of such various nature and temperament can be ensured

Vulgar prejudice stigmatizes large orchestras as *noisy*· but if they be well constituted, well practised, and well conducted, if they perform sterling music, they should be called *powerful*, and certainly, nothing is more dissimilar than those two expressions A trumpery little vaudeville orchestra may be *noisy*, when a large body of musicians properly employed shall be of extreme softness, and shall produce—even in their loudest effects—sounds the most beautiful Three ill-placed trombones will seem *noisy*, insufferable and the instant after, in the same room, twelve trombones will strike the public by their noble and *powerful* harmony

Moreover, unisons acquire real value only when multiplied beyond a certain number. Thus, four violins of first-rate skill playing together the same part will produce but a very poor—nay, perhaps, even detestable effect, while fifteen violins of ordinary talent shall be excellent This is why small orchestras—whatever the merit of the performers who compose them—have so little effect, and consequently so little value

But in the thousand combinations practicable with the vast orchestra we have just described would dwell a wealth of harmony, a variety of tone qualities, a succession of contrasts, which can be compared to nothing hitherto achieved in Art, and above all, an incalculable melodic, expressive, and rhythmical power, a penetrating force of unparalleled strength, a prodigious sensitiveness for gradations in aggregate and in detail Its repose would be majestic as the slumber of ocean, its agitations would recall the tempest of the tropics, its explosions, the outbursts of volcanos, therein would be heard the plaints, the murmurs, the mysterious sounds of primeval forests, the clamours, the prayers, the songs of triumph or of mourning of a people with expansive soul, ardent heart, and fiery passions its silence would inspire awe by its solemnity, and organizations the most rebellious would shudder to behold its *crescendo* spread roaringly,—like a stupendous conflagration!

The Orchestral Conductor

Theory of his Art.

Music appears to be the most exacting of all the Arts the most difficult to cultivate, and that of which the productions are most rarely presented in a condition which permits an appreciation of their real value, a clear view of their physiognomy, or discernment of their real meaning and true character Of producing artists, the composer is almost the only one, in fact, who depends upon a multitude of intermediate agents between the public and himself, intermediate agents, either intelligent or stupid, devoted or hostile, active or inert, capable—from first to last—of contributing to the brilliancy of his work, or of disfiguring it, misrepresenting it, and even destroying it completely

Singers have often been accused of forming the most dangerous of these intermediate agents, but, in my opinion, without justice The most formidable, to my thinking, is the conductor of the orchestra A bad singer can spoil only his own part, while an incapable or malevolent conductor ruins all Happy, also, may that composer esteem himself when the conductor into whose hands he has fallen is not at once incapable and inimical For nothing can resist the pernicious influence of this person The most admirable orchestra is then paralysed, the most excellent singers are perplexed and rendered dull, there is no longer any vigour or unity, under such direction the noblest daring of the author appears extravagance, enthusiasm beholds its soaring flight checked, inspiration is violently brought down to earth, the angel's wings are broken, the man of genius passes for a madman or an idiot, the divine statue is precipitated from its pedestal and dragged in the mud And, what is worse, the public, and even auditors endowed with the highest musical intelligence, are reduced to the impossibility (if a new work be in question, and they are hearing it for the first time) of recognising the ravages perpetrated by the orchestral conductor—of discovering the follies, faults, and crimes he commits If they clearly perceive certain defects of execution, not he, but his victims, are in such cases made responsible If he have caused the chorus-singers to fail in taking up a point in a finale, if he have allowed a discordant wavering to take place between the choir and the orchestra, or between the extreme sides of the instrumental body, if he have absurdly hurried a movement, if he have allowed it to linger unduly, if he have interrupted a singer before the end of a phrase, they exclaim "The singers are detestable! The orchestra has no firmness, the violins have disfigured the principal design, everybody has been wanting in vigour and animation the tenor was quite out, he did not know his part, the harmony is confused; the author is no accompanist, the voices are——" &c, &c, &c

Except in listening to great works already known and esteemed, intelligent hearers can hardly distinguish the true culprit, and allot to him his due share of blame, but the number of these is still so limited that their judgment has little weight, and the bad conductor—in presence of the public who would pitilessly hiss a *vocal accident* of a good singer—reigns, with all the calm of a bad conscience, in his baseness and inefficiency Fortunately, I here attack an exception, for the malevolent orchestral conductor—whether capable or not—is very rare

The orchestral conductor full of goodwill, but incapable, is, on the contrary, very common. Without speaking of innumerable mediocrities directing artists who, frequently, are much their superiors, an author, for example, can scarcely be accused of conspiring against his own works Yet how many are there who, fancying they are able to conduct, innocently injure their best scores!

Beethoven, it is said, more than once ruined the performance of his symphonies, which he would conduct, even at the time when his deafness had become almost complete. The musicians, in order to keep together, agreed at length to follow the slight indications of time which the concertmeister (first violin-player) gave them, and not to attend to Beethoven's conducting-stick Moreover, it should be observed, that conducting a symphony, an overture, or any other composition whose movements remain continuous, vary little, and contain few nice gradations, is child's play in comparison with conducting an opera, or like work, where there are recitatives, airs, and numerous orchestral designs preceded by pauses of irregular length

The example of Beethoven, which I have just cited, leads me at once to say that if the direction of an orchestra appear to me very difficult for a blind man, it is indisputably impossible to a deaf one, whatever may have been his technical talent before losing his sense of hearing.

The orchestral conductor should *see* and *hear*, he should be *active* and *vigorous*, should know the *composition* and the *nature* and *compass* of the instruments, should be able to *read* the score, and possess—besides the especial talent of which we shall presently endeavour to explain the constituent qualities—other almost indefinable gifts, without which an invisible link cannot establish itself between him and those he directs, the faculty of transmitting to them his feeling is denied him, and thence power, empire, and guiding influence completely fail him. He is then no longer a conductor, a director, but a simple beater of the time,—supposing he knows how to beat it, and divide it, regularly

The performers should feel that he feels, comprehends, and is moved· then his emotion communicates itself to those whom he directs, his inward fire warms them, his electric glow animates them, his force of impulse excites them, he throws around him the vital irradiations of musical art If he be inert and frozen, on the contrary, he paralyses all about him, like those floating masses of the polar seas the approach of which is perceived through the sudden cooling of the atmosphere

His task is a complicated one He has not only to conduct, in the spirit of the author's intentions a work with which the performers have already become acquainted, but he has also to give them this acquaintance when the work in question is new to them. He has to criticise the errors and defects of each during the rehearsals, and to organise the resources at his disposal in such a way as to make the best use he can of them with the utmost promptitude. For, in the majority of European cities nowadays, musical artizanship is so ill distributed, performers so ill paid, and the necessity of study so little understood, that *economy of time* should be reckoned among the most imperative requisites of the orchestral conductor's art.

Let us now see what constitutes the mechanical part of this art.

The power of *beating the time,* without demanding very high musical attainments, is nevertheless sufficiently difficult to secure, and very few persons really possess it. The signs that the conductor should make—although generally very simple—nevertheless become complicated, under certain circumstances, by the division and even the subdivision of the time of the bar.

The conductor is, above all, bound to possess a clear idea of the principal points and character of the work of which he is about to superintend the performance or study; in order that he may, without hesitation or mistake, at once determine the time of each movement desired by the composer. If he have not had the opportunity of receiving his instructions directly from the composer, or if the *times* have not been transmitted to him by tradition, he must have recourse to the indications of the metronome, and study them well; the majority of composers, nowadays, taking the precaution to write them at the head, and in the course of, their pieces. I do not mean to say by this that it is necessary to imitate the mathematical regularity of the metronome; all music so performed would become of freezing stiffness, and I even doubt whether it would be possible to observe so flat a uniformity during a certain number of bars. But the metronome is none the less excellent to consult in order to know the original time, and its chief alterations.

If the conductor possess neither the author's instructions, tradition, nor metronome indications,—which frequently happens in the ancient masterpieces, written at a period when the metronome was not invented,—he has no other guide than the vague terms employed to designate the time to be taken, and his own instinct, his feeling—more or less distinguishing, more or less just—of the author's style. We are compelled to admit that these guides are too often insufficient and delusive. Of this we have proof in seeing how old operas are given in towns where the traditional mode of performance no longer exists. In ten different kinds of time, there will always be at least four taken wrongly. I once heard a chorus of *Iphigenia in Tauride* performed in a German theatre *allegro assai, two in the bar*, instead of *allegro non troppo, four in the bar;* that is to say, exactly twice too fast. Examples might be multiplied of such disasters, occasioned either by the ignorance or the carelessness of conductors of orchestras; or else by the real difficulty which exists for even the best-gifted and most careful men to discover the precise meaning of the Italian terms used as indications of the time to be taken. Of course no one can be at a loss to distinguish a Largo from a Presto. If the Presto be two in a bar, a tolerably sagacious conductor, from inspection of the passages and melodic designs contained in the piece, will be able to discern the degree of quickness intended by the author. But if the Largo be four in a bar, of simple melodic structure, and containing but few notes in each bar, what means has the hapless conductor of discovering the true time? And in how many ways might he not be deceived? The different degrees of slowness that might be assigned to the performance of such a Largo are very numerous; the individual feeling of the orchestral conductor must then become the sole authority; and, after all, it is the author's feeling, not his, which is in question. Composers therefore ought not to neglect placing metronome indications in their works; and orchestral conductors are bound to study them closely. The neglect of this study on the part of the latter, is an act of dishonesty.

I will now suppose the conductor to be perfectly well acquainted with the times of the different movements in the work of which he is about to conduct the performance or rehearsals; he wishes to impart to the musicians acting under his orders the rhythmical feeling within him, to decide the duration of each bar, and to cause the uniform observance of this duration by all the performers. Now, this precision and this uniformity can only be established in the more or less numerous assemblage of band and chorus by means of certain signs made by their conductor.

These signs indicate the principal divisions, the accents of the bar, and, in many cases, the subdivisions, and the half-accents. I need hardly here explain what is meant by the 'accents' (accented and unaccented parts of a bar); I am pre-supposing that I address musicians.

The orchestral conductor generally uses a small light stick, of about a foot in length, and rather whitish than of a dark colour (it is seen better), which he holds in his right hand, to make clearly distinct his mode of marking the commencement, the interior division, and the close of each bar. The bow, employed by some violinist-conductors (leaders), is less suitable than the stick. It is somewhat flexible, and this want of rigidity, together with the slight resistance it offers to the air, on account of its appendage of hair, renders its indications less precise.

The simplest of all times—two in a bar—is beaten simply.

The arm and the stick of the conductor being raised, so that his hand is on a level with his head, he marks the first beat, by dropping the point of his stick perpendicularly (*bending his wrist* as much as possible; and not lowering the whole arm), and the second beat by raising the stick by a contrary gesture.

2

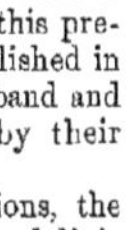

1

The time—one in a bar—being in reality, and particularly for the conductor, but the time of an extremely rapid two in a bar, should be beaten like the preceding. As the conductor is obliged to raise the point of his stick, after having lowered it, he necessarily divides this into two portions.

In the time—four in a bar—the first gesture, or down beat, is universally adopted for marking the first accented part, the commencement of the bar.

The second movement made by the conducting-stick, from right to left, rising, indicates the second beat (first unaccented part). A third, transversely, from left to right, indicates the third beat (second accented part); and a fourth, obliquely, from down to up, indicates the fourth beat (second unaccented part). The combination of these four gestures may be figured thus :—

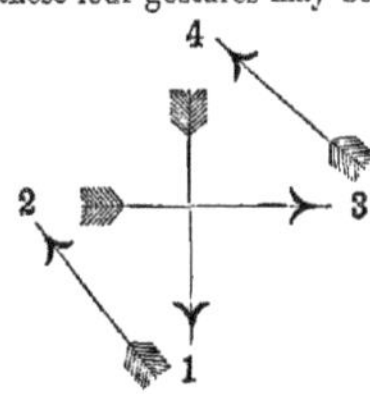

It is of importance that the conductor, in thus delivering his different directions, should not move his arm much; and consequently, not allow his stick to pass over much space; for each of these gestures should operate nearly instantaneously; or at least, take but so slight a movement as to be imperceptible. If the movement become perceptible, on the contrary, and multiplied by the number of times that the gesture is repeated, it ends by throwing the conductor behind in the time he is beating, and by giving to his conducting a tardiness that proves injurious. This defect, moreover, has the result of needlessly fatiguing the conductor, and of producing exaggerated evolutions, verging on the ridiculous, which attract the spectators' attention, and become very disagreeable to witness.

In the time, three in a bar, the first gesture made, from up to down, is likewise universally adopted for marking the first beat; but there are two ways of marking the second. The majority of orchestral conductors indicate it by a gesture from left to right; thus :—

Some German Kapel-meisters do the contrary; and carry the stick from right to left; thus :—

This way has the disadvantage—when the conductor turns his back to the orchestra, as in theatres—of permitting only a small number of musicians to perceive the very important indication of the second beat; the body of the conductor then hiding the movement of his arm. The other method of proceeding is preferable; since the conductor stretches his arm *outwards*, withdrawing it from his chest; and his stick, which he takes care to raise slightly above the level of his shoulder, remains perfectly visible to all eyes. When the conductor faces the players, it is immaterial whether he mark the second beat to the right, or to the left.

However that may be, the third beat of the time, three in a bar, is always marked like the last of the time, four in a bar; by an oblique movement upwards.

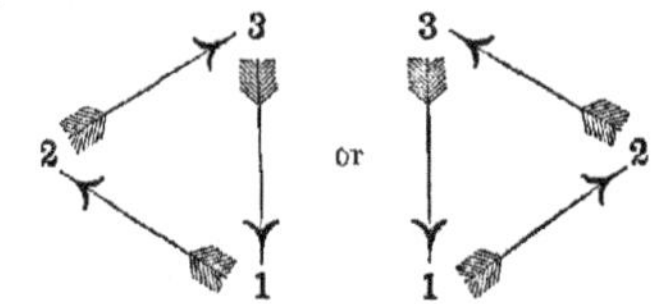

The times,—five and seven in a bar,—would be more comprehensible for the performers, if, instead of indicating them by a particular series of gestures, they were treated as though the one were composed of three and two in a bar, and the other composed of four and three.

Then, these times would be beaten thus :—

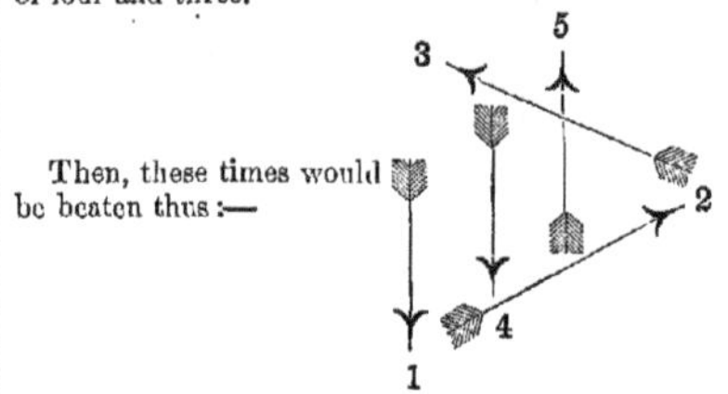

Example of seven in a bar :—

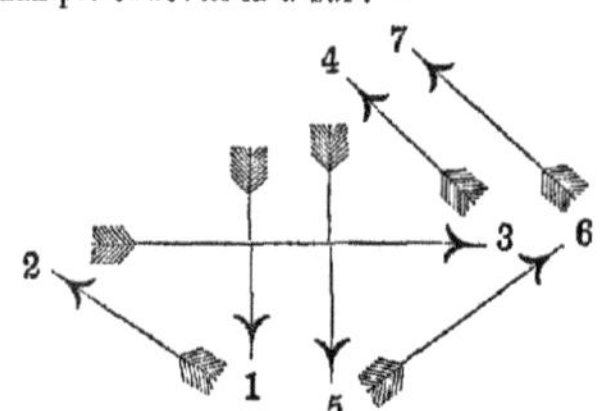

These different times, in order to be divided in this way, are assumed to belong to movements of moderate measure. The advice would not hold good, if their measure were either very quick or very slow.

The time, two in a bar, I have already signified, cannot be beaten otherwise than as we have before seen—whatever its degree of rapidity. But if, as an exception, it should be very slow, the conductor ought to subdivide it.

A very rapid four in a bar, on the contrary, should be beaten two in a bar; the four accustomed gestures of a moderate movement becoming then so hurried as to present nothing decided to the eye, and serving only to confuse the performer instead of giving him confidence. Moreover,—and this is of much more consequence,—the conductor, by uselessly making these four gestures in a quick movement, renders the pace of the rhythm awkward, and loses the freedom of gesture which a simple division of the time into its half, would leave him.

Generally speaking, composers are wrong to write, in such a case, the indication of the time as four in a bar. When the movement is very brisk, they should never write any other than the sign 𝄵, and not that of 𝄴, which might lead the conductor into error.

It is exactly the same for the time, three in a bar, fast $\frac{3}{4}$, or $\frac{3}{8}$. Then the conductor must omit the gesture of the second beat, and, by remaining the period of a beat longer on the first, only raise the stick at the third.

3

1 & 2

It would be absurd to attempt to beat the three in a bar of one of Beethoven's scherzos.

In slow movements the rule for these two times is like that for two in a bar. If the movement be very slow, each time must be divided; and consequently eight gestures must be made for the time, four in a bar, and six for the time, three in a bar, repeating (and shortening) each of the principal gestures we have before instanced.

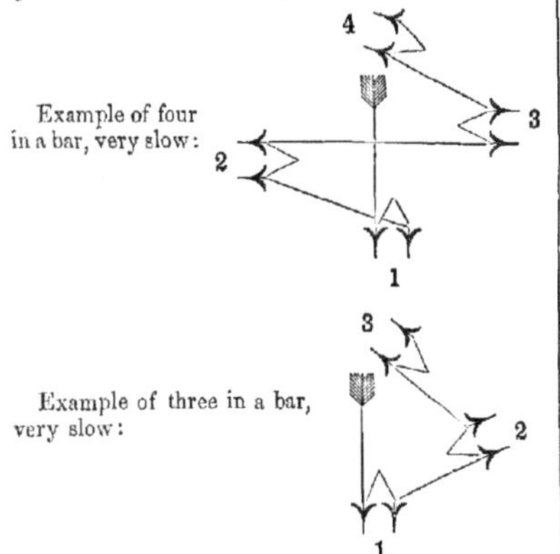

Example of four in a bar, very slow:

Example of three in a bar, very slow:

The arm should take no part in the little supplementary gesture indicating the subdivision of the bar; merely the wrist causing the stick to move.

This division of the different times is intended to prevent the rhythmical divergences which might easily take place among the performers during the interval which separates one beat from the other. The conductor not indicating anything during this period (rendered somewhat considerable by the extreme slowness of the movement), the players are then entirely left to themselves, *without conductor;* and as the rhythmical feeling is not the same with all, it follows that some hurry, while others slacken, and unity is soon destroyed. The only exception possible to this rule is that of a first-rate orchestra, composed of performers who are well acquainted with each other, are accustomed to play together, and know almost by heart the work they are executing. Even then, the inattention of a single player may occasion an accident. Why incur its possibility? I know that certain artists feel their self-love hurt when thus kept in leading-strings (like children, they say); but with a conductor who has no other view than the excellence of the ultimate result, this consideration can have no weight. Even in a quartet, it is seldom that the individual feeling of the players can be left entirely free to follow its own dictates. In a symphony, that of the conductor must rule. The art of comprehending it, and fulfilling it with unanimity, constitutes the perfection of execution; and individual wills—which can never agree one with another—should never be permitted to manifest themselves.

This being fully understood, it will be seen that subdivision is still more essential for very slow times; as those of $\frac{6}{4}$, $\frac{6}{8}$, $\frac{9}{8}$, $\frac{12}{8}$, &c.

But these times—where the triple rhythm plays so important a part—may be divided in various ways.

If the movement be brisk or moderate, it is rarely well to indicate other than the simple beats of these times, according to the procedure adopted for the analogous simple times.

The times of $\frac{6}{8}$ allegretto, and of $\frac{6}{4}$ allegro, therefore, are to be beaten like those of two in a bar: —𝄵 = or 2 = or $\frac{2}{4}$; the time, $\frac{9}{8}$ allegro, should be beaten like that of three in a bar—$\frac{3}{4}$ moderato, or like that of $\frac{3}{8}$ andantino; and the time, $\frac{12}{8}$ moderato or allegro, like the time, simple four in a bar. But if the movement be adagio, largo assai, or andante maestoso, either all the quavers, or a crotchet followed by a quaver, should be beaten, according to the form of the melody, or the predominant design.

It is unnecessary, in this three in a bar, to mark all the quavers; the rhythm of a crotchet followed by a quaver in each beat suffices.

As to the subdivision, the little supplementary gesture for simple times should be made; this subdivision will however separate each beat into two unequal portions, since it is requisite to indicate visibly the value of the crotchet, and that of the quaver.

If the movement be still slower, there can be no hesitation; the only way to ensure unity of execution is to beat all the quavers, whatever be the nature of the written bar.

Taking the three measures shown above in order, the conductor must beat three quavers down, and three up, for the time of $\frac{6}{8}$:—

Three down, three to the right, and three up, for the time of $\frac{9}{8}$:—

Three down, three to the left, three to the right, and three up, for the time of $\frac{12}{8}$:—

A dilemma sometimes presents itself when certain parts—for the sake of contrast—are given a triple rhythm, while others preserve the dual rhythm.

If the wind-instrument parts in the above example be confided to players who are good musicians, there will be no need to change the manner of marking the bar, and the conductor may continue to subdivide it by six, or to divide it simply by two. The majority of players, however, seeming to hesitate at the moment when, by employing the syncopated form, the triple rhythm clashes with the dual rhythm, require assurance, which can be given by easy means. The uncertainty occasioned them by the sudden appearance of the unexpected rhythm, contradicted by the rest of the orchestra, always leads the performers to cast an instinctive glance towards the conductor, as if seeking his assistance. He should look at them, turning somewhat towards them, and marking the triple rhythm by very slight gestures, as if the time were really three in a bar, but in such a way that the violins and other instruments playing in dual rhythm may not observe the change, which would quite put them out. From this compromise it results that the new rhythm of three-time, being marked furtively by the conductor, is executed with steadiness; while the two-time rhythm, already firmly established, continues without difficulty, although no longer indicated by the conductor. On the other hand, nothing, in my opinion, can be more blamable, or more contrary to musical good sense, than the application of this procedure to passages where two rhythms of opposite nature do not co-exist, and where merely syncopations are introduced. The conductor, dividing the bar by *the number of accents he finds contained in it*, then destroys (for all the auditors who see him) the effect of syncopation; and substitutes a mere change of time for a play of rhythm of the most bewitching interest. If the accents be marked, instead of the beats, in the following passage from Beethoven's Pastoral Symphony, we have the subjoined—

whereas the four previously maintained display the syncopation and make it better felt :—

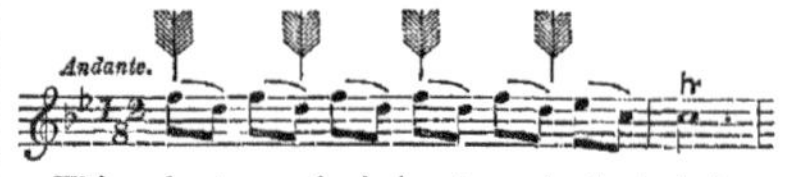

This voluntary submission to a rhythmical form *which the author intended to be thwarted* is one of the gravest faults in style that a beater of the time can commit.

There is another dilemma, extremely troublesome for a conductor, and demanding all his presence of mind. It is that presented by the super-addition of different bars. It is easy to conduct a bar in dual time placed above or beneath another bar in triple time, if both have the same kind of movement. Their chief divisions are then equal in duration, and there needs only to divide them in half, marking the two principal beats :—

But if, in the middle of a piece slow in movement, there be introduced a new form brisk in movement, and if the composer (either for the sake of facilitating the execution of the quick movement, or because it was impossible to write otherwise) have adopted for this new movement the short bar which corresponds with it, there may then occur two, or even three short bars super-added to a slow bar :—

Three bars to one.

The conductor's task is to guide and keep together these different bars of unequal number and dissimilar movement. He attains this by dividing the beats in the andante bar No. 1, which precedes the entrance of the allegro in $\frac{6}{8}$, and by continuing to divide them; but taking care to mark the division more decidedly. The players of the allegro in $\frac{6}{8}$ then comprehend that the two gestures of the conductor represent the two beats of their short bar, while the players of the andante take these same gestures merely for a divided beat of their long bar.

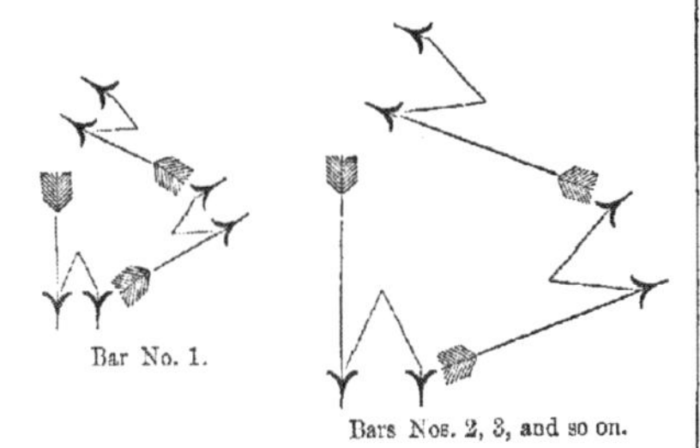

It will be seen that this is really quite simple because the division of the short bar, and the subdivisions of the long one, mutually correspond. The following example, where a slow bar is super-added to the short ones, without this correspondence existing, is more awkward :—

Here, the three bars allegro-assai preceding the allegretto are beaten in simple two-time, as usual. At the moment when the allegretto begins, the bar of which is double that of the preceding, and of the one maintained by the violas, the conductor marks *two divided beats* for the long bar, by two equal gestures down, and two others up :—

The two large gestures divide the long bar in half, and explain its value to the hautboys, without perplexing the violas, who maintain the brisk movement, on account of the little gesture which also divides in half their short bar.

From bar No. 3, the conductor ceases to divide thus the long bar by four, on account of the triple rhythm of the melody in $\frac{6}{8}$, which this gesture interferes with. He then confines himself to marking the two beats of the long bar; while the violas, already launched in their rapid rhythm, continue it without difficulty, comprehending exactly that each stroke of the conductor's stick marks merely *the commencement* of their short bar.

This last observation shows with what care dividing the beats of a bar should be avoided when a portion of the instruments or voices has to execute triplets upon these beats. The division, by cutting in half the second note of the triplet, renders its execution uncertain. It is even necessary to abstain from this division of the beats of a bar just before the moment when the rhythmical or melodic design is divided by three, in order not to give to the players the impression of a rhythm contrary to that which they are about to hear :—

In this example, the subdivision of the bar into six, or the division of the beats into two, is useful; and offers no inconvenience *during bar No.* 1, when the following gesture is made:

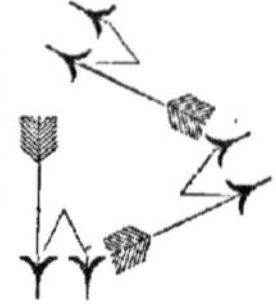

But from the beginning of bar No. 2 it is necessary to make only the simple gestures—

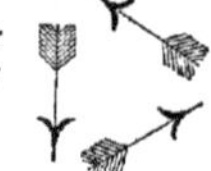

on account of the triplet on the third beat, and on account of the one following it, which the double gesture would much interfere with.

In the famous ball-scene of Mozart's *Don Giovanni*, the difficulty of keeping together the three orchestras, written in three different measures, is less than might be thought. It is sufficient to mark downwards each beat of the *tempo di minuetto*:—

Once entered upon the combination, the little allegro in $\frac{3}{8}$, of which a whole bar represents one third, or one beat of that of the minuetto, and the other allegro in $\frac{2}{4}$, of which a whole bar represents two thirds, or two beats, correspond with each other and with the principal theme; while the whole proceeds without the slightest confusion. All that is requisite is to make them come in properly.

A gross fault that I have seen committed consists in enlarging the time of a piece in common-time, when the author has introduced into it triplets of minims:—

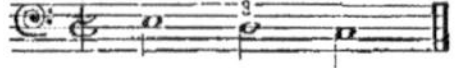

In such a case, the third minim adds nothing to the duration of the bar, as some conductors seem to imagine. They may, if they please, and if the movement be slow or moderate, make these passages by beating the bar with three beats, but the duration of the whole bar should remain precisely the same. In a case where these triplets occur in a very quick bar in common-time (allegro-assai), the three gestures then cause confusion, and it is absolutely necessary to make only two,—one beat upon the first minim, and one up upon the third. These gestures, owing to the quickness of the movement, differ little, to the eye, from the two of the bar with two equal beats, and do not affect the movement of those parts of the orchestra which contain no triplets.

We will now speak of the conductor's method of beating in recitatives. Here, as the singer or the instrumentalist is reciting, and no longer subject to the regular division of the bar, it is requisite, while following him attentively, to make the orchestra strike, simultaneously and with precision, the chords or instrumental passages with which the recitative is intermingled; and to make the harmony change at the proper instant, when the recitative is accompanied either by holding-notes or by a tremolo in several parts, of which the least apparent, occasionally, is that which the conductor must most regard, since upon its motion depends the change of chord:

Example, not kept time to.

Violins.

Violas & Basses.

In this example, the conductor, while following the reciting part, not kept time to, has especially to attend to the viola part, and to make it move, at the proper moment, from the F to the E, at the commencement of the second bar; because otherwise, as this part is executed by several instrumentalists playing in unison, some of them would hold the F longer than the rest, and a transient discord would be produced.

Many conductors have the habit, when directing the orchestra in recitatives, of paying no heed to the written division of the bar, and of marking an up beat before that whereon a brief orchestral chord occurs, even when this chord comes on an unaccented part of the bar:—

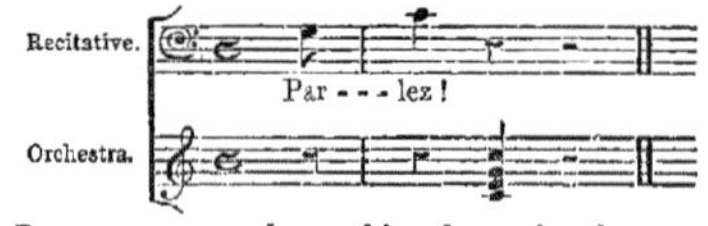

In a passage such as this, they raise the arm at the rest which commences the bar, and lower it at the time of the chord.

I cannot approve such a method, which nothing justifies, and which may frequently occasion accidents in the execution. Neither do I see why, in recitatives, the bar should not be divided regularly, and the real beats be marked in their place, as in music beaten in time. I therefore advise—for the preceding example—that the first beat should be made down, as usual, and the stick carried to the left for striking the chord upon the second beat; and so on for analogous cases; always dividing the bar regularly. It is very important, moreover, to divide it according to the time previously indicated by the author, and not to forget,—if this time be *allegro* or *maestoso*, and if the reciting part have been some time reciting unaccompanied,—to give to all the beats, when the orchestra comes in again, the value of those of an allegro or of a maestoso. For when the orchestra plays alone, it does so generally in time; it plays without measured time only when it accompanies a voice or instrument in recitative.

In the exceptional case where the recitative is written for the orchestra itself, or for the chorus, or for a portion of either orchestra or chorus, it being then requisite to keep together, whether in unison or in harmony, but without regular time, a certain number of performers, *the conductor himself becomes the real reciter*, and gives to each beat of the bar the duration he judges fit. According to the form of the phrase, he divides and subdivides the beats, now marks the accents, now the semiquavers, if there be any, and, in short, indicates with his stick the melodic form of the recitative.

It is an understood thing that the performers, knowing their parts almost by heart, keep their eye constantly upon him, otherwise, neither security nor unity can be obtained.

In general, even for timed music, the conductor should require the players he directs to look towards him as often as possible.

An orchestra which does not watch the conducting-stick has no conductor. Often, after a pedal-point for instance, the conductor is obliged to refrain from marking the decisive gesture which is to determine the coming in of the orchestra until he sees the eyes of all the performers fixed upon him. It is the duty of the conductor, during rehearsal, to accustom them to look towards him simultaneously at the important moment.

If the rule just indicated were not observed in the above bar, of which the first beat, marking a pedal-point, may be prolonged indefinitely, the passage—

could not be uttered with firmness and unity; the players, not watching the conductor's stick, could not know when he decides the second beat and resumes the movement suspended by the pedal-point.

The obligation upon the performers to look at their conductor necessarily implies an equal obligation on his part to let himself be well seen by them. He should,—whatever may be the disposal of the orchestra, whether on rows of steps, or on a horizontal plane,—place himself so as to form the centre of all surrounding eyes.

To place him well in sight, a conductor requires an especial platform, elevated in proportion as the number of performers is large and occupies much space. His desk should not be so high as that the portion sustaining the score shall hide his face. For the expression of his countenance has much to do with the influence he exercises, and if there be no conductor for an orchestra that does not and will not watch him, neither is there any if he cannot be well seen.

As to the employment of noises of any kind whatever, produced by the stick of the conductor upon his desk, or by his foot upon the platform, they call for no other than unreserved reprehension. It is worse than a bad method; it is a barbarism. In a theatre, however, when the stage evolutions prevent the chorus-singers from seeing the conducting-stick, the conductor is compelled—to ensure, after a pause, the taking up a point by the chorus—to indicate this point by marking the beat which precedes it by a slight tap of his stick upon the desk. This exceptional circumstance is the only one which can warrant the employment of an *indicating noise*, and even then it is to be regretted that recourse must be had to it.

While speaking of chorus-singers, and of their operations in theatres, it may here be observed that chorus-masters often allow themselves to beat time at the side-scenes, without seeing the conductor's stick, frequently even without hearing the orchestra. The result is that this time, beaten more or less ill, and not corresponding with that of the conductor, inevitably induces a rhythmical discordance between the choral and instrumental bodies, and subverts all unity instead of tending to maintain it.

Another traditional barbarism lies within the province of an intelligent and active conductor to abolish. If a choral or instrumental piece be performed behind the scenes, without accompaniment from the principal orchestra, another conductor is absolutely essential. If the orchestra accompany this portion, the first conductor, who hears the distant music, is then strictly bound to *let himself be guided* by the second, and to follow his time *by ear*. But if—as frequently happens in modern music—the sound of the chief orchestra hinders the conductor from hearing that which is being performed at a distance from him, the intervention of a special conducting mechanism becomes indispensable, in order to establish instantaneous communication between him and the distant performers. Many attempts, more or less ingenious, have been made of this kind, the result of which has not everywhere answered expectations. That of Covent Garden Theatre, in London, moved by the conductor's foot, acts tolerably well. But the *electric metronome*, set up by Mr. Van Bruge in the Brussels Theatre, leaves nothing to be desired. It consists of an apparatus of copper ribbons, leading from a Voltaic battery placed beneath the stage, attached to the conductor's desk, and terminating in a movable stick fastened at one end on a pivot before a board at a certain distance from the orchestral conductor To this latter's desk is affixed a key of copper, something like the ivory key of a pianoforte, it is elastic, and provided on the interior side with a protuberance of about a quarter of an inch long. Immediately beneath this protuberance is a little cup, also of copper, filled with quicksilver At the instant when the orchestral conductor, desiring to mark any particular beat of a bar, presses the copper key with the forefinger of his left hand (his right being occupied in holding, as usual, the conducting-stick) this key is lowered, the protuberance passes into the cup filled with quicksilver, a slight electric spark is emitted, and the stick placed at the other extremity of the copper ribbon makes an oscillation before its board The communication of the fluid and the movement are quite simultaneous, whatever be the distance traversed

The performers being grouped behind the scenes, their eyes fixed upon the stick of the electric metronome, are thus directly subject to the conductor, who could, were it needful, conduct, from the middle of the Opera orchestra in Paris, a piece of music performed at Versailles.

It is merely requisite to agree beforehand with the chorus-singers, or with their conductor (if, as an additional precaution, they have one), the way in which the orchestral conductor beats the time—whether he mark all the principal beats, or only the first of the bar—since the oscillations of the stick, moved by electricity, being always from right to left, indicate nothing precise in this respect

When I first used, at Brussels, the valuable instrument I have just endeavoured to describe, its action presented one objection. Each time that the copper key of my desk underwent the pressure of my left forefinger, it struck, underneath, another plate of copper, and, notwithstanding the delicacy of the contact, produced a little sharp noise, which, during the pauses of the orchestra, attracted the attention of the audience, to the detriment of the musical effect

I pointed out the fault to Mr Van Bruge, who substituted for the lower plate of copper the little cup filled with quicksilver, previously mentioned Into this the protuberance so entered as to establish the electric current without causing the slightest noise

Nothings remains now, as regards the use of this mechanism, but the crackling of the spark at the moment of its emission. This, however, is too slight to be heard by the public.

The metronome is not expensive to put up it costs £16 at the most Large lyric theatres, churches, and concert-rooms should long ago have been provided with one. Yet, save at the Brussels Theatre, it is nowhere to be found This would appear incredible, were it not that the carelessness of the majority of directors of institutions where music forms a feature is well known, as are their instinctive aversion from whatever disturbs old-established customs, their indifference to the interests of art, their parsimony wherever an outlay for music is needed, and the utter ignorance of the principles of our art among those in whose hands rests the ordering of its destiny

I have not yet said all on the subject of those dangerous auxiliaries named chorus-masters Very few of them are sufficiently versed in the art to conduct a musical performance or so that the orchestral conductor can depend upon them. He cannot therefore watch them too closely when compelled to submit to their coadjutorship

The most to be dreaded are those whom age has deprived of activity and energy. The maintenance of vivacious times is an impossibility to them Whatever may be the degree of quickness indicated at the head of a piece confided to their conducting, little by little they slacken its pace, until the rhythm is reduced to a certain medium slowness, that seems to harmonize with the speed at which their blood flows, and the general feebleness of their organization

It must in truth be added, that old men are not the only ones with whom composers run this risk There are men in the prime of life, of a lymphatic temperament, whose blood seems to circulate *moderato* If they have to conduct an allegro assai, they gradually slacken it to *moderato*; if, on the contrary, it be a largo or an andante sostenuto, provided the piece be prolonged, they will, by dint of progressive animation, attain a *moderato* long before the end. The *moderato* is their natural pace, and they recur to it as infallibly as would a pendulum after having been a moment hurried or slackened in its oscillations

These people are the born enemies of all characteristic music, and the greatest destroyers of style May Fate preserve the orchestral conductor at any cost from their co-operation.

Once, in a large town (which I will not name), there was to be performed behind the scenes a very simple chorus, written in $\frac{6}{8}$, allegretto. The aid of the chorus-master became necessary. He was an old man

The time in which this chorus was to be taken having been first agreed upon by the orchestra, our Nestor followed it pretty decently during the first few bars, but, soon after, the slackening became such that there was no continuing without rendering the piece perfectly ridiculous It was recommenced twice, thrice, four times, a full half-hour was occupied in ever-increasingly vexatious efforts, but always with the same result The preservation of allegretto time was absolutely impossible to the worthy man At last the orchestral conductor, out of all patience, came and begged him not to conduct at all; he had hit upon an expedient —He caused the chorus-singers to simulate a march-movement, raising each foot alternately, without moving on This movement, being in exactly the same time as the dual rhythm of the $\frac{6}{8}$ in a bar, allegretto, the chorus-singers, who were no longer hindered by their director, at once performed the piece as though they had sung marching, with no less unity than regularity, and without slackening the time.

I acknowledge, however, that many chorus-masters, or sub-conductors of orchestras, are sometimes of real utility, and even indispensable for the maintenance of unity among very large masses of performers. When these masses are obliged to be so disposed as that one portion of the players or chorus-singers turn their back on the conductor, he needs a certain number of sub-beaters of the time, placed before those of the performers who cannot see him, and charged with repeating all his signals. In order that this repetition shall be precise, the sub-conductors must be careful never to take their eyes off the chief conductor's stick for a single instant. If, in order to look at their score, they cease to watch him for only three bars, a discrepancy arises immediately between their time and his, and all is lost.

In a festival where 1200 performers were assembled under my direction, at Paris, I had to employ four chorus-masters, stationed at the four corners of the vocal mass, and two sub-conductors, one of whom directed the wind-instruments, and the other the instruments of percussion. I had earnestly besought them to look towards me incessantly; they did not omit to do so, and our eight sticks, rising and falling without the slightest discrepancy of rhythm, established amidst our 1200 performers the most perfect unity ever witnessed.

With one or more electric metronomes, it seems no longer necessary to have recourse to this means. One might, in fact, thus easily conduct chorus-singers who turn their back towards the chief conductor; but attentive and intelligent sub-conductors are always preferable to a machine. They have not only to beat the time, like the metronomic staff, but they have also to speak to the groups around them, to call their attention to nice shades of execution, and, after bar-rests, to remind them when the moment of their re-entry comes.

In a space arranged as a semicircular amphitheatre, the orchestral conductor may conduct a considerable number of performers alone, all eyes then being able to look towards him. Nevertheless, the employment of a certain number of sub-conductors appears to me preferable to individual direction, on account of the great distance between the chief conductor and the extreme points of the vocal and instrumental body.

The more distant the orchestral conductor is from the performers he directs, the more his influence over them is diminished.

The best way would be to have several sub-conductors, with several electric metronomes beating before their eyes the principal beats of the bar.

And now,—should the orchestral conductor give the time standing or sitting down?

If, in theatres where they perform scores of immense length, it be very difficult to endure the fatigue of remaining on foot the whole evening, it is none the less true that the orchestral conductor, when seated, loses a portion of his power, and cannot give free course to his animation, if he possess any.

Then, should he conduct reading from a full score, or from a first violin part (leader's copy), as is customary in some theatres? It is evident that he should have before him a full score. Conducting by means of a part containing only the principal instrumental cues, the bass and the melody, demands a needless effort of memory from a conductor; and, moreover, if he happen to tell one of the performers, whose part he cannot examine, that he is wrong, exposes him to the chance of the reply: "How do you know?"

The disposal and grouping of the players and chorus-singers come also within the province of the orchestral conductor; particularly for concerts. It is impossible to indicate arbitrarily the best method of grouping the performers in a theatre or concert-room; the shape and arrangement of the interior of these places necessarily influence the course to be taken in such a case. Let us add, that it depends, moreover, upon the number of performers requiring to be grouped; and, on some occasions, upon the style of composition adopted by the author whose work is to be performed.

In general, for concerts, the following disposal of the orchestra seems best:—An amphitheatre of eight, or at least, five rows is indispensable. The semicircular form is the best for the amphitheatre. If it be large enough to contain the whole orchestra, the entire mass of instrumentalists will be disposed of along these rows; the first violins in front on the right, facing the public; the second violins in front on the left; the violas, in the middle, between the two groups of violins; the flutes, hautboys, clarinets, horns, and bassoons behind the first violins; a double rank of violoncellos and double-basses behind the second violins; the trumpets, cornets, trombones, and tubas behind the violas; the rest of the violoncellos and double-basses behind the wooden wind instruments; the harps in the foreground, close to the orchestral conductor; the kettle-drums, and other instruments of percussion behind or in the centre of the brass instruments; the orchestral conductor, turning his back to the public, at the base of the orchestra, and near to the foremost desks of the first and second violins.

There should be a horizontal flooring, or stage, more or less wide, extending in front of the first rows of the amphitheatre. On this flooring the chorus-singers should be placed, in form of a fan turned three-quarters towards the public, so that all shall be able easily to see the motions of the orchestral conductor. The grouping of the chorus-singers, in consonance with their respective order of voice, will differ according as the author has written in three, four, or six parts. At any rate, the women—sopranos and contraltos—should be in front, seated; the tenors standing behind the contraltos; and the basses standing behind the sopranos.

The solo-singers should occupy the centre, and foremost, part of the front stage, and should always place themselves in such a way as to be able, by slightly turning the head, to see the conducting-stick.

For the rest, I repeat, these indications can be but approximate; they may be, for many reasons, modified in various ways.

At the Conservatoire, in Paris, where the amphitheatre is composed of only four or five rows, not circular, and cannot therefore contain the whole orchestra, the violins and violas are on the stage; while the basses and wind instruments alone occupy the rows; the chorus is seated on the front of the stage, facing the public, and the women, sopranos and contraltos, turning their backs directly upon the orchestral conductor, are utterly unable to see his motions. The arrangement is very inconvenient for this portion of the chorus.

It is everywhere of the greatest consequence that the chorus-singers placed on the front of the stage shall occupy a plane somewhat lower than that of the violins; otherwise they would considerably deaden the sound of these instruments.

For the same reason, if there are not other rows for the choir in front of the orchestra, it is absolutely needful that the women should be seated, and the men remain standing up; in order that the voices of the tenors and basses, proceeding from a more elevated point than those of the sopranos and contraltos, may come forth freely, and be neither stifled nor intercepted.

When the presence of the chorus-singers in front of the orchestra is not necessary, the conductor will take care to send them away; since this large number of human bodies injures the sonority of the instruments. A symphony, performed by an orchestra thus more or less stifled, loses much of its effect.

There are yet other precautions, relative especially to the orchestra, which the conductor may also take, to avoid certain defects in performance. The instruments of percussion, placed, as I have indicated, upon one of the last rows of the orchestra, have a tendency to modify the rhythm, and slacken the time. A series of strokes on the long drum struck at regular intervals in a quick movement, like the following:—

will sometimes lead to the complete destruction of a fine rhythmical progression, by checking the onward bound of the rest of the orchestra, and destroying the unity. Almost always, the long drum player, through not observing the original time given by the conductor, is somewhat behindhand in striking his first stroke. This retardment, multiplied by the number of strokes which follow the first one, soon produces—as may be imagined—a rhythmical discrepancy of the most fatal effect. The conductor,—all whose efforts to re-establish unanimity are then in vain—has only one thing left to do; which is, to insist that the long drum player shall count beforehand the number of strokes to be given in the passage in question, and that, knowing his part, he shall no longer look at his copy, but keep his eyes constantly fixed upon the conducting-stick; by which means he will follow the time without the slightest want of precision.

Another retardment, arising from a different cause, frequently takes place in the trumpet-parts; it is when they contain a quick flow of passages such as this:—

The trumpet-player, instead of taking breath *before* the first of these three bars, takes breath at their commencement, during the quaver-rest, A; and, not counting for anything the short time it has taken him to breathe, gives its whole value to the quaver-rest, which thus becomes superadded to the value of the first bar. The result of this is the following:—

an effect all the worse because the final accent, struck at the commencement of the third bar by the rest of the orchestra, comes a third of the time too slow in the trumpets, and destroys unity in the striking of the last chord.

To obviate this, the conductor must first previously warn the players against such inexactness, into which they almost all are led to fall unawares; and then, while conducting, must cast a glance towards them at the decisive moment, and *anticipate a little*, by beating the first beat of the bar where they come in. It is incredible how difficult it is to prevent trumpet-players from doubling the value of a quaver-rest thus placed.

When a long *accelerando, little by little*, is indicated by the composer, for passing from an allegro moderato to a presto, the majority of orchestral conductors hurry the time *by jerks*, instead of quickening it equally throughout, by an insensible onward rate. This should be carefully avoided.

The same remark applies to the converse proposition. It is even more difficult to slacken a quick time smoothly, and without checks, so as to transform it little by little into a slow time. Often, from a desire to testify zeal, or from defect of delivery in his musical feeling, a conductor demands from his players *an exaggeration of nice gradations*. He comprehends neither the character nor the style of the piece. The gradations then become so many blemishes; the accents, yells; the intentions of the poor composer are totally disfigured and perverted; while those of the orchestral conductor—however politely meant they may be—are none the less injurious: like the caresses of the Ass in the fable, who crushed his master while fondling him.

And now let us instance many deplorable abuses that have obtained in almost all the orchestras of Europe—abuses which reduce composers to despair, and which it is the duty of conductors to abolish as soon as possible.

Performers playing stringed instruments will rarely give themselves the trouble to play a *tremolo*; they substitute for this very characteristic effect, a tame repetition of the note, half, and sometimes three-quarters slower than the one whence results the tremolo: instead of demisemiquavers, they make triple or double ones; and in lieu of producing sixty-four notes in a bar in four-time (adagio), they produce only thirty-two, or even sixteen. The action of the arm necessary for producing a true tremolo, demands from them too great an effort. This idleness is intolerable.

Many double-bass players permit themselves—from idleness, also, or from a dread of being unable to achieve certain difficulties—to simplify their part. This race of simplifiers, be it said, has existed for forty years; but it cannot endure any longer. In ancient works, the double-bass parts were extremely simple; therefore there can be no reason to impoverish them still more: those in modern scores are rather more difficult, it is true; but, with very few exceptions, there is nothing in them impossible of execution; composers, masters of their art, write them with care, and as they ought to be executed. If it be from idleness that the simplifiers pervert them, the energetic orchestral conductor is armed with the necessary authority to compel the fulfilment of their duty. If it be from incapacity, let him dismiss them. It is his best interest to rid himself of instrumentalists who cannot play their instrument.

Flute-players, accustomed to be above the other wind instruments, and not admitting that their part can be written below that of clarinets or hautboys, frequently transpose entire passages an octave higher. The conductor, if he do not carefully peruse his score, if he be not thoroughly acquainted with the work he is conducting, or if his ear lack keenness, will not perceive the strange liberty thus taken. Nevertheless, multitudes of such instances occur, and care should be taken to banish them entirely.

It happens everywhere (I do not say in some orchestras only)—it happens everywhere, I repeat, that violinists, who have, as is well known, to play—ten, fifteen, twenty of them—the same part in unison, do not count their bars' rest; each, always from idleness, relying on the others doing it. Whence it follows that scarcely the half of them come in again at the right moment; while the rest still hold their instrument under their left arm, and look about them. Thus the point is greatly weakened, if not entirely missed. I invoke the attention and rigour of orchestral conductors to this insufferable habit. It is, however, so rooted that they will only ensure its extirpation by making a large number of violinists amenable for the fault of a single player; by inflicting a fine, for example, upon a whole row, if one of them misses coming in. Even were this fine no more than half-a-crown, I will answer for it that each of the violinists would count his rests, and keep watch that his neighbours did the same, since it might be inflicted five or six times upon the same individuals in the course of one performance.

An orchestra, the instruments of which are not in tune individually, and with each other, is a monstrosity; the conductor, therefore, should take the greatest care that the musicians tune accurately. But this operation should not be performed in presence of the public; and, moreover, every instrumental noise—every kind of preluding between the acts—constitutes a real offence to all civilized auditors. The bad training of an orchestra, and its musical mediocrity is to be inferred from the impertinent noise it makes during the periods of quiet at an Opera or Concert.

It is also imperative for a conductor not to allow clarinet-players to use always the same instrument (the clarinet in *B*♭), without regard to the author's indications; just as if the different clarinets—those in *D* and in *A*, particularly—had not a special character of their own, of which the intelligent composer knows the exact value; and as if the clarinet in *A* had not moreover a low semitone more than the clarinet in *B*♭,—the C♯, of excellent effect,

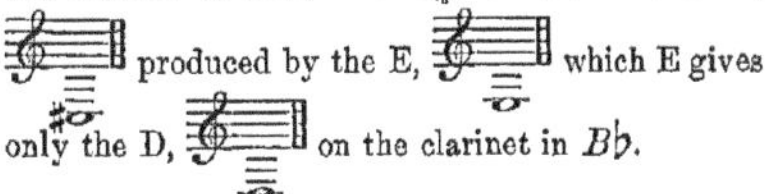

A habit as vicious, and still more baneful, has crept into many orchestras since the introduction of horns with cylinders and pistons: it is that of playing *in open sounds*, by means of the new mechanism adapted to the instrument, those notes intended by the composer to be produced *in closed sounds*, by means of the right hand within the bell. Moreover, the horn-players nowadays, on account of the facility afforded by the pistons or cylinders for putting their instrument into different keys, use only the *horn in F*, whatever may be the key indicated by the author. This custom gives rise to a host of inconveniences, from which the conductor should use all his efforts to preserve the works of composers *who know how to write*. As to those of others, it must be confessed, the disaster is of much less consequence.

He should also set his face against the economical fashion adopted by certain theatres—called lyric—of causing the cymbals and the long drum to be played by the same performer. The sound of the cymbals when attached to the long drum—as they must be to render this economy feasible—is an ignoble noise, fit only for bands at tea-gardens. This custom, moreover, leads mediocre composers into the habit of never employing one of these instruments without the other, and of considering their use as solely confined to forcibly marking the accented parts of the bar. This is an idea fruitful in noisy platitudes; and one that has brought upon us the ridiculous excesses beneath which, if a stop be not put to them, dramatic music will sooner or later sink.

I conclude by expressing sincere regret at beholding choral and orchestral studies still so badly organized. Everywhere, for grand choral and instrumental compositions, the system of rehearsals in the mass is maintained. They make all the chorus-singers study at once, on the one hand; and all the instrumentalists at once, on the other. Deplorable errors, innumerable mistakes, are thus committed—particularly in the intermediate parts—errors which the chorus-master and the conductor do not perceive. Once established, these errors degenerate into habits, and become part and parcel of the execution.

The hapless chorus-singers, moreover, are by far the worst treated of all the performers during their studies, such as they are. Instead of giving them *a good conductor*, knowing the times of the different movements accurately, and proficient in the art of singing, to beat the time, and make critical observations; *a good pianist*, playing *from a well-arranged pianoforte score*, upon *a good piano;* and *a violinist*, to play in unison or in octave with the voices as each part is learned alone—instead of these three *indispensable artists*, they commit them (in two-thirds of the lyric theatres of Europe) to the superintendence of a single man, who has no more idea of the art of conducting than of that of singing, who is generally a poor musician, selected from among the worst pianists to be found, or who cannot play the pianoforte at all—some old superannuated individual, who, seated before a battered out-of-tune instrument, tries to decipher a dislocated score which he does not know, strikes false chords, major when they are minor, or vice-versa, and, under the pretext of conducting and of accompanying by himself, employs his right hand in setting the chorus-singers wrong in their time, and his left hand in setting them wrong in their tune.

One might believe oneself in the Dark Ages, on witnessing such an exhibition of Gothish economy.

A faithful, well-coloured, clever interpretation of a modern work, even when confided to artists of a higher order, can only be obtained, I firmly believe, by partial rehearsals. Each part of a chorus should be studied singly until it be thoroughly known, before combining it with the others. The same step should be taken with regard to the orchestra, for a symphony at all complicated. The violins should first be practised alone; the violas and basses by themselves; the wooden wind instruments (with a small band of stringed instruments, to fill in the rests, and accustom the wind instruments to the points of re-entrance) and the brass instruments the same; and very often it is necessary to practise the instruments of percussion alone; and lastly, the harps, if they be numerous. The studies in combination are then far more profitable, and more rapid; and there is then good hope of attaining fidelity of interpretation, now, alas, but too rare.

The performances obtained by the old method of study are merely *approaches* to achievement; beneath which so very many masterpieces have succumbed. The superintending conductor, after the butchering of a master, none the less serenely lays down his stick with a satisfied smile; and if some few misgivings remain with him as to the mode in which he has fulfilled his task, should no one venture at the close to dispute its accomplishment, he murmurs aside: "Bah! væ victis!"

HECTOR BERLIOZ.

THE END.

CONTENTS.

ILLUSTRATIONS.

Printed in the USA
CPSIA information can be obtained
at www.ICGtesting.com
LVHW012350270823
756425LV00005B/298